Silver by the ton

The History of Ilford Limited, 1879–1979

Figure 1   Alfred Hugh Harman, 1841–1913, founder of the company.

Silver by the ton
The History of Ilford Limited, 1879–1979

Robert J. Hercock
and George A. Jones

McGraw-Hill Book Company (UK) Limited

London · New York · St Louis · San Francisco · Auckland · Bogotá · Beirut · Düsseldorf
Johannesburg · Lisbon · Lucerne · Madrid · Mexico · Montreal · New Delhi · Panama
Paris · San Juan · São Paulo · Singapore · Sydney · Tokyo · Toronto

Published by McGraw-Hill Book Company (UK) Limited
MAIDENHEAD · BERKSHIRE · ENGLAND

British Library Cataloguing in Publication Data
Hercock, Robert J
    Silver by the ton.
    1. Ilford Limited – History
    I. Title II. Jones, George A
    338.7′61′770941   HD9999.P54I/   78–41221

ISBN 0–07–084525–5

12345J&S81079

PRINTED AND BOUND IN GREAT BRITAIN

Contents

Foreword

The history of the one hundred years of Ilford Limited tells the story of a business enterprise and how several generations of dedicated men and women paved the way for what is now an important part of the photographic industry.

While it would have been fitting for the company to celebrate its centenary at its birthplace, the once tiny village of Ilford, I feel certain that the founder, Alfred Harman, would have approved of the company's expansion and its many facilities which today, from its headquarters at Basildon, span the globe.

He and his colleagues were pioneers; experimentation and innovation are just as important today as they were to Harman's young company. His successors continue the search for new and improved products to meet twentieth-century demands, and this book records Ilford's successes—and its hardships—during its first century.

A. A. S. Rae
Chairman

Preface

Modern photography, both monochrome and colour, relies upon the light-sensitive properties of silver halide salts.

When in 1879 Alfred Harman started the manufacturing business which was to become Ilford Limited, he probably used a few thousand ounces of silver nitrate. Total usage of metallic silver for all purposes, including the coinage, was about 7 000 000 oz a year. The average price of fine silver that year was 51d per oz. Owing to the general depression in trade, bank failures, and a terrible famine in India, the price had dropped from a peak of 62d twenty years before.

By the early 1900s, the company was using 250 000 oz of silver nitrate annually. The price of fine silver had dropped to under 24d per oz in 1902 and stayed below 30d until the end of the First World War; it shot up in 1920 to a peak of 89·5d.

In 1930, Ilford used 1 000 000 oz (31 tons), though total usage of silver in the United Kingdom had hardly risen since 1880. The business slump caused the price to fall in 1931 to the lowest ever recorded: 12d per oz.

Since then, both demand and price have increased by leaps and bounds. In 1968, the country imported nearly 114 000 000 oz, and the price reached 259d, then regarded as sufficiently high to pose a threat to the industry. Ten years later, Ilford was using over 4 000 000 oz (126 tons) a year, of which two-thirds were purchased and one-third recovered from processing solutions and waste materials. The price was steadily approaching £3 per oz.

Acknowledgements

The authors wish to thank the many Ilford employees, past and present, who have given so much of their time to provide firsthand information for this book. We owe an especial debt to Mr Sam Welford, who carried out much painstaking historical research for us, who wrote Chapters 9 and 10, and who contributed to Chapter 11. Finally, we thank the Ilford board for permission to refer to documents in their archives, including the minute books of the many companies concerned, their annual reports, and remaining account books.

1. Introduction

If the ancient Greeks or Romans had developed photography, we might have known what Helen of Troy, or Cleopatra, really looked like. We might have a picture of Caesar crossing the Rubicon or Nero playing his lyre while Rome burned. As it is, although the ancients knew something of the principles on which photography is based, they did not develop the technology needed to invent it. They certainly knew metallic silver, which they valued for the ease with which it could be worked, for its lustre and for its rust-free qualities. They also knew that light could affect materials. Aristotle concluded that the green colour of plants was due to exposure to sunlight, since plants bleached in the dark turned green again when brought into light. There is, however, no evidence that they were familiar with the effect of light on compounds of silver—the factor on which all photography depends.

Nevertheless, one other main ingredient of photography was known both to the Greeks and Romans and to the Chinese. This was the *camera obscura*—the Latin phrase for 'dark room' used to describe the phenomenon that light shining into a room through a chink in the shutters produces an inverted image of the scene outside on the opposite wall. Convex lenses were also known in antiquity, since some were found at Nineveh, Pompeii, and elsewhere. They appear to have been used both as magnifiers and burning glasses: the Romans used glass lenses to light sacred fires and to cauterize flesh.

The first detailed description of the *camera obscura* (or pinhole camera) appears in Leonardo da Vinci's notebooks, written in about 1500 AD, but not published until 1797. The first published description appeared in 1553. It was written by Giovanni Battista della Porta who also described the use of a concave mirror to improve the brightness of the image. This effect was, in fact, known before the sixteenth century. The properties of lenses and mirrors were fully described by Roger Bacon in *Opus Magnus*, published in the thirteenth century. Bacon was also familiar with the properties of combinations of lenses.

The *camera obscura*, regarded for centuries mainly as an entertainment, was put to practical use during the Renaissance when artists attached increasing importance to achieving correct perspective. The *camera obscura* was used to study the formation of the three-dimensional scene on a flat surface. It was further developed in 1665, when Johann Zahn constructed a portable *camera obscura*. It consisted of a box with a lens at one end and, at the other, a slanting mirror which threw the image on a translucent screen at the top.

This development came into its own at the end of the eighteenth century when accomplished gentlefolk were expected to be able to write poetry, play musical instruments, and to sketch. To compensate for lack of skill in sketching, many used a portable *camera obscura*. A sheet of thin paper was placed over the screen and the view was traced with a pencil.

The idea of permanently recording the view was clearly an attractive one and must have occurred to many people. But it was not until the nineteenth century, with the growth of chemistry, that success came.

The first step had already been taken in 1545 when Geber is credited with discovery of the fact that silver dissolves in nitric acid to form silver nitrate.

The observation that silver chloride, which occurs naturally as hornsilver in silver mines, darkened on exposure to light, is generally attributed to Georg Fabricius, in 1565, although one authority gives the credit to Giacomo Battista Beccaria, in 1757.

Angelo Sala reported that silver nitrate turned black on exposure to sunlight in 1614. This effect was more thoroughly investigated by Johann Schulze in 1727. He suspended chalk in a silver nitrate solution and found that, when he placed a flask containing the suspension in sunlight, the chalk on the side towards the light turned deep purple, whereas the side away from the light was unchanged. He exposed the flask to the heat of a fire and obtained no results, showing that it was light, not heat, which caused the change. He wrapped opaque paper stencils around bottles containing his solution and exposed them to light: on removing the stencils, the patterns were clearly visible.

Carl Wilhelm Scheele announced in 1777 that silver chloride was blackened more effectively by the violet end of the solar spectrum than by the red, and that the blackening was due to the formation of particles of silver.

As far as is known, the first person to set out deliberately to devise a process to record images was Thomas Wedgwood, son of Josiah, the potter. It is said that Wedgwood's attention was directed to photography by an order to the pottery from the Czar of Russia for a large dinner service, each piece to carry the picture of a different English mansion or castle. It occurred to Wedgwood that the job would be much simplified if the image in a *camera obscura* could be captured by some light-sensitive process.

Dr William Lewis, in his book *History of Colours*, described both the work of Schulze and his own experiments with wood and ivory in 1763. When he died, his notebooks were bought by Josiah Wedgwood who also engaged Lewis's assistant, Alexander Chisholm, as secretary, chemical assistant, and tutor to Thomas. Further, Dr Joseph Priestley, who had also described Schulze's work in his *History of Discoveries Relating to Vision, Light and Colours*, was a member of the Lunar Society which met in Josiah Wedgwood's house. He was thus well known to Thomas, and it was probable that from these coincidences he knew of the effect of light on silver nitrate.

Wedgwood moistened sheets of white paper and white leather with silver nitrate solution and placed over them a drawing in ink on glass. He obtained a reverse image of the drawing after a few minutes' exposure to direct sunlight, and found that treated leather was more sensitive than treated paper, probably because of the presence of gallic acid in the leather.

Humphry Davy, who communicated the results of Wedgwood's experiments to the Royal Institution in 1802, found that sensitivity was improved by converting the silver nitrate to silver chloride. He did so by immersing the paper or leather, already impregnated with silver nitrate, in dilute hydrochloric acid, but neither Davy nor Wedgwood discovered a method of fixing the images, which had, therefore, to be kept away from the light to prevent the unexposed portions of the image from darkening. Moreover, none of the materials which they prepared was sensitive enough to record the image in a *camera obscura*. Wedgwood thus failed to achieve his original objective, and ill health seems to have prevented him from continuing the research; he died, in 1805, at the age of 31.

First to capture the image in a *camera obscura* was Joseph Nicéphore Niepce, who did so in 1826. He used metallic plates coated with Syrian bitumen, normally soluble in oil of lavender, but insoluble when exposed to light. He could therefore fix his image by dissolving the unaffected bitumen in oil of lavender after exposure in the camera. Syrian bitumen or 'bitumen of Judea' was found to be more sensitive than material from Trinidad or elsewhere.

Niepce's process required an exposure of several hours in bright sunlight and it fell to Jacques Daguerre to invent a more practical process. Initially, Daguerre used a plate of polished silver or silver-plated copper exposed to iodine vapour in a box, thus forming a thin layer of silver iodide on the surface of the plate. When exposed in a camera for 4 to 5 hours only a faint image was visible; but he found that if, after exposure, the plate was exposed to fumes from mercury, a strong image could be obtained with only 10 minutes' exposure. He fixed the image by bathing in salt solution.

In 1839, in return for the publication of his process, the French government granted Daguerre an annual pension of 6000 francs. Public reaction was extraordinarily enthusiastic and within 5 months, 25 editions of his publication had been printed in seven countries.

In 1840, John Frederick Goddard of London and Franz Kratochwila of Vienna found that the sensitivity of the Daguerre plate could be increased by using both iodine and bromine vapours for sensitization. This improvement, together with the Petzval portrait lens made in 1840 by Voigtlander, enabled portraits to be obtained in about 20 seconds with a good light.

The Daguerre process suffered from the disadvantage that the opaque metal support prevented the production of prints by transmitted light. Hence, Daguerreotypes were unique and could not be used for multiple copies. This difficulty was overcome by Henry Fox Talbot.

Like Wedgwood, Talbot was spurred to work on photography by a desire to record the image in a *camera obscura*, which he used for sketching. He devised a process which consisted of treating paper first with a solution of sodium chloride and, when dry, with a solution of silver nitrate so that silver chloride was formed within the paper with silver nitrate in excess. He found that to treat the paper in this order was essential to obtain sensitivity; if the process was reversed, with silver nitrate first and sodium chloride second so that the latter was in excess, the paper was very insensitive. In fact, he actually used sodium chloride or potassium iodide solution to fix his picture.

At first Talbot's pictures were produced in the camera by printing-out and the tone values were reversed—black became white and vice versa. In other words, the record was a negative, but with him originated the idea of converting the negatives to positives, that is printing them by placing the negative in contact with a freshly sensitized piece of paper and exposing through the negative.

On the announcement of Daguerre's process in 1839, Talbot took steps to publicize his own results and arranged for Michael Faraday to read a paper before the Royal Institution, three weeks later.

Talbot's next discovery was a process which he called 'Calotype'. This process employed a developer and was described before the Royal Society in 1841. A sheet of paper was treated with silver nitrate solution and then with potassium iodide. When dry, this paper kept almost indefinitely. Before exposure, the paper was sensitized by floating on a solution of gallic acid, silver nitrate, and acetic acid. It was then exposed for a short time in a camera to form a latent image which was not visible until it had been developed in the same solution as that used for sensitizing. By this means, Talbot could obtain pictures in strong sunlight in one minute with a lens aperture of f/15.

For the next fifteen years there was much rivalry between proponents of Talbot's process, which yielded many prints from one exposure, and Daguerre's, which yielded only one positive per exposure, but of a much better quality and finer definition. Nevertheless, many fine Calotypes have survived.

Both processes were quickly superseded by Frederick Scott Archer's wet collodion process of 1851. It combined the definition of the Daguerreotype with the facility of printing of the Calotype and was faster than either. He dissolved collodion, a material similar to guncotton, in a mixture of alcohol and ether to which he added ammonium iodide. This mixture was coated on glass and the solvents allowed to evaporate, leaving a thin, tacky layer. The plate was then immersed in strong silver nitrate solution to form silver iodide, drained and immediately exposed in the camera, developed thereafter in pyrogallic acid or acid iron sulphate solution, and fixed in hypo. To be successful, the plates had to be prepared, exposed, and developed before they dried, which meant in about ten minutes. This may not have been too difficult in a studio, but outdoors a portable darkroom was a necessity.

Scott Archer's process became popular almost overnight and led to the formation, in 1853, of the Photographic Society of London, which later became the Royal Photographic Society; to the formation of the Société Française de Photographie in 1854, and to the establishment of the *British Journal of Photography* in 1854 and of the *Photographic News* in 1853.

Attempts were made to make dry collodion plates by W. B. Bolton and B. J. Sayce who produced an emulsion of silver bromide in collodion and coated it on glass. These plates kept well but they were much slower than wet collodion; they were manufactured by the Liverpool Dry Plate Co. from 1867 onward. The negatives were usually printed-out on albumen (obtained from white of eggs) silver chloride paper invented by Louis Blanquart-Evard in 1850. This paper continued to be used for about thirty years until replaced by collodion or gelatin print-out papers.

The era of the gelatin dry plate was inaugurated by an article published in 1871 in the *British Journal of Photography* by Dr Richard L. Maddox. This development opened the way for plates to be manufactured commercially. Maddox added silver nitrate solution to a hot, slightly acidified gelatin solution containing cadmium bromide to obtain a suspension of silver bromide in gelatin, now generally known as an 'emulsion'. This was coated on a warm glass plate and allowed to cool and dry. After exposure the plate was developed in a plain pyro-gallol solution and fixed with hypo. Sixteen years later Maddox listed his reasons for experimenting with gelatin as: the cost of collodion, the health hazards of breathing ether and alcohol, which are solvents for collodion, and dissatisfaction with existing dry plates. Before deciding upon gelatin, he had tried various resins, and albumen and isinglass.

Maddox's emulsion was extremely crude. No attempt was made to wash out the cadmium nitrate formed during the preparation of the silver bromide and silver nitrate was present in excess. As a result, the plates did not keep well and were slow and foggy. In the next few years, many experimenters strove to improve upon Maddox's emulsion and were so successful that by 1880 dry plates, faster than wet collodion ones, were in regular commercial production.

In 1873, J. Burgess was offering for sale dry plates at 2s 6d per dozen quarter-plates ($3\frac{1}{4}$ in $\times$ $4\frac{1}{4}$ in) and also gelatin-bromide emulsion for photographers to coat their own plates. The latter, being in a wet state, soon decomposed so Richard Kennett introduced pellicles of dried emulsion in 1874, which the user could soak in water and melt for coating his own plates.

In the same year both J. King and J. Johnston emphasized the importance of removing the unwanted salts from the emulsion after it had been prepared. The former used dialysis and the latter shredded the emulsion jelly after it had set and washed it in cold water.

In 1874 Peter Mawdsley pointed out the value of preparing paper coated with a gelatino-bromide emulsion, which could be chemically developed in a similar way. Mawdsley founded the Liverpool Dry Plate and Photographic Printing Co., probably the first large-scale producer of both photographic dry plates and papers. It was said (by Burgess) that he used Burgess's emulsion formula.

During 1877 J. Johnston suggested the addition of ammonia to the emulsion during preparation to increase speed and F. Wratten discovered that the emulsion could be separated from the unwanted salts by the addition of alcohol, which precipitated the gelatin and silver bromide together and the solution containing the unwanted salts could be poured off. The spongy mass containing the silver bromide was then redispersed in water. Both these discoveries had profound implications for later emulsion making.

Joseph Swan was a partner with John Mawson, his brother-in-law, in Mawson and Swan, a firm of chemists and druggists. Swan became interested in photography very early and Mawson and Swan were selling special collodion for photography in 1856. By 1864 he had perfected a process for printing with carbon which was taken up by the Autotype Co. He also interested himself in methods of using photographs to illustrate books and periodicals. In 1865 he patented the halftone process (Patent No. 1791) which is still in use today and, in 1866, a method of producing electrotypes from carbon prints which was adapted to intaglio copper-plate printing (Patent No. 239).

In 1877 Swan, who was also the co-inventor with Edison of the electric light bulb, became interested in dry plates and started experimenting. He was plagued by the variability of speed of his materials, which he discovered was due to the need to control temperature in order to obtain consistent results. He built a factory at Low Fell, near Newcastle-upon-Tyne, and started selling dry plates by the end of the year.

The first to publish his work regarding the effect of heat on speed was Charles Bennett in 1879. After preparing his emulsion he stewed it for 5 to 10 days at 32 °C (90 °F). This process was carried to its logical conclusion a year later by Mansfield who *boiled* his emulsion for 10 to 15 minutes. Both of these processes caused a deterioration of the gelatin which was overcome by using a suggestion, made by W. B. Bolton in 1874, to add more gelatin at the end of the ripening period.

The heating is nowadays carried out in two stages, which gives better control. After emulsification, during which a suspension of fine crystals of silver bromide is formed (in gelatin), the emulsion is ripened, often in the presence of ammonia as suggested by Johnston and Monckhoven, at a high temperature during which period the crystals grow in size. The emulsion is then set and washed and remelted. Substances are then added to the liquid emulsion which is then digested at a high temperature for an hour or so. During this period the crystals do not grow, but they do increase in sensitivity.

Another discovery of vital importance to the future of photography, optical sensitization, was made by H. W. Vogel in 1873. Until then, all materials using silver compounds were sensitive only to blue and violet light. He found that when a yellowish-red dye, Coralline, was added to a collodion emulsion, it became sensitive to green light as well as to blue and violet. Later (1884) he discovered that a mixture of basic dyes, Quinoline Red and Quinoline Blue, sensitized collodion plates to green, yellow and orange. He sold a solution of these two dyes under the name of Azaline to plate manufacturers, but it suffered from the disadvantage that the sensitization was weak, compared with the strong inherent blue sensitivity of the silver halide, and exposures had to be made through a strong yellow filter to correct this, thus reducing the speed.

The photographic process had made enormous strides in 40 years. Not only were the images clearer but sensitivity to light had been increased 2000-fold, as shown by Table 1.

Process	Date	Exposure
Daguerreotype (silver iodide)	1839	30 min
Calotype with development	1841	3 min
Wet collodion plate	1851	10 sec
Gelatin-silver bromide plate	1878	0·005 sec

Table 1

In 1879, six years after Vogel's discovery, Alfred Hugh Harman founded the nucleus of Ilford Limited.

2. Alfred Hugh Harman

Many people have made a contribution to the development of photography into a major industry which has profoundly influenced the way in which we live and work. It would be very difficult indeed, as technical improvements have followed each other, to single out one which, by itself, might be said to be the all-important one. It is, however, possible to establish the date on which photography first moved out of the state of being an interesting, if rather erratic pursuit of amateurs into a truly commercial, professional operation. There is little doubt, either, over the identity of one of the men who brought about this transformation. He is Alfred Hugh Harman, who made his first appearance in photographic and industrial history in 1863 when, at 22, an advertisement appeared in the *British Journal Photographic Almanac* for Dages and Harman, photographic printers, of 3 Albert Cottages, Hill Street, Peckham, London, where he also lived.

Very little is known of his early life. His father was a bootmaker and Alfred was born in 1841. At the age of 19, on 7 April 1860, he married Amelia Ann Taylor, the daughter of a greengrocer, by whom he had four sons and three daughters. Two of the sons, Alfred and Percy, emigrated to Australia and founded the Harman Engineering Co. in Melbourne.

Harman's second wife, with whom he settled in Ilford, was Nina Octavia Helvetia du Gué, the daughter of Auguste Louis Benjamin du Gué, a Swiss who had emigrated from Lausanne to Dublin and there married Julie Knobel in 1825. Alfred and Nina Harman had no children.

By 1864, he had set up in business on his own at Gunnersbury Villas, Albert Road, later called Harders Road, Peckham, London. An advertisement in the *Almanac* for that year claimed that his enlargements 'are acknowledged the best' and offered a service of printing and copying and the production of slides or large transparencies for decorative purposes from photographers' own negatives. Harman further undertook to provide a specimen stereo slide, in exchange for 6s either in stamps or as a postal order.

Stereo slides were very popular at the time and many Victorian parlours had their stereoscopic viewer. Harman's specimen offer was, therefore, not particularly remarkable. But his offer to provide photographers with copies and enlargements was unusual. At the time, photography, even for professionals, was still very much a do-it-yourself businesss. Negatives and slides would probably have been made by the wet collodion process, with prints on albumenized paper. Harman would therefore have been among the first to offer such a service.

It is not known how he obtained his experience in photography or how he financed his business. He appears, however, to have met with early success: a year later, he was again advertising in the *Almanac*, this time claiming that because of numerous improvements in printing and because of the introduction of machinery in the printing process he was able to offer prints from negatives at 'very low prices for good work'.

His claim seems to have been fully justified: he offered to provide *cartes-de-visite* (visiting cards $2\frac{1}{4}$ in $\times$ $3\frac{1}{2}$ in carrying a portrait of the owner) at 1s 2d per dozen or 12s per gross. A decade earlier, a dozen *cartes-de-visite* cost a guinea. Moreover, parcels of negatives could be sent by rail from any part of the country or by Omnibus or Telegraph Despatch from all parts of London; so it is clear that Harman's business was no longer local, but nationwide.

By 1867, he was advertising in the *Almanac* a service providing enlargements by solar camera and artificial light. 'An exceedingly effective enlargement, half-life size, and beautifully finished in water colours' cost 30s including a cut-out mount and supporting strut. A year later he moved to more commodious premises at 79 High Street, Peckham, near his old premises at Gunnersbury Villas and also opened another studio at 110, Ewell Road, Surbiton, Surrey, to which address he transferred his household.

In 1873, Harman advertised enlargements by the collodion transfer process. This probably referred to a process of stripping the image in a collodion film and applying it to another surface such as canvas. One technique for doing this was to coat the collodion surface with gelatin and to allow it to dry. The combined film was then stripped from the glass by cutting round the edges with a sharp knife and peeling off the layer.

Another *Almanac* advertisement in the following year was addressed 'to all photographers desirous of gaining a reputation for good and permanent work!!' It offered enlargements printed in Autotype (carbon process) on paper, artist's canvas, or opal glass. In this and subsequent advertisements he styled himself Alfred Harman & Co.

Two events at this time help to illuminate Harman's character. The first was a law suit, heard at the Lambeth County Court before Pitt Taylor on 18 July 1873, when Harman sued a Mr D. H. Cussons of Southport, dealer in photographic goods, for the value of an enlarged photograph coloured with oil paint. In July 1872, Cussons sent Harman a *carte-de-visite* of a freemason in full regalia and asked for it to be enlarged and coloured at a fee of seven guineas. Upon completion, Cussons sent an insulting letter of complaint to Harman suggesting alterations which would have necessitated repainting the picture.

Harman replied on 20 August, asking for the picture to be returned saying that he would keep it and not let Cussons have it at any price. When the picture arrived back the following day, however, he wrote again to Cussons saying that unless the fee were paid he would sue Cussons for the amount. Cussons replied to both these letters accepting the terms offered in Harman's letter of 20 August.

The main point at issue was that the picture had been painted without white gloves which Cussons said were visible in the *carte-de-visite*. However, the judge ruled that the gloves were not visible and that the colour of the gloves had not been stated on the order. Harman won his case and costs of £4.

The second incident was a letter to *Photographic News* in 1877 in which he stated that 'if any person engaged in photography were always to take a substantial meal in the middle of the day, we should hear less of the cry that it is an unhealthy occupation'. In later years, after the establishment of his plate factory, he was still concerned that his employees should be able to obtain hot meals during the day.

In 1878, he applied for a provisional patent for a process of retouching negatives to give the appearance of being finished by hand. During this period he must also have been experimenting with the new dry plate emulsions described by Maddox in 1871 for, in 1879, he decided to give up his photographic business and concentrate on the manufacture of dry plates.

Having made the decision, Harman sought a site

Figure 2   Ilford Broadway, 1880. An engraving from a contemporary photograph. The country road ahead led to Romford and Brentwood. Cranbrook Road, where Harman started the business in his private house, leads off to the left of the picture. The cottages he subsequently bought, on the site where the Ilford factory was situated for 95 years, lies to the right. (Courtesy: Central Library, London Borough of Redbridge.)

close to London with a clean, dust-free atmosphere. He settled on the then small village of Ilford (Figure 2), east of London in the county of Essex, and acquired a house called 'Elmhurst' on the corner of Park Avenue and Cranbrook Road. There, he set up the Britannia Works (see Appendix 1).

Limited, employing thousands of people.

In the cellar and ground floor of 'Elmhurst' Harman, with two men and three boys, made dry plates. Helped in busy times by his wife and housekeeper, he drove daily to London in a horse and trap to deliver his latest consignment of dry plates.

> When Harman began to manufacture dry plates in 1879, his small staff included three boys: J. P. Coyle, known as Peter, H. Gosling and William Rowlinson. Peter stayed with the firm until he retired in the early 1930s. One of his descendants, E. C. Coyle, was employed until 1972. H. Gosling left the firm when it moved to the Clyde Estate; he joined Boots, the chemists, as a photographer, but was re-engaged as an emulsion maker when Selo Limited was formed after the First World War. William Rowlinson left to join the Co-operative Society. H. E. Gosling, a nephew of H. Gosling, and P. Juniper, a grand-nephew of Rowlinson, still work at the Basildon site of Ilford Limited.

The formation of this company was one of the vital steps which took photography out of the hands of amateurs and set it firmly on the path to becoming a major, highly skilled and professional industry. The plates made by the Britannia Works were soon to be renamed 'Ilford' and the company's birth, 100 years ago, provided the foundation for the modern Ilford

The Britannia Works prospered and very soon Harman rented a cottage for 10s a week on the Clyde Estate, south of the High Road, where plates were coated with emulsion made in Cranbrook Road. Almost immediately afterwards, Harman purchased houses in Grove Terrace (later Uphall Road). Thereafter, the emulsion was made in the cottage and

Figure 3   The trademark Harman introduced in 1886.

Figure 4   Edward Ball Knobel (1841–1930) was a man of many parts; he studied law and geology before working as a chemist with Bass and Co., brewers, of Burton-on-Trent, becoming head brewer. He transferred to Courtaulds, as chief dye chemist, before joining Harman at the Britannia Works Co. in 1893, at the age of 52. Knobel published a number of papers on astronomy, including English translations of ancient Persian, Greek, and Latin manuscripts. He was an accomplished violinist, playing in many concerts at the Crystal Palace, London.

coated, packed, and stored in the Grove Terrace houses (see Appendix 1).

By 1883, only four years after its foundation, the business had expanded so well that a special factory was built on the Clyde Estate for plate manufacture. Two years later, Harman quarrelled with Marion and Co. and terminated their agreement. In 1886, he tried to obtain an injunction to prevent their using the name 'Britannia'. Harman lost his case: Mr Justice Chitty ruled that, as Marion and Co. had registered the mark, they were entitled to use it. Harman reacted to the decision by changing the name of his plates from 'Britannia' to 'Ilford' and the name Britannia Works to the Britannia Works Company. He also introduced the paddle steamer trademark (Figure 3) and reduced his prices. For example, the price of one dozen Ordinary quarter–plates ($3\frac{1}{4}$ in $\times$ $4\frac{1}{4}$ in) was reduced from 2s to 1s.

The business continued to expand and in 1888, he engaged a chemist, Joseph J. Acworth who left two years later and ultimately became managing director of the Imperial Dry Plate Company, which was purchased by Ilford in 1918. In 1889, he engaged Andrew Agnew to supervise the quality of the plates produced. One reason for Harman's success, in a business in which so many others failed, was his insistence that only plates of the finest quality left his factory. In the same year, he engaged John Howson as business manager: he was responsible for a more active advertising campaign and he introduced *Photographic Scraps*, the *Ilford Manual of Photography* and other useful publications for promoting Ilford products.

In 1891, when he was 50, Harman converted the Britannia Works Co. into a private limited company and introduced a profit-sharing scheme for his employees.

Harman by now began to contemplate retirement because of ill health, but before he could do so he had to find a competent person to run the factory. In June 1893, he engaged Edward Ball Knobel as a scientific expert. Within a month, Knobel was appointed a director. Shortly afterwards Harman took a holiday and spent six months touring Europe and North Africa.

On his return, in 1894, Harman bought Lower Grayswood House (later Grayswood Place) near Haslemere, Surrey. This large house was built for Mrs Humphry Ward, the novelist, in 1890 with the proceeds of her first novel (£3200). She sold it two years later because she said it was too new and too noisy. It is said that Harman actually bought the house from Dame Adelina Patti, but documents relating to the house for that period are missing.

Knobel was made managing director in December 1894, and Harman's attendances at board meetings became less frequent. However, as when he was on holiday, an almost daily correspondence was carried on with Knobel concerning the running of the factory.

On 10 March 1898 a special board meeting was called at which Harman announced that negotiations had been going on for two months for the creation of a public company. The disposal of the private company realized £380 000; £260 000 was paid in cash, the rest in 60 000 £1 preference shares and 60 000 £1 ordinary shares. As the major shareholder, 80 per cent of this sum went to Harman. However, he refused a directorship in the new company and ceased to have an active interest in its day-to-day running, but he did not sever the connection entirely and it seems that he was consulted on various matters.

In June 1898, he offered a camera which he had patented to the company, but withdrew the offer three weeks later for unspecified reasons. A year later he offered to do experimental emulsion-making for the company provided that they bore the expense of an assistant and the rental and the cost of fitting up of a suitable laboratory. This offer was not taken up immediately, but meanwhile he was advising Knobel on emulsion-making matters. In a letter dated 18 April 1900, he apologized for not being able to test a trial plate which he had been sent, on account of the presence of visitors in the house and he made suggestions for the improvement of Rapid plates.

However, in January 1901 a house at 2 Museum Hill, Haslemere, was rented for three years for £40 per annum and an assistant, R. S. Potter, was engaged at £200 per annum. In October 1901, Harman was instructing Knobel on the preparation of a warm-toned paper and three months later he reported the results of work done at Haslemere which he claimed would be of great value to the company. No record of these results has survived.

On 1 December 1902 he wrote that he found the new Special Rapid plates coated at Ilford identical to the original SR plate and 'very much behind those made here by the formula given you. I consider it a great mistake to have dropped the method given you from here'. His letter continued:

> We have experimented with the dye sent to Potter by Renwick, we find it the best in every respect we have yet tried. It gives plates equal to Cadetts and is far and away superior to our usual dye for the reds, while the yellow and greens do not suffer in the least. It gives a slight fog which we are trying to get over. I shall be glad if you will let me have the name and address of the man who supplied it.

We shall be glad to do something for the Bromide paper but as you have not yet reported on the formula given you about 6 months ago, it is disheartening as we are left in the dark as to whether our work is of utility or otherwise. These remarks apply to the suggestion for Alpha emulsions given you a few weeks ago and to many other things.

It is obvious from this letter that the company was experimenting with the production of panchromatic plates and also that the relationship between the company and Harman was not running as smoothly as might be wished. In the event, it was later agreed to terminate the lease of the Haslemere laboratory on 25 March 1904, the reason given being that Potter's services were required at Ilford.

In addition to his experimental work, Harman was also advising the company on other matters. He approved the purchase of a plot of land at Brentwood for a new plate factory in December 1899 and in January 1901 was asked to approach the Ilford Gas Company about sulphurous fumes which affected plate production. Three months later he was consulted on the advisability of increasing discounts and raising the price of plates: he advised against doing so and his advice was accepted.

On 27 November 1902, he was elected a director of the company; he held the appointment until 3 February 1904, when ill health forced him to resign.

As his working life drew to a close Harman appears to have taken an increasing interest in local affairs. In 1898, he decided to finance and endow a church and vicarage for Grayswood provided that a new parish was formed. This was done by taking parts of the Chiddingfold, Haslemere, Thursley, and Witley parishes. Lord Derby donated one and a half acres of land beside the main Haslemere–Guildford Road. The church was built during 1900 and 1901 with local stone in an Early Gothic style at a cost of £4200. The architect was a Swede named Axel Herman Haag, later changed to Haig, who lived in Grayswood.

The vicarage was built some distance from the church near the grounds of Grayswood Place for £2000 and the Rev. John Sherlock Leake, a friend of Harman, was appointed the first vicar. The living was in the gift of the Bishop of Winchester and endowed with £279 per annum by Harman and £21 per annum by the Ecclesiastical Commission.

The church, which had the dedication of All Saints, was consecrated on 11 February 1902; the first person to be buried in the churchyard was Harman's second wife Nina Octavia Helvetia who died in January 1902.

At the north end of the transept is a window,

dedicated to Knobel L. B. du Gué who died at St Leonards-on-Sea on 22 August 1890, which was donated by his most loving sister Nina O. H. Harman. There is reason to believe that Edward Knobel was distantly related to Harman's wife, hence the occurrence of Knobel as a Christian name of Louis du Gué and possibly the preferment of Edward Knobel by Harman.

After his wife's death in 1902, he adopted Margaret Knobel, one of Edward Knobel's daughters. She changed her name to Knobel-Harman by deed poll in September 1902 and went to live at Grayswood.

Harman's presence in Grayswood made sufficient impact on the inhabitants that G. R. Rolston in his *Haslemere 1850–1950* thought fit to mention him driving a smart four-in-hand down Haslemere High Street. He contributed to various local causes and when his gardener retired Harman presented him with a sum of money sufficient to enable him to erect two semi-detached cottages for himself and his family.

He died, at the age of 72, on 23 May 1913 and is buried beside his wife in Grayswood churchyard. There is a memorial, surrounded by chains, to them both against the east wall of the church and a tablet to Harman inside the church from the parishioners of Grayswood.

He left £266 000, after paying duties of £66 000. Of this, £50 000, the house and grounds, stable and lodges, waterworks and water tower of Grayswood Place, together with all furniture, silver plate, pictures, jewellery, horses, and carriages and motors were bequeathed to his adopted daughter, Margaret. The sum of £200 was left in trust with the Vicar and churchwardens of All Saints to maintain his grave. To Mrs Antoinette Lees and to Mrs Ada du Gué, the sister and sister-in-law respectively of his wife, Nina, went annuities of £1000 per annum.

The remainder of his estate was distributed in bequests to his friends and acquaintances and charities, many of which were for boys and orphans. His domestic servants (and they appeared to have been many, indoor and outdoor, coachman, motor driver, groom, gardener, and mechanic being noted) received £5 for each year of service.

The house was put up for sale for £9800 in 1916 but no buyer appeared. It was instead let to a Mrs Graham Cooper in 1920 and finally sold in 1922 to J. S. Whatton. The solicitor handling the transaction was Alfred Dinn who had been associated with Harman since the early days of the Britannia Works Company. The house has since been divided into two and other houses have been built in the grounds.

Harman is said to have been a friendly man. He did

not seek publicity for himself and took little part in the activities of the various photographic societies which flourished in and around London at the time, as did other manufacturers such as J. B. B. Wellington and Alexander Cowan.

On only two occasions has it been recorded that Harman took part in the meetings of the London and Provincial Photographic Association, both held at the beginning of 1887 at Masons' Hall Tavern in the City of London. At the first, when a lecture was given by J. B. B. Wellington on 'Orthochromatic Photography', Harman stated that he had no experience of ortho plates which he did not make. He thought that it was a good material to use especially in large towns and dim light and that the use of a yellow screen was a disadvantage. He did not consider them much good unless they kept well. He presided at the second meeting a week later and during the discussion stated that collodio-chloride prints were more stable than albumen prints. The best way of keeping sensitized paper was to cut it to size and store in wide-mouthed, stoppered bottles. (Printing papers at the time were sold in rolls and were cut to the required size by the user.)

He was clearly an astute business man, who insisted on quality, but kept a careful watch on wastage. He was reluctant to spend money on factory improvements until it was absolutely necessary. Towards the end of his active control of the company, when the business had become well established, he became even more cautious and unwilling to accept innovations, the usual reason he gave being that 'the time is premature'.

Although it is not known whether he received any scientific training, it is obvious that he was a very practical man, good at empirical research. During the first nine years of the company's existence, as far as is known, he was responsible for devising and controlling during manufacture, all the emulsions produced.

His attitude to his employees seems to have been one of strict benevolent Victorian paternalism. He treated them generously by the standards of the time and cared for their general welfare. In some respects, his ideas on industrial relations seem to have been in advance of his time. Concern for the well being of employees was by no means a universal factor of Victorian industry.

But, perhaps because he did not court publicity, Harman remains a rather shadowy figure. The two court cases recorded here—one of them over what might seem a relatively trivial disagreement—indicates that he was a determined man not lightly deterred from any course of action he considered right.

The bequests in his will indicate that he was a warm, family man with a typical, Victorian awareness of the duties of his position as a wealthy manufacturer.

But on the size and value of Harman's contribution to the development of photography, there can be no doubt at all.

IN 1879 . . .

In the year in which Alfred Harman decided to manufacture dry plates, most of the things which are commonplace today did not exist. The whole world of electronics and nuclear physics was in the future, as was the discovery of alpha, beta, gamma, and X-rays.

Because there were no cinemas, no record players, no radio or television receivers, people thought and behaved differently. They worked longer hours: they were more self-contained, more self-reliant. Ideas and new concepts took longer to percolate through society: government played a much less pervasive role in the country's life.

But affairs were on the move. As the industrial revolution gained momentum, invention had followed invention. The great improvement in transport and communications, which took place in Queen Victoria's reign, had produced a network of railways which was probably more extensive than that of today. In the years between 1850 and 1897, the length of track grew from 6600 to 21 000 miles.

Road transport, however, still depended upon the horse. The main roads were metalled, but many minor ones were in bad condition. (In 1893, Harman complained to the local authority about the condition of the road leading to his factory. The authority agreed to pave the road with wood—presumably wooden blocks—if the firm paid half the cost.)

The first street railway had been opened in 1860 in Birkenhead by Francis Train: it covered $2\frac{1}{2}$ miles. Each coach was drawn by two horses and carried up to 30 passengers at between 7 and 8 mph. The electric tram, which first appeared in Germany in 1883, did not become commonplace in Britain until near the end of the century. The Metropolitan Railway, forerunner of the underground system, using a broad gauge and steam engines, had been opened in 1863, covering the $3\frac{1}{2}$ miles from Paddington to Holborn Hill.

At sea, steam was replacing sail. The paddle steamer *The Great Western*, which was the first designed to cross the Atlantic, had been launched in 1837. By 1840, there were 600 steamers totalling 95 000 tons (3 per cent of total tonnage): the number increased to 8500, totalling 6 million tons (two-thirds of the total) by 1897. The tonnage in sail remained constant: the whole of the increase in tonnage in this period was in steam.

Although the telegraph system existed in 1879, the telephone, invented three years previously, had not yet been developed commercially. The Post Office, however, offered a service which seems fantastic by today's standards. There were eleven deliveries of letters daily in London: six in the suburbs. Letters posted before 6 pm were guaranteed delivery the same evening within a radius of 6 miles: answers to letters addressed to London from Ilford were received the following day. All of this was for 1d per ounce.

Modern photographers would have been most inconvenienced by the lack of artificial light sources. The arc lamp and the limelight existed, but they were very intense sources of illumination. Furthermore, the former needed an electric generator, driven by a steam or gas engine: there was no electric-mains network. To run a limelight, the operator had to make his own oxygen and store it in bags. If no gas mains supply was available, gas had to be stored in the same way. For other purposes, only candles, oil lamps, or gas jets were available. In the days of collodion dissolved in ether and alcohol, the fire hazards were considerable.

The carbon filament lamp had been invented in 1878, but for many years to come either primary batteries or a private electric generator had to be installed before they could be used.

Income tax in 1879 was 5d in the £ and it varied between 2d and 8d in the £ for the rest of the century. No tax was paid on incomes below £150 per annum and an abatement of £120 was allowed on incomes of between £150 and £400 per annum. This meant that most workers paid no income tax: a skilled engineer earned £80, and a labourer £25, per annum.

The range of goods available was narrower and people's needs and expectations were lower, but there is no doubt that the workman of the late nineteenth century lived more comfortably than his forebears. It is difficult to equate the value of the pound then with that of 1979, but its purchasing power was probably at least twenty times greater. A man's earnings were therefore worth considerably more than today.

He could buy a good business suit in Scots tweed for £2.15s: a pair of trousers cost him 15s. He paid less than 1d per pint for beer, 3s 6d for a bottle of whisky and 2s 6d for a bottle of either gin or rum. For about £10 he could, if he wished, buy a gold watch: for £2.15s he could buy a silver one—or a good sewing machine. A company could give its employees an exceptionally fine dinner, with local transport thrown in, for around £1 per head, while an ordinary simple meal could be had for a few pence.

Bricks cost 9s per 1000 and a substantial red brick house could be built for less than £300. Such a house would be let at between 7s and 9s a week.

During Queen Victoria's reign, Britain had become more and more prosperous and some of this prosperity had filtered downwards, especially to skilled and semi-skilled workers, although it brought little joy to the really poor.

In 1879, more was yet to come: between then and the end of the century, the real value of wages was to increase by 80 per cent as earnings rose and prices, especially of food, fell, thanks to the principles of free trade and the repeal of the Corn Laws. It was not a particularly exceptional year for Britain. But it was one in a period of continuing Victorian expansion: a thrusting period in which there seemed little limit to what the British might do and the Empire seemed likely to last forever.

3. A flying start (1879-1891)

The summer of 1879 was the wettest of the century: it was followed by a winter which enveloped London in a thick, yellow fog. Industry, in general, was in a period of stagnation. It was not the most favourable time in which to start the manufacture of gelatin dry plates or photographic materials of any kind. Furthermore, in the eight years since Maddox had published his note on gelatin dry plates, a number of companies had begun to manufacture them commercially. By 1879, there were over twenty brands on the market. Harman had four main competitors: the Liverpool Dry Plate and Photographic Printing Company, Wratten and Wainwright (both of London), Mawson and Swan (Newcastle) and Samuel Fry (Kingston-on-Thames).

Harman was clearly undeterred by either current circumstances or by the competition. At 38, he was probably confident that he had the business and professional experience needed to make a success of manufacture.

When Harman started his enterprise, emulsion making was still a craft and very poorly understood; but the basic principles had been established and published. They were:

1. There had to be an excess of bromide solution during making.
2. Light sensitivity could be enhanced by ripening at a high temperature.
3. Ripening could be carried out at a lower temperature in the presence of ammonia solution.
4. Unwanted salts had to be removed before coating.
5. Colour sensitivity could be improved by the addition of certain dyes.

However, many discoveries and refinements remained to be unearthed before the quality of modern materials could be achieved.

At first, the basement of the Harmans' house, 'Elmhurst', in Cranbrook Road, Ilford, was used for emulsion making and coating; the ground floor was used for the remaining operations. Help was provided by two men and three boys. The boys did the lighter work and washed the glass, the latter being obtained initially from the iron-mongers, Young and Marten of Stratford, London.

Harman did the emulsion making, possibly assisted by his wife, thereby preserving the secrecy of the operation. At first, he made only one type of plate, the 'Britannia' Dry Plate, the formula for which has been lost. The procedure was probably as follows:

Gelatin was dissolved in hot water and a solution of potassium bromide was stirred in. Silver nitrate solution was then added slowly, the mixture being stirred vigorously all the time, to form a cream-coloured liquid with silver bromide crystals in suspension; this was called an 'emulsion'. When all the silver nitrate had been added, the liquid was kept hot for a specified time to improve its sensitivity to light, then cooled to form a stiff jelly. The jelly was broken up and washed in cold water to remove the unwanted nitrates. It was then remelted to enable it to be coated on glass plates.

To coat a plate with emulsion, Harman's staff used a teapot. The plate was held on the finger-tips of the left hand and liquid emulsion poured from the teapot into the centre. The plate was then tilted gently in all directions to ensure it was completely covered. When this was accomplished, the coated plate was left on a chilled plate of glass, carefully levelled, to set. Thus a uniform layer of emulsion was obtained. The choice of a teapot for coating was deliberate; the emulsion was drawn from the bottom of the pot, leaving behind the froth, which floated.

When set, the plates were placed in racks in a cupboard and dried with warm air. The dry plates were packed in boxes of a dozen, labelled and delivered to London by Harman himself in a dog cart drawn by two ponies in tandem.

The success of gelatin dry plates was due to the unique properties of gelatin, which swells in cold water without going into solution. This property greatly assists the penetration of the solutions used for developing and fixing into the layer of emulsion on a dry plate. Moreover, on heating, swollen gelatin goes into solution and becomes a liquid, enabling the silver bromide crystals to be dispersed uniformly during making. It also helps to keep the very fine crystals of silver bromide in suspension at this and subsequent

Figure 5   Thomas Hughes joined Harman in 1882 as factory manager and was a director of the company formed in 1891, of the Britannia Works Co. of 1898 and of Ilford, Limited, from 1900 to 1903.

stages. After making, gelatin sets to a firm jelly on cooling and this can be broken up for easier and quicker washing in cold water. After washing, it can be remelted for coating and then cooled to form a firm layer on glass, ready for drying.

Another property of gelatin, which neither Harman nor anybody else suspected at the time, is that it contains certain impurities which impart to the emulsion a sensitivity much greater than ever achieved with the wet collodion process.

Harman, however, like many other manufacturers of that time, may well have had some unrevealed methods. He surrounded his emulsion-making processes with secrecy and no record of them has survived from the early days. Since the new enterprise was successful almost immediately, his processes must have been effective and certainly seem to have produced products which appealed to his customers.

To begin with, it is likely that he supplied professional photographers known to him from the old days. But as business expanded he appointed Marion & Co. of 22–23, Soho Square, London, as his agent. Since Marions placed an advertisement for Britannia Dry Plates in the 1881 edition of the *British Journal Photographic Almanac* they must already have become Harman's agents in 1880—the year following the opening of his new venture. In the following year they also advertised various papers under the 'Britannia' trademark. These were probably not made by Harman, as he appears to have had insufficient space in 1881 in which to produce papers. Their use of the trademark was to lead to a dispute later. Marions also advertised cameras, including a miniature one at 42s with an instantaneous shutter, holding twelve dry plates $1\frac{1}{4}$ inch square; Harman seems to have had no interest in that side of the business.

Expansion came very quickly. Indeed, it was probably also in 1880 that Harman extended his premises by renting (for 10s a week) a cottage on the Clyde Estate, just south of the crossroads which were at the centre of the village of Ilford.

In the cottage, plates were coated with the emulsion which, in the continuing requirement to preserve secrecy, was still made in Elmhurst. Light-tight jars containing the emulsion were transported down the road to the cottage on a hand-cart which sometimes overturned in one of the many pot holes with the consequent loss of emulsion, to Harman's fury.

But the cottage quickly became inadequate for Harman's growing business, since very shortly after renting it he bought seven houses in Grove Terrace, later known as Uphall Road. Thereafter, emulsion was made in the cottage and coated, packed and

stored in the Grove Terrace houses.

Harman's business continued its rapid expansion for, in 1882, he engaged Thomas Hughes as factory manager. A year later a special factory was built for the manufacture of dry plates: the factory incorporated one of the Grove Terrace houses. Hughes remained with the firm until 1919, when he retired at the age of 72.

In 1885, Harman and Marions quarrelled and the agreement between them was terminated. In the following year, Harman sought an injunction to prevent Marions from using the name 'Britannia' for their products. Harman lost the case because it was judged that as Marions had registered the mark they were entitled to use it. In their advertisements prior to this date they had listed Britannia plates without reference to the Britannia Works.

Harman reacted by changing the name of his plates from Britannia to Ilford. He also registered his company as the Britannia Works Company, introduced the paddle-steamer trademark, and reduced the price of his plates. The price of one dozen Ordinary quarter-plates ($3\frac{1}{4}$ in $\times$ $4\frac{1}{4}$ in) was reduced from 2s to 1s. Marions, in their turn, opened a new factory at Southgate in 1887 to manufacture Britannia plates.

As business increased, Harman was forced to increase his staff. As far as is known, Harman had always done his own experimental work, but in 1888 he engaged a chemist Joseph J. Acworth, who seems to have had a private income. He had published a series of articles in the *British Journal of Photography* on touring the Continent with a camera. He was born in Rochester, Kent, in 1853, and became a Fellow of the Chemical Society in 1875 and a Fellow of the Institute of Chemistry in 1878. His association with Harman was short-lived; he left in 1890, after only two years, to go to Erlangen University where he obtained a doctorate for work on the dye sensitization of emulsions. Returning to England in 1892, he built a private laboratory at Cricklewood for experimental emulsion research. This developed into the Imperial Dry Plate Company of which he was a managing director. He died in 1927 at the age of 74.

A year after engaging Acworth, Harman engaged Andrew Agnew, who continued to be associated with the company until 1937 to supervise the quality of materials produced by the new factory. The story is that Harman was visiting Glasgow to inspect an automatic printing and developing machine, which was demonstrated by a young Scottish photographer, who so impressed Harman that he remarked, perhaps rather deviously, that he always advertised for staff in the *British Journal of Photography* under the initials

*Figure 6   John Howson, Harman's first business manager, who joined the company in 1889. He wrote
and published the first Ilford magazines and books, including* Photographic Scraps, *the* Ilford
Manual of Photography, *and the* Ilford Year *book.*

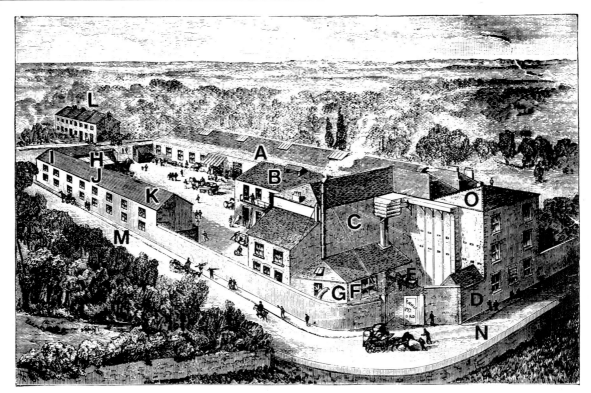

Figure 7   The Britannia Works Company's factory at Ilford, 1888: an engraving which appeared in the British Journal of Photography, *June 29. A Coating rooms; B POP stores; C POP emulsion and cutting; D Covered passage with ice-well beneath; E Covered way to emulsion room; F Engine room; G Lamp room; H Stores; I Glass washing; J Glass drying; K Glass examining; L Magdala cottages; M Private road; N Grove Terrace (later Uphall Road); O One of the original three-storey houses. The far gate opened onto a lane, later an internal way between the technical service building and central engineering department, leading into Roden Street. The yard inside the gates was afterwards covered over. Napier Cottages, not shown, were to the right of Magdala Cottages (L); Clyde cottages were further to the right. The engraving involved the use of artistic licence, presumably to show the rural setting of the factory.*

XYZ. A week later an advertisement appeared, Agnew replied and was engaged. Agnew's job was to reject any batches of material which he considered to be substandard, a task which he took seriously.

In the same year, 1889, Harman engaged John Howson as business manager. Howson, who stayed with the firm until 1900, was responsible for a much more active advertising campaign and toured the country lecturing on, and demonstrating, Ilford materials. He also initiated in September 1889 *Photographic Scraps*, a free monthly leaflet giving hints on photography and promoting Ilford materials. The publication continued until it was stopped by the First World War. Howson also introduced the *Ilford Manual of Photography*, which ran to many editions, as well as a range of leaflets promoting Ilford materials.

Very little documentary evidence has survived about the factory between 1879 and 1891 but the engraving in Figure 7 shows a view of it at the time. Harman refused to allow any outside visitors and an

account of the early years has to draw heavily on fragmentary recollections of early employees written down many years later. However, other manufacturers of the time were not as secretive, and they have left descriptions of their works in articles in photographic journals. Two such manufacturers were William Cobb and R. W. Thomas. Their factories were probably typical of the time and the following brief accounts of their operations may throw some light on Harman's own factory.

William Cobb's factory was established in a converted chapel behind his portrait studio in Wellington Street, Woolwich, and employed 60 people. Cobb's son, a chemist and a Fellow of the Chemical Society, was in charge of the technical side of the business.

The glass was cleaned by girls ('of a somewhat superior class') and then 'subbed' with a solution to ensure that the emulsion adhered to the glass.

Coating was done in the vaults by hand as Cobb

believed that better quality could thus be obtained than by machine coating.

Four men could coat 12 000 whole-plates ($8\frac{1}{2}$ in × $6\frac{1}{2}$ in) per day. The coated plates were conveyed on endless bands through the drying room on the floor above to the packing room.

The plates were cut to size on Cowan's (of Marions) centre cutting boards. These automatically centred the plates to ensure that the two halves were identical in size. It was easier and more efficient to coat large plates, either by hand or by machine, and then cut them into halves or quarters than to coat smaller ones. Thus, four quarter-plates ($4\frac{1}{4}$ in × $3\frac{1}{4}$ in) were cut from one whole-plate and halves ($4\frac{3}{4}$ in × $6\frac{1}{2}$ in) were cut from double-halves ($9\frac{1}{2}$ in × $6\frac{1}{2}$ in). By making the halves larger than half a whole-plate, much the same aspect ratio (about 1.35:1) was preserved for all three plate sizes.

Two packers were associated with each cutter. The first dusted the plates with a soft brush to remove any glass particles, inserted edge slips to separate the plates and wrapped them in paper. The second put the wrapped plates in boxes, made on the premises. Three cutters and six packers could account for fifty to sixty gross of quarter-plates per day.

Spoiled plates were stacked in racks and immersed in one or other of two coppers of hot water. The recovered glass was repolished and reused. What happened to the emulsion is not known. (At Ilford the washed-off emulsion was discharged into the River Roding until it was realized that the silver could be recovered. Most maufacturers seem to have been slow to economize by recovering waste silver.)

R. W. Thomas's factory was situated near the station at Thornton Heath. Power was provided by a Cornish boiler and an 8 hp steam engine which also drove a Siemens dynamo for charging the storage batteries used for lighting.

The glass was cleaned by a sulphuric acid and potassium chromate solution, washed, and then polished. After preparation, the emulsion was 'cooked' in steam-jacketed jars. Instead of washing, the emulsion was centrifuged, three jars at a time, to remove the unwanted salts in solution. It was then redispersed in gelatin for coating.

The plates were coated on an Edwards coating machine capable of producing 12 000 12 in × 10 in plates per day and dried by air drawn over anhydrous calcium chloride. A portrait studio was attached to the works for testing the plates produced.

Electric lighting was installed at Thomas's factory. Marions' new factory at Southgate, built in 1887, also used electric lighting. This innovation does not seem to have been installed at Ilford until 1895.

By 1891, Harman's factory was claiming to be the largest manufacturer of photographic plates in the world and listed materials for sale as shown in Tables 2 and 3.

Camera plates	Introduced	Relative speed
Ordinary (yellow label)	1879	1
Rapid (white label)	1886	1.25
Special Rapidity (red label)	1888	2
Isochromatic Instantaneous	1891	2

Table 2

Printing materials	Introduced	Relative exposure 1ft from gas jet
Rapid Bromide paper, Rough or Smooth	1884	1
Slow Bromide paper, Rough or Smooth		20–40
Rapid Bromide Opals ⎤ same emulsion		
⎬ as Bromide		
Slow Bromide Opals ⎦ papers		
Alpha paper	1884	100
Alpha Lantern plates, same emulsion as paper	1889	
Special Lantern ρlates	1891	10
Printing-Out Paper (POP)	1891	

Table 3

The Isochromatic plate differed from the others in that it was sensitive to green and yellow light as well as to blue and blue-green light. In 1873, Vogel had discovered that the addition of Coralline dye to a collodion emulsion increased its sensitivity to green and yellow light, but was unsuccessful in applying this effect to gelatin plates. In 1883, Pierre Alphonse Attout (alias Tailfer) and John Clayton of a company called Tailfer and Clayton of Paris applied for a British patent (no. 101) for the sensitization of gelatin plates with Eosin. Waterhouse discovered the effect of Eosin (tetrabromofluorescein) in collodion emulsion in 1876 and Eder in 1883 had found that Erythrosin (tetraiodofluoresein) was a better sensitizer than Eosin. The innovation introduced in Attout's patent was to dissolve the Eosin in ammonia solution and add it to the emulsion during making. Alternatively, the finished plates could be bathed in Eosin dissolved in ammoniacal alcohol, but for commercial production the first method was simpler.

A plate manufacturer B. J. Edwards of The Grove, Hackney, London, applied for, and obtained, a licence to use Attout's process in Britain and the colonies and started making Isochromatic plates in 1888. Later, Harman came to an agreement with Edwards for the use of the patent. The patent covered the use of Erythrosin and Rose Bengal as well as Eosin, but although Edwards seems to have preferred to use Eosin, Harman chose Erythrosin.

The Rapid Bromide paper was designed for enlarging and the Slow Bromide paper for contact printing. Opals were opal glasses coated with the same emulsions used for bromide paper and were supposed to give improved image tones.

Alpha paper and Alpha Lantern plates were coated with a special emulsion which enabled image tones from red through to black to be obtained by varying the exposure time and the development.

Special Lantern plates were coated with a bromide emulsion about twice as fast as Slow Bromide paper and one-fortieth of the speed of Ordinary plates.

Printing-Out Paper was designed to replace albumen papers and required no development. The paper was exposed behind a negative and the exposure, usually in daylight, continued until the image became visible. The print was then washed, toned in gold solution, washed, and fixed.

All these materials were available in a wide range of sizes except the Lantern plates which were $3\frac{1}{4}$ inches square. Typical prices are shown in Table 4.

Material	Price per dozen	Size
Ordinary	1s	quarter-plate
Rapid	1s 3d	quarter-plate
Special Rapid	1s 6d	quarter-plate
Isochromatic		
Instantaneous	1s 6d	quarter-plate
Lantern	1s	($3\frac{1}{4}$ in × $3\frac{1}{4}$ in)
Opals	13s	whole-plate
Bromide paper	2s 3d	whole-plate sheet
Alpha paper	1s 9d	whole-plate sheet
POP	7s 6d	sheet $24\frac{1}{2}$ in × 17 in

Table 4

4. Britannia becomes Limited (1891-1898)

Towards the end of 1891, Harman decided to convert the Britannia Works Company into a private limited company and to offer the company's employees facilities for sharing in its success. It is possible that his motivation for this move was to prepare for retirement.

The new company, The Britannia Works Company Limited, was registered (regn. no. 35433) on 17 December 1891, with a capital of £120 000 divided into 24 000 £5 shares. The initial subscribing shareholders, each with one share, were:

Alfred Hugh Harman
Thomas Hughes (factory manager)
John Howson (business manager)
F. J. Jenks (company secretary)
James Lewis (emulsion maker)
Henry Newman (manager)
William Underwood (engineer)

Shortly before registration Harman issued a notice to the company's employees; it is summarized below:

1. The only shareholders in the new company would be Harman and his employees.
2. Each employee would receive one £5 share for 5 years service or two £5 shares for 10 years service.
3. Employees could buy as many shares as they could afford, provided they did not borrow money for the purpose. For those who could not pay for the shares at once, clubs could be formed to purchase shares by weekly or monthly subscriptions.
4. Employees were given the option of receiving payment for services in terms of profit-sharing instead of fixed wages. In practice, this meant being paid wages in terms of the dividend on a fixed number of shares.

The final sentence of the notice said:

It is earnestly hoped that a large number of employees will avail themselves of these advantages and that their increased attention to duties will lead to increased profits, for the benefit of themselves and the business generally.

In the event, the first clause of the notice was not strictly applied, since Harman's friends and business acquaintances were allowed to purchase shares almost from the company's beginning.

When the Articles of Association were published, restrictions were placed on the employee's shares; he could sell them only to other of the company's employees, to Harman or, if Harman's holding fell below £30 000, to the directors. An employee's share certificate is shown in Figure 9.

At the new company's first board meeting on 2 December 1891, Harman assumed the title of governing director and he appointed Thomas Hughes as director and works manager at a salary equal to the dividend on 880 shares. John Howson was appointed director and business manager (750 shares) and Frederick J. Jenks, secretary (500 shares). As the dividend for the first year of the new company was declared at 20 per cent tax paid, the share allocations were equivalent to annual salaries of £880, £750, and £500 respectively.

Harman received 23 540 of the new shares plus £2300 in lieu of the remaining 460 shares; 120 of these were acquired by Hughes, 60 by Howson, 84 by Jenks, and 150 by Lewis, all presumably by purchase. Thus, 4 people held 414 shares out of the 460 not held by Harman. The remaining 46 were held in ones and twos by other employees.

By the end of the year, the holdings had altered slightly and the number held by other employees had increased by 14 to 60 shares. This seems a small number but, in 1892, employees numbered less than 100, of whom more than half were probably boys. The names can be identified of 16 employees who, between them, held 42 shares worth £210. In present-day terms this equals about £4200, an average holding of some £260, with a spread of between £100 and £900.

One of the first items of business of the new board concerned a patent (no. 18349) obtained by Harman three years previously in 1888 for a glass-washing machine through which glass plates were conveyed by endless bands and rollers.

Harman, typically, was engaged in litigation with W. J. Wilson (Paget Prize Plate Company) over the patent. Its inclusion in the board's agenda was simply in order to transfer the action from Harman to the

Figure 8   F. J. Jenks. With Harman in the early days, Jenks was appointed secretary to the 1898 company. He was persuaded to act as cashier and accountant in 1904, when J. Drummond-Robertson was appointed secretary. After three years, Drummond-Robertson left the company and Jenks was restored to his old position of secretary. He was appointed managing director in 1915.

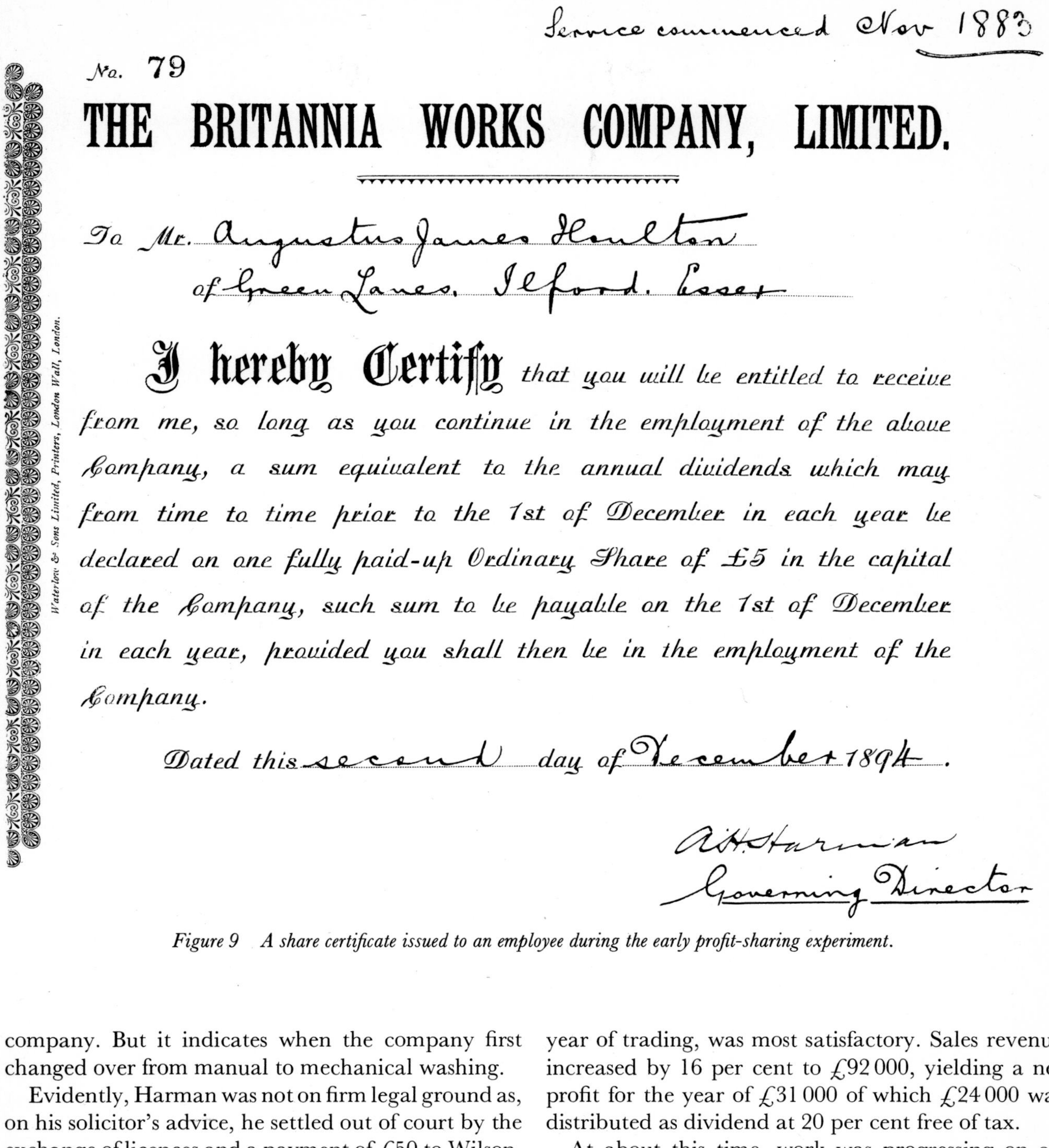

Service commenced Nov 1883

No. 79

THE BRITANNIA WORKS COMPANY, LIMITED.

To Mr. Augustus James Houlton
of Green Lanes. Ilford. Essex

I hereby Certify that you will be entitled to receive from me, so long as you continue in the employment of the above Company, a sum equivalent to the annual dividends which may from time to time prior to the 1st of December in each year be declared on one fully paid-up Ordinary Share of £5 in the capital of the Company, such sum to be payable on the 1st of December in each year, provided you shall then be in the employment of the Company.

Dated this *second* day of *December 1894*.

A.H.Harman
Governing Director

Waterlow & Sons Limited, Printers, London Wall, London.

Figure 9   A share certificate issued to an employee during the early profit-sharing experiment.

company. But it indicates when the company first changed over from manual to mechanical washing.

Evidently, Harman was not on firm legal ground as, on his solicitor's advice, he settled out of court by the exchange of licences and a payment of £50 to Wilson.

Towards the end of 1892 Hughes demonstrated some flat films, which had probably been coated by sticking the film down on long glass plates and coating them on a plate-coating machine. Harman was sufficiently impressed to agree to visit B. J. Edwards at Hackney to see a film-coating machine that Edwards had constructed. After the visit Harman reported that he had decided not to market films; it was agreed to leave the matter in abeyance indefinitely.

The company's annual report for 1892, the first year of trading, was most satisfactory. Sales revenue increased by 16 per cent to £92 000, yielding a net profit for the year of £31 000 of which £24 000 was distributed as dividend at 20 per cent free of tax.

At about this time, work was progressing on an exposure calculator designed in 1882 by Professor V. A. Scott of Dublin (patent no: 17642). The first was made in aluminium, but Harman suggested the use of vulcanite. The calculator consisted of four concentric circles of different diameters rotating on a central pivot. Alternate circles were made of light or dark brown material. The central pivot was marked with plate speeds. The first circle had numbers related to the month and time of day provided by associated tables, the next carried f/numbers, the next the type of

Figure 10   Hughes, Howson, and Jenks walking along Back Lane (later Roden Street) to collect money from the bank, 1895. The wall on their left is of St Mary's Hospital

scene and the outermost showed the correct time of exposure. The calculator was sold, with instructions and a leather case, for 5s. Examples of both the aluminium and the vulcanite versions are kept at the Science Museum, London.

At the end of 1892, Harman raised with the board the question of employing a scientific expert to replace Acworth. On obtaining its assent, he produced a letter from Edward Ball Knobel, a dye chemist at the Courtaulds factory at Braintree, Essex, offering his services. It was agreed to offer Knobel the post at an annual salary equal to the dividends on 1200 shares.

Knobel joined the company on 23 June 1893. A week later he was appointed a director at the same salary: 18 months later he was made managing director. There is some evidence to suggest that Knobel was distantly related to Harman's wife and this may help to explain his engagement and subsequent rapid promotion. There is, however, no

doubt that he deserved his position; he was an outstanding man, far in advance technically of any of his colleagues.

During his first year with the Britannia Works Company, in addition to his work as director and analytical chemist, he was engaged upon the development of pink and mauve POP, matt POP, and Bromide papers; improvements to the Isochromatic plate and in the use of formaldehyde solution as a hardening agent for gelatin. During this period, he discovered he could improve the whiteness of Bromide papers and POP by adding a small quantity of a violet dye, Regina Purple. He was also asked to attempt to use magnesium flash powder instead of a limelight for testing POP and to devise a means of collecting the fumes from the flash. The need to control these fumes well illustrates the difficulties of early testing.

By the beginning of 1893, sales of POP had so increased that the advisability was considered of a building to house a new paper-coating machine. Hughes estimated that he could produce £2000 worth (400 000 ft²) of paper per month without difficulty, £3000 worth with a wider paper, and £4500 worth with a night shift. As a result, no action was taken to build a new coating machine.

It was also decided at about this time to purchase outright, for £725, three plate-coating machines previously hired from B. J. Edwards for £200 per annum. It is not known when Harman started coating plates mechanically, but Edwards had patented his machine in 1884 and was soon making them for other plate manufacturers. Machines based on his design, with slight modifications, were in use at Ilford until the close of the site in 1975, and were used almost universally by plate manufacturers throughout the world. There was evidently an interchange of machine designs between the various manufacturers, as the episode with Wilson in 1891 illustrates. Edwards seems to have been particularly successful with his inventions, though not with his business as a whole.

In June 1893, Henry Newman, a founder member of the new company and a sub-manager in the factory, was taken seriously ill. The company's attitude was humane. It agreed to give him three months' leave on full pay and when, after two months, it became obvious that Newman would probably be unable to continue work, it was decided to terminate his agreement at the end of the three months, but to allow him to live rent free and to pay him £1 per week. He died on 16 August. Condolences were sent to his widow and his 12 company shares were transferred to her. In his place, W. C. Shepherd was appointed and awarded a bonus of £10 for the extra duties he had performed during Newman's absence; the basis of his salary was raised from 55 to 80 shares.

The year 1893 was another good one for the company. Sales rose by 21 per cent to £113 000 yielding a net profit of £40 000. The dividend was, however, kept unchanged at 20 per cent. The improvement in sales, despite a business recession due to a coal strike, was attributed to the introduction of POP. In furtherance of paper sales, Howson arranged to tour the British Isles demonstrating POP and the newly introduced matt POP and Bromide paper.

By this time, Harman evidently trusted Knobel and left in December 1893 for a four month holiday in Europe and North Africa. He kept closely in touch with the business, however, by means of letters and telegrams. Almost his first communication was an objection to Howson's proposal to promote POP, disapproving of sample packets and of demon-

strations. The board braved Harman's displeasure and continued the demonstrations because of increased competition, though they dropped the distribution of samples.

The competition came from Paget, who also challenged Ilford's use of POP as a trademark. The company replied that it did not claim to be the sole makers of printing-out paper and had merely registered the mark POP, having a paddle steamer within the letter 'O'. It fought the business challenge by raising dealer discounts from 15 to 20 per cent on plates in Britain and from 21 to 45 per cent on paper in Australia.

However, in spite of stiff competition, the demand for Ilford products grew and steps were taken to enlarge the works and offices. The company secretary, F. J. Jenks, first bought a small strip of land to the east of the factory, although attempts to buy more foundered because the vendor, the Marquis of Salisbury, tried to insist on a wall seven feet high along the new boundary.

Plans for a new factory were completed by January 1894 and were sent to Harman, who insisted on 'personal consultation'. Knobel joined him in Algiers during February and obtained his agreement.

At the beginning of March, excitement engendered by the proposed extension was dampened slightly by an outbreak of smallpox in the village; some of the company's employees were infected. The board decided that all the employees should be vaccinated at the company's expense. A Dr Shimeld was engaged to do the vaccinations; he undertook to use only calf lymph vaccine and not vaccine prepared from infected children.

As the proposed extension meant that 5 Grove Terrace, which had been used as a mess room for the employees, would no longer be available for that purpose, Harman agreed to buy land and build a new Institute at a cost not exceeding £2000 provided that the company was made responsible for its maintenance. A plot of land was purchased from Dr Shimeld on the east side of Barking Lane (Ilford Lane) opposite the factory: the new Institute was opened by the end of 1895.

Meanwhile, work was progressing on the new factory. Buildings were being erected to house a new boiler and steam engine to drive the machinery and a smaller engine and dynamo to light the factory and offices by electricity. Provision was also made to house a new plate-coating and a paper-coating machine; a Furnival steam-powered guillotine for cutting paper and means for drying straw used for packing. The packing shed was to be enlarged to enable plates for

Figure 11   The Britannia Works Institute, 1895.

Figure 12   The Britannia Works, 1895; a view from the west across what is now Uphall Road. The allotments in the foreground later became the site of the Renwick research laboratory, after the houses built there had been destroyed by bombing in the Second World War.

export to be packed in a warm, dry atmosphere, and the central yard was to be paved and roofed.

In November 1894, Harman saw a machine made by Wilson of Paget Prize Plate for cutting large plates into smaller ones. Although the machine had certain defects, he thought it would be cheaper than hand cutting. The price asked was £130 down with a yearly royalty of £50, but Harman wanted to make an outright purchase at a reasonable price. Knobel approached R. W. Munro Ltd, who guaranteed to make a machine to Wilson's pattern for £130 with a single royalty payment to Wilson of £200. A year later this machine was installed and working well. Two more were ordered in January 1896 at the same price with a royalty of £100 to Wilson on each machine. Improved machines of this type, together with some early Munro machines, were still working when the factory closed in 1975.

The factory was completed sometime early in 1895 and J. Field Dodgson was appointed manager and chief emulsion maker. Electric light had been installed, but candles or oil lamps must still have been used, possibly in safelight lanterns, since a man was employed to watch the lamps to reduce the risk of fire.

Knobel, who had been made managing director in December 1894, had his salary increased from 1200 to 1500 shares equivalent in May 1895.

Shortly afterwards, Harman summoned the directors by telegram to a meeting at Knobel's home, 1 Tavistock Square, London. He proposed the engagement of Austin Edwards, B. J. Edwards' son, as manager of the new factory coupled with the purchase of Austin Edwards' factory in Willoughby Lane, Tottenham, London. This was a curious suggestion as Edwards' business was much smaller than Britannia's, though it did produce films as well as plates; this may have aroused Harman's interest in spite of his rejection of films in 1892. Edwards made films for the Beck Frena magazine camera, which took up to forty flat films with notched edges, exposed successively by operating a lever outside the camera. Frena was an acronym for 'For Rapidly Exposing Negatives Automatically'.

Edwards was employed on trial, on the understanding that if he proved able to produce 'the article' (*sic*) an agreement would be signed. It was also decided that Britannia would like to see the following points in the agreement.

37

1. Employment to be terminable at one month's notice on either side.
2. Edwards must invest in the company.
3. His position would be subordinate to the governing and managing directors.
4. Satisfactory declaration of secrecy.
5. To be an employee and not a director.
6. Salary: dividend on 750 shares (50 per cent more than Dodgson was receiving).
7. Compensation for films and process plates to be settled by governing director on evidence of books.
8. Full disclosure of all his secrets to the governing and managing directors.

Edwards, perhaps not unnaturally, rejected most of these points and it was finally decided that only the declaration of secrecy was necessary. Edwards started on 1 May at the proposed salary plus £1000 for his business, goodwill, and stock; the company paid £900 and Harman £100 of this sum. Edwards also bought 200 Britannia shares.

Having appointed Edwards, the board was now concerned with the fate of Dodgson who had only just been appointed to the same post. He was offered the position of demonstrator of POP and bromide paper at his old salary of 400 shares equivalent, with out-of-pocket expenses. Howson thought this would be beneficial to the company, as only 50 per cent of photographers were using gelatin papers and Dodgson was a capable man with experience of travelling. It is recorded that Dodgson gladly accepted his new appointment, but this was probably not a true expression of his feelings.

A press notice stated:

> The Britannia Works Company Limited, beg to announce that they have purchased the business and goodwill of Mr Austin Edwards, makers of 'Queen' plates and films and that they will henceforth manufacture Ilford 'Artist' and 'Special' films and 'Process' plates.

Edwards' appointment as manager was not revealed.

Soon after the announcement, The London Stereoscopic Company of Regent Street, London, objected to the use of the name 'Artist' as they had been using it for films for two years; the name was changed to 'Empress'.

In May it was decided to transfer everything to Ilford and to close the Tottenham works. Seven women employees were also transferred including a forewoman; she was paid £1 10s per week and the others 10s to 18s.

It was resolved to sell the Edwards films and plate under their new labels at the following prices:

Process plates	1s per dozen $\frac{1}{4}$-plates
Empress films	1s 6d per dozen $\frac{1}{4}$-plates
Rapid films	2s per dozen $\frac{1}{4}$-plates
Frena Empress films No. 1	1s 8d for 20
Frena SR films No. 1	1s 10d for 20

Arguments over the value of Edwards' business continued until August; the following figures give Jenks' and Edwards' estimates of the business position:

	Jenks	*Edwards*
Debtors	£528	£500
Creditors	£716	£550
Balance at bank	£168	£160
Cash	£186	—
Plant	£114	£400
Stock	£200	£411
Goodwill	£500	—

At the beginning of September, Harman, Knobel, and Hughes held a special meeting at Haslemere to discuss 'the fearful losses at the new factory and Edwards' inability to produce SR and Iso. plates'. Whether this was the true cause of their dissatisfaction is not known, but it must be remembered that the new factory had been operational for only five months and Edwards had been in charge for only four. It was to be another twelve months before Knobel could announce that all plates could be made in either the new or old factories. Furthermore, the profit for the year was down only 10 per cent despite disruptions caused by building the new factory.

Following the meeting, matters quickly came to a head. On 11 September 1895, Edwards was invited to lunch with Knobel, who informed him of their dissatisfaction and requested his resignation. He was not to be allowed in the factory again and the terms concluded would take account of the 'frightful loss' to the business. Knobel reported that Edwards was upset, but that the latter had thanked him for his kindness and consideration and had left on friendly terms. However, Edwards later met Harman and complained of Knobel's unkindness.

No letter of resignation was received and the board was concerned about Edwards' 200 shares and the lease of the Tottenham house used by him as a factory. Knobel had to terminate the agreement and matters were settled by the end of October 1895. Edwards received £511 and sold his shares to Harman. He retained the house and was soon advertising Austin Edwards plates and films again from there. He later moved to Warwick.

Dodgson accepted reinstatement as factory

manager with some hesitation. He had not been able to take up his proposed appointment as traveller and demonstrator because there had been so much testing to do in Agnews' department that he had been asked to assist him.

A proposal for extending the company's offices had been discussed for some two years and, at the end of 1895, Harman agreed to purchase nearby land on which to build new offices. Accordingly, land with cottages was bought from Chennell for £750 and the tenants were paid £1 each to obtain vacant possession.

An estimate of £2065 from Joscelyne and Young, builders, for the new offices, with walls and gates, was accepted at the beginning of March. It was stipulated that the work be completed by 1 June, although the Bricklayers' Union had already given notice of a strike in May.

The floors of the offices, but not the corridors, were to be covered with inlaid linoleum tiles at £25. Office furniture was supplied by Hill of Forest Gate for £110. The offices were heated by steam radiators at £36 by Crittall & Co. and lit by electric light installed by Jeffrey Hughes & Co. for £49.

The offices were completed by October 1896. Harman withdrew his usual objections to publicity and allowed a description of them to be published in the *British and Colonial Printer and Stationer* for 1 October 1896. They comprised offices for the manager (with a special typewriter room next door) and for the company secretary, a board room, and a large room illuminated with north lights containing desks for 30 clerks (of which only 20 were used). All the latest improvements were adopted including electric light, as well as gas in case of an emergency, steam heating, and pneumatic bells which the firm considered more reliable and preferable to electric bells. At the back of the building were coal stores and some excellent lavatories.

In the factory, a second well was sunk at a cost of £300. It was $8\frac{1}{2}$ in in diameter, 300 ft deep, and delivered 2900 gal/h by means of a 7 in pump and a 3 hp vertical engine.

During this period, the company appears to have pursued a non-diversification policy, perhaps reflecting Harman's original decision to concentrate on plate making. For example, in July 1895, Dr John Joly offered the firm a screen-plate process of photography in natural colours for £25 000 cash and £25 000 in shares. Knobel rejected the offer saying that, although the idea was ingenious, the price was too high and as it was out of the firm's line, he doubted whether it would be possible to make a financial success of it.

In the same year, the firm was offered the land, on which stood Magdala and Napier cottages, for £1580. Howson suggested offering £1500, but Harman decided 'we need not trouble about the purchase of cottage property for the present' and the offer was declined. Many of the employees had been born and lived in the cottages. They were let at 5s to 6s a week. They were acquired in due course, however, and a despatch building, which later housed the technical service department was built on the site of the Magdala cottages in about 1930. The Napier cottages, built in 1868, survived until the factory closed in 1975.

By June 1896, requests had been received for rollable films and Guiterman's traveller left a sample of celluloid which was available in lengths of 600 to 700 ft. Eastman was selling rollable films $1\frac{5}{8}$ in wide and 70 ft long for £1 3s 0d. Tests had shown that the Ilford emulsions were not suitable for rollable films and the machines available had not been adapted to coat film. Nevertheless, 29 ft of celluloid-coated film $8\frac{1}{2}$ in wide were sold to Elliot & Sons, Barnet, for £1 9s in July 1896; it is not known how the film was coated. The manager of Elliots, Birt Acres, was an early pioneer of cinematography.

Glaveski, inventor of the Animatograph, also wanted film. Harman thought it premature to consider making long lengths of film, but he believed that they should be ready to go to market at short notice. Knobel wondered whether it was worth while making films at all in view of the poor sales and the increase of fire insurance premiums needed because of the presence of celluloid on the premises. The production of flat films was, however, continued.

Howson raised the question of producing rollable films again in 1898 saying that he thought that the time was now ripe, but once again it was resolved that no steps should be taken. The main objection to doing so seemed to be that if Ilford made films Eastman might make plates.

The introduction of celluloid, even on a limited scale, had brought its problems. Great difficulty was experienced in disposing of the coated celluloid waste. Johnson and Matthey refused to handle it, but finally Matthews & Co. agreed to accept it and recover the silver.

The presence of celluloid on the premises also inspired the formation of a works fire brigade at the beginning of 1896.

At the end of 1896 it was decided to stop making Frena films and to sell the residual stock to Beck at 10 per cent reduction. The films had never sold as well as was anticipated, and Miss Lindley, in charge of the girls who had come from Tottenham, had been dismissed in the previous year.

39

FIRE FIGHTING

At the end of 1895, Knobel ordered a supply of hand grenades from Young and Martens of Stratford, London. These were not explosive devices for curbing an insurrection, but glass bottles for tossing onto fires to help extinguish them. At the beginning of the following year the local fire brigade made trials with an engine and found insufficient water supply from the mains for the use of a 1 in nozzle. With a $\frac{1}{2}$ in nozzle and 110 lb steam pressure, a jet could be thrown over the highest building, but the water supply was still insufficient and the hose burst in several places. The company formed its own fire brigade with a secondhand engine, bought for £210, but found it to be inadequate and obtained a new one.

In order to test the new brigade, Knobel crept into the factory unobserved one dark September evening at 8.30 pm and raised the fire alarm with the night watchman. The time at which the alarm was sounded and the times of arrival of the brigade members were all carefully recorded in Knobel's notebook:

> Matt and Riches appeared almost immediately. Grover, who lived at the Magdala cottages, arrived within 4 minutes and got out the engine and lit the fire under the boiler. Within the next 8 minutes, M. Poole, Tillet, Underwood and White arrived from the Institute and G. Poole, Pulfer, Murrell and Lindsell within the next 10 minutes. The last arrival was Willatt who took 26 minutes, as he lived further from the factory. Three men were known to be absent. 20 minutes after the signal, full steam was raised, two hoses totalling 350 ft, with $\frac{5}{8}$ in nozzles, were laid and water was playing full stream.

Knobel records that he was well satisfied with the test. He arranged for the brigade members to be paid a gratuity of £2 at the end of the first year of the brigade's existence.

The Urban District Council, the local fire brigade, and the police, however, were not so pleased and insisted that the works brigade captain should inform the police and the fire superintendent when drills were to take place. Knobel replied that the whole object would be lost if the fire captain was told, but agreed that the police should be informed on all occasions, the last being an unfortunate lapse.

George Eastman, seeking a manufacturing base for his company in England, approached Harman in November 1897 with the proposal that the two companies amalgamate, but Harman and the board rejected the offer.

The company can certainly not have felt any urge to amalgamate as 1897 was again a good year showing a net profit of £47 000, the same as the previous year. This result amounted to a return of almost 40 per cent on the invested capital, the best the firm has so far achieved in its hundred years of existence. A dividend of 27½ per cent was declared for the year. Howson proudly announced that all manufacturers had had a bad year with the exception of the Britannia Works. He had also heard that the Eastman Company of London were amalgamating with the Eastman Company of America to form a new company with a capital of £2 million and thought that the Britannia

Works should congratulate itself on their good fortune in not amalgamating with Eastman of London.

Shortly afterwards, Knobel managed to dissuade the Ilford District Council from applying to the Local Government Board for permission to erect a 'dust destructor' adjacent to the company's works on the ground of the harmful effects it might have upon the factory's products.

As a consequence of this event, the board agreed that Hughes should stand as a candidate in the forthcoming district council elections in order to look after the firm's interests. Harman consented to the proposal, provided he undertook to resign as councillor if council business interfered too much with factory business. Hughes was returned as member for the central ward and the firm agreed to pay his election expenses of £32 18s, on Harman's recommendation. This item of business was the last minute entered for the private company's last board meeting, since on 10 March 1898, at a special meeting of the board, Harman announced that negotiations had been going on for two months to convert the Britannia Works from a private to a public company.

Harman had had this idea before, soon after the formation of the private limited company in 1891, when he had entered into negotiations with a well-known financier, Osborne O'Hagan. At that time, Turquand Youngs & Co. had prepared a statement covering five years trading and Ashurst, Morris and Crisp, solicitors, had been instructed to register the new company and draw up the necessary documents. The plan collapsed, however, because O'Hagan had insisted that Harman assume managerial responsibility for the new company, whereas Harman's motive in going public was to be able to retire.

In the 1898 negotiations, Harman granted an option on his company to E. T. Hooley, another financier, who passed the option to a Birmingham stockbroker. A contract was prepared providing for a deposit of £40 000 on signature and O'Hagan again appeared as promoter.

All the directors and George Dinn, solicitor, were present at the special meeting. Harman announced that £382 000 was to be paid for the company including the reserve fund of £65 000. The new company would issue 380 000 £1 shares, half ordinary and half 6 per cent preference of which 120 000, half ordinary and half preference, would be used to purchase the company. Each existing shareholder would receive five £1 new shares for one old £5 share plus £11 per share in cash. Employees' shares were to be included in this arrangement and Harman pointed out that the new shares would be marketable and not locked up as previously. Interest at the rate of 5 per cent would be paid on the purchase money until the new company came into existence. Employees in the profit-sharing scheme would be paid at 20 per cent from 1 November 1897 until 31 October 1898.

Knobel was to remain as managing director, but Harman said the promoters insisted on a new board of directors 'of first-class City people' and although the services of Hughes and Howson would be retained they would not be directors. In the event, however, they both retained their seats on the board. Harman himself retired.

The purchase money was guaranteed by the City of London Contract Corporation Ltd and the Chicago Contract Corporation Ltd. A special resolution that: 'having regard for the Agreement for Sale of the Company's undertakings, the Company would be wound up voluntarily and that Alfred George Dinn of 1 Gresham Buildings, London E.C. 2, would be appointed liquidator' was put to an extraordinary general meeting of the shareholders at the Institute on 7 June 1898, and carried. The final meeting took place on 14 September 1898, when the old company ceased to exist and the new company, the Britannia Works Company (1898) Ltd came into being. Harman retired to Grayswood, although he served the company in a consultative capacity for a number of years. He realized about £200 000 in cash and 90 000 shares in the new company by the disposal of his shares in the old company.

Despite the upheaval, work in the factory continued and a decision was taken to strengthen the scientific staff. In April 1898, Edwin Banks was engaged as a chemist to assist Knobel; only the third chemist in 20 years. An Edwin Banks had written a series of articles in the *British Journal of Photography* in 1883 on photographic chemistry and processes, and an Edwin Banks had been employed by the Gem Dry Plate Co. of Willesden Green in the previous year. Whether these were the same man is not known, but it is probably so, as he was said to be a man of experience. He was paid £300 per annum. A letter written to Knobel by Harman on the occasion of Banks' engagement is of interest for the light it sheds on Harman's attitude to secrecy.

> With reference to Banks, I have seen nothing of him except his portrait in a group that Howson sent; that did not represent a strong man to my mind. He appeared to have an unhealthy corporation. At the same time he might be useful to us and if *you* are fully convinced of this you had better come to terms with him. I understood from Howson that he had been a teacher of chemistry at a college in the country. I did not know that he had been a photographer. If you engage him give him £300 per annum on an agreement which should clearly set forth that he gives us his whole time and that his researches are to be absolutely for our benefit without further payment. That all his notes belong to us and be written in plain English in books which are our property and are not to be taken away. *I strongly recommend* that he takes *no part whatever* in the work of the factory and that he is made to keep to his own room and not have access to the factory. I would if I were you at once start a new rule, that is to make all employed in the Laboratory Building pass in and out of the door in the wall opening onto the Terrace, the one close to the Laboratory, and give each a key and stop all of them crossing the yard. If you let Banks into the factory that will be the initial stage of trouble.

Three months later Frank Forster Renwick, who ultimately became an outstanding research director, was engaged.

5. Turbulent years (1898-1918)

The board of the new company, 'The Britannia Works (1898) Limited', met for the first time on 17 May 1898. It comprised four newcomers, all new to the manufacture of photographic materials, and three old hands, with a well-established record of success behind them.

The newcomers were: The Earl of Crawford (chairman), Major General G. F. Blake (deputy chairman), Charles J. Cox, and the Hon. Derek Keppel. The old hands were Messrs Knobel (managing director), Howson, and Hughes.

An early decision was that '1898' be dropped from the new title which thus reverted to the old form, 'The Britannia Works Company Limited'. The name was changed again after two more years. Since 1886, 'Ilford' had been used for the products and not the original 'Britannia'. In October 1900, Knobel suggested that the company take the name Ilford Limited. The Ilford Urban District Council at first objected to the proposal, but finally agreed, provided that 'Limited' was spelt in full with a comma between Ilford and Limited. The new name was adopted in 1901; the comma removed in 1951.

At the same time that the name of the company was changed to Ilford, Limited, a subsidiary company was formed to protect the name 'Britannia Works Company Limited' with the same directors as Ilford, Limited. The name Britannia Works Co. Ltd has been used ever since to conduct many subsidiary activities.

The new board soon decided to terminate Harman's profit-sharing scheme and, in November 1898, a new bonus scheme was announced. If the dividend on ordinary shares was 6 per cent or over, employees were entitled to a percentage, equal to one-half of the dividend, of their wages as bonus; for dividends of less than 6 per cent there was no bonus. Employees had to have six months continuous employment to qualify for the bonus, but no deduction was made for absence caused by sickness unless it exceeded a total of two months in one year. The bonus could be withdrawn for lack of interest, wastefulness, carelessness, negligence, or other sufficient reason. It was payable up to the date of leaving, if service was terminated satisfactorily by notice on either side, by illness, accident, or death.

The reasons given for not paying the bonus in individual cases are interesting and sometimes amusing: conspiring to strike, dismissal for indiscipline and hitting boys, bad timekeeping, playing cards and football during working hours, hiding in a bin and falling asleep, or leaving without giving notice.

However, by 1904, Knobel formed the opinion that the bonus scheme had failed in its objectives and suggested an alternative system of rewards for skill, devotion, and careful work. Under the new scheme, introduced in November 1904, all sub-managers, chemists, clerks, and other employees, were paid monthly a fixed five per cent of their wages, provided they had discharged their duties satisfactorily during the previous month. The bonus was paid only for time worked and not for holidays or for sickness longer than one week; it formed no part of the terms of engagement.

Lord Crawford resigned in May 1900 because of ill health and recommended Major General James Waterhouse as a new member of the board. He was elected in July. Major General Blake was made chairman and Charles Cox became deputy chairman.

Another director left in July of the same year. The board had resolved that Howson should make periodic promotional visits to the main towns in Britain; although he had done this many times before, on this occasion Howson refused. The board terminated his agreement as director. Howson resigned his employment with the firm, but offered to remain as commercial manager until a replacement was found. The board refused to agree and he left with one month's salary after twelve years' service. However, he was soon offered a post by Acworth of Imperial Dry Plate, whom he had known from the early days at Ilford.

This had unfortunate repercussions for George Grigs who was an accounts clerk and Howson's stepson. As Howson was with Imperial, the board decided to dismiss Grigs with two months' salary plus one month in lieu of notice. It was later discovered that a record of customers' names and particulars of the shipment of orders was missing. Grigs was suspected of taking it, but he denied having done so and offered to supply as much of the information as he could from memory. Knobel threatened to issue a writ if the record was not returned, but what happened thereafter has not been recorded. Howson was replaced as commercial manager by Henry Charles Zerffi in September at an annual salary of £500.

In February 1901, Derek Keppel, who was equerry to the Duke of Cornwall and York, applied for leave of absence for six months to accompany the Duke on a tour of the colonies. He promised that during the tour he would endeavour to further the interests of the company to his utmost. He resigned a year later because the pressure of his outside interests prevented him from attending board meetings.

At the time of Lord Crawford's resignation, Blake and Knobel had asked Harman to take over as chairman; he declined because of ill health. A second approach was made on Keppel's departure and this time Harman accepted a seat on the board, which he

held until February 1904 when ill health again intervened. During this period (1901–1904) Harman established a laboratory at Haslemere, with R. S. Potter as an assistant, for experimental emulsion research.

In December 1902, George Eastman of Kodak set in train an important series of events. He approached Knobel with a second offer of amalgamation of the two companies. Special meetings of the board were held, but no agreement was reached on how to proceed.

A circular was issued to shareholders on 18 May. It was signed by Harman, Hughes, Knobel, and Waterhouse (directors), and others and recommended acceptance of the scheme. Three days later Harman called a meeting of the major shareholders, a majority of whom voted to support the proposal.

The circular explained that Kodak had recently acquired two of the largest plate manufacturers in the United States and proposed to make dry plates in England. This, the circular said, would lead to

---

THE EARL OF CRAWFORD

James Ludovic Lindsay, 26th Earl of Crawford and 9th Earl of Balcarres, was born on 28 July 1847. He was a man of many interests. After Eton and Trinity College, Cambridge, he became very interested in astronomy and, like Knobel, became an astronomer of renown. Throughout his life, he founded or supported observatories. After observing the 1870 eclipse of the sun from Cadiz, he established, with the help of his father, the famous observatory at Dun Echt in Aberdeenshire. This became a well-known centre for astronomical research.

Lord Crawford lived at Dun Echt, taking part in its work, until he inherited his uncle's property at Balcarres. During this time, he built up a fine library of 11 000 volumes, including many ancient and rare works on astronomy and some important Latin manuscripts.

When he inherited the Balcarres estate, he thought of moving the observatory there. However, he heard that the small observatory on Carlton Hill, Edinburgh, was in danger of closing through lack of support and offered his books and instruments as the nucleus for a new Scottish observatory. Thus originated the Royal Observatory of Scotland on Blackford Hill, opened in 1896.

His interest in astronomy led him to a keen interest in photography. In 1872, he published a paper with G. Cowper Ranyard entitled *On Photographic Irradiation in Over-exposed Plates*. In this, he described the phenomenon of halation, caused by reflection of light from the rear surface of a glass plate, and demonstrated that it could be avoided by a light-absorbing backing layer. He was elected President of the Royal Astronomical Society in 1878 and 1879; a Fellow of the Royal Society in 1878; President of the Royal Photographic Society from 1896 to 1900; and President of the Royal Philatelic Society in 1910.

As James Lindsay he sat in the House of Commons as M.P. for Wigan from 1874 to 1880 and then, as Lord Wigan, in the House of Lords.

Although he sat on the Britannia Works board for only just over two years, he was clearly able to make a useful contribution because of his specialized knowledge. He left, owing to ill health, in 1900. He died in January 1913.

increased competition for Ilford, Limited and, as a consequence, increased expenditure by both companies and a reduced dividend for shareholders. On the other hand, a merger would benefit Ilford because of Kodak's facilities for worldwide distribution.

At the time, Kodak's share capital was $35 million (£7 million at the current exchange rate) of which $24 million had been issued. The profit for the second half of 1902 was $1.5 million and a 6 per cent dividend was paid on the preference and ten per cent on the ordinary shares. The comparable figures for Ilford, Limited for the whole of 1902 were; capital £380 000; profits £51 500; 6 per cent dividend on preference and 12½ per cent on ordinary shares.

Publication of this circular was closely followed by a statement issued by the anti-amalgamation directors, G. F. Blake (chairman) and C. J. Cox (deputy chairman), attacking both Harman's document and Kodak's offer. Perhaps more realistically, they talked of the *absorption* of Ilford, Limited by Kodak and not of amalgamation. They were not satisfied that the proposal would be to the advantage of the shareholders and maintained that it was impossible for the board to arrive at a decision in the absence of Kodak's detailed accounts and balance sheet for 1902 and without an expert opinion on the relative positions of the two companies.

Blake and Cox said that the Kodak offer was too low and dismissed Harman's fear of increased competition, suggesting that it was more likely that Kodak wished to absorb Ilford in order to eliminate competition and improve their own position. They insinuated that arrangements had been made for the transfer of the services of Knobel and Hughes, but said that they were ignorant of the terms of transfer. Finally, they regretted it had not been possible to submit both sides of the question simultaneously.

News of the proposal had been published by Kodak before the two documents appeared and it was immediately taken up by the press with headlines such as 'The Ilford-Kodak Raid' (*Investors Guardian*), 'Ilford's Climb Down' (*Daily Mail*), 'Hauling down the Colours' (*Pall Mall Gazette*). The articles without exception opposed the proposal and expressed outrage both at the takeover of British industry by American companies and at what they said was the unfairness of the Kodak offer. These items were followed by letters to the editors: 'To surrender at once . . . seems a weak and timid action' ('Broker', *Pall Mall Gazette*); 'If the present directors are so puerile as to wish to sacrifice a splendid business because an American company threatens to bully them, by all means let them resign and we will put in their place some Englishmen with

some backbone, which they appear to lack.' ('Sick of Americans', *Financial Times*.)

The next step was taken by H. T. Brice, H. E. Goodison, H. J. Philpot and W. D. Tupe, who wrote to shareholders calling for a committee to consider the matter; to oppose 'the present unjust and wholly inadequate offer by Eastman Kodak' and to obtain better terms.

Further circulars were issued to shareholders by both factions. Harman's group gave more details of the deliberations of the board on receiving the Kodak proposal. They said that counter-proposals had been put forward in January, but certain board members were unwilling to investigate the matter or to receive a motion entertaining the proposal on any terms. The group also said that the Chairman had declined to receive Mr Eastman or to hear the news which Eastman had communicated to Knobel. As a consequence of the deadlock, it had been decided to call a meeting of the principal shareholders; 90 per cent of those at this meeting favoured the exchange. On the other accusations, the question was asked whether those who had spent their lives conducting the business and who had conducted it successfully through many years, or those who spent an hour or two once a month sitting at a table, were best able to decide what was good for the trade. The group concluded by quoting an article in *The Statist* in favour of the merger and supported a call for an impartial committee to enquire into the matter.

In their circular, Blake and Cox claimed that they had received such strong support from the shareholders that they had approached the Harman group and asked them to drop their scheme, in the best interest of Ilford, Limited, but they had refused. It was therefore decided to call an extraordinary general meeting on June 25. The proposal before the meeting was: 'to consider the proposal for the exchange of shares made by the Eastman Kodak Company of New Jersey, USA, and if deemed desirable to appoint a committee to consider the same and report to a further meeting'. It was probably the most 'extraordinary' meeting the company ever held.

The chairman, G. F. Blake, opened by regretting that there was no longer unanimity among either the board or the shareholders. He had welcomed Harman's return to the board the previous year because of his large holding and interest in the company and his long experience of the business. He was not concerned:

to enquire whether his motive in joining us was for the express purpose of endeavouring to put through this proposal that he has advocated with the weight of his very large holding . . . It may be it was so or it may be that the proposal came upon him with the same surprise that it did upon me.

After praising Knobel for his untiring zeal and energy, his great capacity, his unquestioned ability, and high scientific attainments, the chairman said he found himself at a loss to understand how such a man could come to the decision he had. He could only conclude that the very zeal of the man had caused him to overwork and as a result he had lost his nerve and been over-intimidated by the bugbear of competition.

Knobel, in his turn, scolded the chairman for his covert remarks about Harman and himself and again accused him of not taking the Kodak proposals seriously. He hoped the meeting would set up a committee to resolve the matter, which the board had not. The excellence of Ilford products was due to himself and the staff at Ilford and not the board. Blake and Cox were not sufficiently familiar with the details of the business to be able to judge the best course of action.

Cox claimed that the matter had been fully discussed when first raised, but that it was impossible to reach a decision because of lack of information about the purchasing company. When the audited accounts did arrive three months later, he was not satisfied and had asked the auditors to report upon them, but they had not submitted their report so far.

Hughes said that he had worked for the company for 21 years and had a substantial holding in it, which he would not wish to risk. He denied the suggestion that he supported the proposal because he had received an inducement.

The debate rambled on, sometimes acrimoniously, but finally the motion was adopted that a committee of five shareholders be appointed . . .

to consider the existing circumstances of the Ilford company and to consider whether any proposal or suggestions that may be submitted to the committee are likely to prove of benefit to the Ilford company and its shareholders; . . .

The five elected were:

Henry T. Brice (stockbroker)
William Ashmole (auctioneer)
George A. Haslam
Arthur W. Dixon (Atlas Trust Company)
Mark Finch

The committee's report was completed by 12 August 1903. They concluded:

1. The offer was totally inadequate and that no offer should be considered which did not include an alternative of cash; furthermore as the company was American there would be little or no market for its shares in the United Kingdom.

2. It was desirable that the British manufacturers of photographic materials, cameras and lenses, and distributors should combine to meet outside competition.

3. There was no evidence to support the unjust and unworthy suggestions made against individuals and widely but unwisely published. However, one section of the board had pushed the proposal hastily without considering the many interests involved and the other had advanced trifling objections and declined serious discussions. The board as a whole exhibited a want of general business acumen. It had not moved with the times and introduced modern ideas and methods, particularly on the commercial side.

4. The Company had been offering discount rates too small in comparison with those of Eastman Kodak and of British manufacturers.

They recommended:

1. The business should be continued with stronger and more energetic management; to achieve this, changes in the personnel of the board were absolutely necessary.

   Major General Blake should retire as chairman and occupy an ordinary seat on the board. He should be replaced by somebody with a thorough practical knowledge of commercial affairs.

   C. J. Cox should be asked to resign because of his poor state of health.

   Major General Waterhouse should be asked to resign as his experience and lack of knowledge of trade and finance did not qualify him for the post of director.

   Thomas Hughes should be asked to resign since his double role as director and factory manager placed him at a disadvantage. His services as factory manager should be retained.

   The services of Knobel and Harman should be retained in view of the value of their scientific and manufacturing knowledge to the company.

2. Directors' fees were excessive in comparison with those of similar companies and should be reduced to £500 per annum for the chairman and £250 for other directors and that the post of deputy-chairman should be abolished. (Previously: chairman £700, deputy £500, directors £400).

3. The directors should be requested to take the necessary steps to enable shareholders to fill the vacancies occasioned by the suggested retirements.

The adjourned meeting was recalled to consider the committee's report on 25 September. The committee's recommendations were carried. The chairman suggested that the implementation of the resolutions should be left until the annual general meeting, due shortly (December).

Before the meeting, steps were taken to modify the

Figure 13   Major-General Sir Ivor Philipps, KCB, DSO, 1861–1940, was the second son of Rev. Sir James Philipps, vicar of Warminster, Wiltshire, and later a canon of Salisbury Cathedral. Sir James had a Victorian-sized family of six sons and five daughters. Felsted School, Essex, which offered reduced fees to the sons of clergymen, was chosen for Ivor. He entered the Army in 1883, through the Militia, and was promoted rapidly. His DSO was awarded after the relief of Peking in 1900. After leaving the Army in 1906, he became Liberal MP for Southampton.

Ivor Philipps had no practical experience of business and entered it by chance. Ashurst, Morris, and Crisp were for many years solicitors to Ilford, Limited. Philipps happened to meet John Crisp one day in

Articles of Association to bring them in line with the Companies Act 1900 and the shareholders' recommendations. Cox died in October and Hughes and Waterhouse resigned in, November. The board appointed James Kemp-Welch and Robert David Lewis to replace them.

Blake was absent from the annual general meeting, as he had decided not to stand for re-election; Knobel took the chair. Objections were raised at the appointment of two directors so soon before the meeting without reference to the shareholders. Eventually they were accepted by the meeting together with the two nominees put forward by the committee — William Ashmole and Alfred R. Smith.

Ashmole was an auctioneer and chairman of the Ilford Gas Works, Smith was a builder and director of the Costa Rica Railway, Lewis was a colliery air-pipe manufacturer of Bilston, and Kemp-Welch a gentleman of no occupation. The last was elected chairman at the first meeting of the board.

Knobel and Harman were the only remaining members of the old board and the only ones familiar with the business. It may be doubted whether the new board was stronger than the old. The business continued to decline for the next decade. Fortunately, when Harman retired, Lieutenant Colonel (later Sir) Ivor Philipps, who was to play a major part in shaping the company, was appointed in December 1905 and elected chairman in the following month. In the meantime, the company had another problem to deal with: pollution.

When Harman settled in Ilford in 1879, its population was about 7000 and the factory had green fields on all sides except to the north. By 1900 the population had grown to 20,000 and the factory was almost completely surrounded by houses heated by coal fires. Smoke from these fires, plus fumes from a gas works across the river, caused thick, winter fogs which spoiled or 'fogged' the plates in the factory drying rooms.

In April 1899, 25 000 whole-plates were ruined. To meet the difficulty, Knobel suggested building a new factory further out in the country. This suggestion was approved and eight acres of land on Great Warley Common, Brentwood, were purchased for £1700 in September 1901, although there was some opposition to the scheme by local inhabitants. Figures 14–16 show the development of this land.

Plans for the new factory included the boring of a well to deliver 3000 gal per hour, electricity generating plant and refrigeration plant for cooling the water used to set the emulsion on the plate coating machines. It was ready in June, 1904.

R. Field Dodgson was appointed factory manager and F. F. Renwick chief chemist. W. McLaren Smith, senior emulsion maker, was transferred, among others, from Ilford; they were paid allowances for expenses.

In 1903, it was realized that there were not enough houses at Warley to accommodate all the factory employees. Steps were taken to build cottages on the land to the rear of the factory and further land was purchased to enable a new road, christened Britannia Road, to be built for access. The houses were red brick, in two terraces, and let at 9s a week to employees.

From the start, trouble was experienced at Warley in making plates equal in quality to those made at Ilford. A letter written to Renwick by Knobel in November 1905 said:

with reference to your letter of yesterday about the Zenith plates I should like to point out that the Zenith

---

Throgmorton St., London and told him that the Ilford board was unsettled and the shareholders restive. Philipps agreed to take on the job of chairman, knowing that his army training had given him good organizing ability. He quickly restored order and, under his guidance, the company quickly prospered.

During the First World War, he became Parliamentary Secretary to the Ministry of Munitions under Lloyd George.

Four of the Philipps brothers became famous. Three of them were for many years the tallest MPs in the House of Commons: J. W. Philipps, MP for Pembrokeshire (later Lord St Davids) was 6 ft 3 in, Sir Ivor himself was 6 ft 4 in and O. C. Philipps, MP for Pembroke Boroughs (later Lord Kilsant) was 6 ft 7 in. The fourth brother became Lord Milford. One of the sisters, Elsbeth, married Marcus S. Dimsdale; their son, Wilfred H. Dimsdale was a director of Ilford, Limited for many years.

Sir Ivor built up a successful business by bringing together a large part of the very fragmented British photographic industry during the 34 years he was chairman. He was largely responsible for the decision that Ilford should produce films as well as plates and papers.

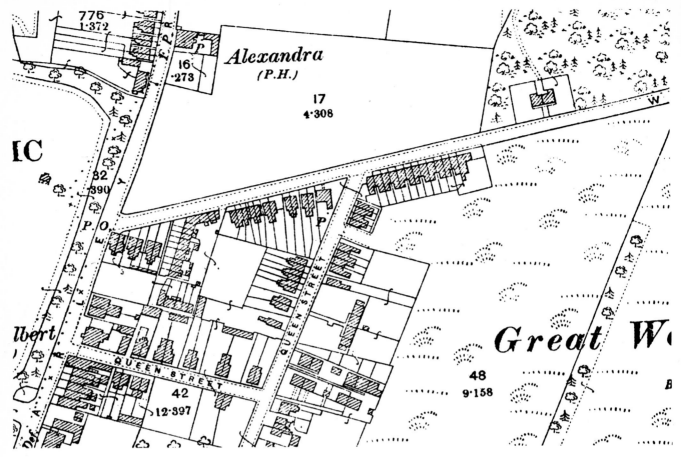

Figure 14   A map of the Warley area of Brentwood, Essex, in 1896.

plate is unfortunately not unique among our plates in the possession of the defects you mention; all our other plates showing the same faults . . .

By then, the demand for Ilford plates had declined and modifications to the drying rooms at Ilford had overcome the problems of atmospheric pollution. There was therefore less reason for the existence of the Warley factory.

In July 1907, the idea was mooted that collodion paper should be produced at Warley, but the motion was discarded when estimates showed it would prove uneconomic. Five months later, the factory manager was authorized to discharge such labour as he thought fit. The factory was finally closed in April 1910. The skilled personnel were moved back to Ilford, leaving a skeleton maintenance staff. Thus ended the first attempt, and a very costly one, to manufacture photographic materials at Warley, but it was not the only one, as will be seen later.

At Ilford, a process for purifying the air for plate-drying rooms was devised with the assistance of a consultant engineer. The air, in addition to being filtered, was washed with water and the water vapour

removed by refrigeration. It was then reheated before being blown into the drying rooms. This method operated satisfactorily in the plate factory from August 1902.

By 1905, the damage caused by the gas works fumes in the old paper factory was estimated to run into thousands of pounds and an air purification system was installed there, similar to that in the plate factory. At the same time, it was decided to use refrigerated water to chill the plates on the coating machines, as at Warley, thus saving £400 a year on ice. The machinery was supplied by the Haslam Foundry Co for £7500.

It became clear by 1908 that the Warley factory was no longer a viable proposition, and plans were drawn up to concentrate the plate and paper factories at Ilford.

Harman, in his later years, had always opposed the purchase of land unless it was needed immediately, but the new company had reversed this policy in 1898. Seven and a half acres of land had been purchased from Lord Salisbury for £5250, stretching from the factory to Ilford Lane in the east and down to the present Bengal Road in the south. After the new

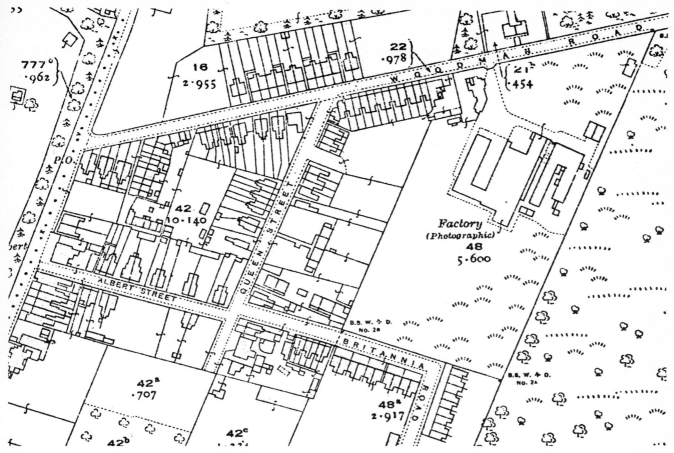

Figure 15   A map 24 years later, showing the first Warley factory of Ilford, Ltd.

Figure 16   The early Warley factory, viewed from Britannia Road, to the south. The building near the left of the picture, which was the main entrance, remained until 1975, together with many of the others visible.

factory at Warley had been started, most of this land was sold to a Stratford builder named George Sharpe for development. The present Uphall Road, along the line of the old Grove Terrace, was built by him in 1907. Sharpe gave his name to a market he erected just to the south of the factory; even after Ilford had built on it, many years later, the site was still generally referred to as 'Sharpe's market'.

Some of the land to the south of the old factory was repurchased from Sharpe in 1908 to build the new plate factory. At the same time, a new two-storey chemistry laboratory was built on the south side of the counting house in Roden Street, together with new studios over the carpenter's shop and a new glass store.

Three printing presses were ordered for the production of sensitized postcards and, a year later, a steam guillotine for cutting paper. The Munro Company were asked to look into the whole question of mechanization of the factory, which led to the installation of a hydraulic press for shredding emulsion prior to washing. An adequate supply of pure water was a constant preoccupation of the management; in 1911, the existing well was deepened by 30 ft and a new 7 in pump, fitted with an engine to drive it, was brought in.

More land was acquired in 1911. The Clyde, Grove, Magdala, Napier, and Salisbury cottages, and land and stables were purchased from Mrs Ashmole and two houses and land in Ilford High Road from William Ashmole, her husband, who was an Ilford director. At that time, Ilford owned all the land between the factory and Ilford Lane.

By 1912, the output of the extended Ilford factory exceeded the combined outputs of the Ilford and Warley factories six years earlier.

In addition to the new factories at Ilford and Warley, consideration had been given from time to time to the establishment of manufacture in other countries such as Germany (1899), Austria (1909), Hungary (1911), and Japan (1906). The first three projects were quickly abandoned, but much effort continued to be put into an attempt to establish a Japanese factory.

Japan had always been a very good market for Ilford products, but in 1906 this business was threatened by the imposition of a heavy duty on imported photographic products. Therefore, Knobel submitted a report to the board on the feasibility and desirability of establishing a factory in that country. The board accepted the report and decided that Knobel should visit Japan to examine the possibilities.

The board's view was that it would be best to form a separate subsidiary company, registered as Japan-

ese, with Ilford as a major shareholder, having a voting majority on the board and in overall control. Knobel was instructed to obtain estimates for plant before leaving England and, on arrival in Japan, to:

1. Negotiate with Japanese firms.
2. Examine and select factory sites.
3. Confer with architects and engineers and to obtain estimates for construction.
4. Obtain legal advice.
5. Consider questions of management and control.

He was then to report back to the board.

Knobel left for Japan on 10 August 1906, taking with him as assistant his son Harry Edward who had been trained as a mining engineer. Even before he left, Kuwada, one of the firms with whom Ilford had been negotiating, said they were not prepared to work with other Japanese houses. However, on arrival he persuaded Kuwada to work with Konishi and Asanuma, although Kuwada still thought that they and Ilford could succeed without other help. But Konishi objected to Kuwada and Asanuma being included, and all three objected to Ilford's request for three-fifths of the share capital.

On 24 October, Knobel cabled that the best arrangement was to form a Japanese company with Ilford representatives on the board; the Japanese involvement was to be £20 000 and Ilford's £30 000. The Japanese companies were each to take 17½ per cent of the profit and Ilford 47½ per cent, the extra 30 per cent being for goodwill and technical know-how.

The Ilford lawyers were very doubtful about the whole arrangement, but the matter was settled by the Japanese companies repudiating the agreement. Knobel was still hopeful of securing alternative sources of Japanese capital, but negotiations collapsed and he sailed for home on 1 November. The board later decided that 'it was not expedient to carry out the scheme'.

The decision was a disappointment for Knobel, but his time with the company was running out. In October 1902, he had signed a five-year contract accepting the position of managing director at £1800 per annum. On 1 October 1907 he wrote to the board; the contents of the letter were not recorded in the company's archives, but the effect was electric. A copy was sent to the firm's solicitors for an opinion and a reply was drafted and sent. Knobel's reply, dated 26 October, was obviously unsatisfactory and it was resolved to remove him from his position as managing director immediately and terminate his employment at six months' notice.

Fortunately, *The Statist* was not as reticent as the

board about what had occurred. That paper reported that in his first letter, Knobel had drawn attention to the fact that his contract was due to expire at the end of the month and at the same time had taken the opportunity to complain of the board's lack of cooperation and vigour in extending the business throughout the world, obviously having in mind the disagreement about the Japanese venture. The board denied these accusations and had asked Knobel for his resignation which he refused to give. It accordingly dismissed him.

Thus departed the last of the four directors of the old company and the board was left without anyone thoroughly familiar with the technical or of other aspects of the business, or anyone employed in a full-time, executive position.

The company profits had reached a maximum of £54 000 in 1901, but had rapidly declined after the Kodak offer of 1903 to £14 000 in 1907. The dividend had also been cut from 12½ to 4 per cent during the same period. The Kodak offer had assumed equality of value of the shares of the two companies. At that time Ilford £1 shares were worth about 35s; by 1907 they had dropped to 5s and the Kodak shares had risen to 50s.

Conventional excuses had been made for the decline of the business; bad weather, increased competition, and the higher discounts paid by the company after the 1903 committee's recommendations, but, as *The Statist* pointed out, these were hardly sufficient reasons. Other companies, Kodak in particular, had been increasing their business at Ilford's expense, implying a lack of enterprise on the part of the Ilford board.

This inadequacy was best illustrated by the board's ambivalent attitude towards the manufacture of roll films. In 1899, it was approached by the European Blair Camera Company, manufacturers of rollable and cinematograph films, with the proposal that the Britannia Works purchase their company. It was agreed to pay £2600 for the concern and to rent the premises for one year at £218 per annum provided that Knobel and Hughes were satisfied with the patents and plant. After their inspection, they concluded that the plant was not worth buying, although the patent for coating and drying film might be useful.

In 1900, they were offered the Goldberg films patent for making base for films for £6000 in cash or £1500 cash and the difference in royalties for Britain and the colonies only. The offer was declined. In 1902, Knobel was empowered to negotiate the purchase of plant for the production of roll films which had been offered to the company, but nothing resulted.

Eighteen months later, the purchase of B. J. Edwards' factory at Ealing, which had a roll-film-making machine, was considered and rejected. At the end of 1903, the whole question of the manufacture of rollable films was discussed and deferred.

The plunge into roll film was not taken until 1912 when two Germans, A. Trumm and P. Lehmann, were engaged to make film base and coat films at the empty Warley factory. A description of the proposed methods has not survived, but it can be guessed at from the new plant which was ordered. The proposal was to coat a thin layer of a solution of cellulose nitrate on the circumference of a large, rotating drum. When the solvents had evaporated the thin layer of celluloid was slit and rolled up. This film was coated by stretching it out on a long slab of glass and applying the emulsion from a hopper which ran along rails on both sides of the glass slab. As the original boilers and plant at Warley had been sold or transferred to Ilford when the factory was closed, it meant starting virtually from scratch.

The specialized equipment for making roll films was ordered from P. Soffge, Potschappel, Dresden, Germany. Cronin & Sons, a well-known Brentwood building firm, was engaged to make alterations to the factory. Sixty sleepers from the Great Eastern Railway were among the items ordered, presumably to carry the rails along which the emulsion hopper ran.

Two years later, in April 1914, Trumm submitted roll films to Agnew for tests. He had hoped that films would be ready for sale in May, but they were not available even at the end of June.

When the First World War started in August 1914, Trumm and Lehmann were listed as undesirable aliens and asked to leave Brentwood, as it was a proscribed area. They gave up their houses, stored their furniture, and sent their wives and families back to Germany. Ilford, Limited paid the costs of moving the furniture from Warley to Ilford and of storing it, and granted Trumm £10 and Lehmann £5 towards the cost of sending their families home. It was also resolved that their salaries should be paid, even if they were interned. As far as is known, the factory continued to produce films until at least April 1915, because applications for the post of film expert at Warley were then being considered, which suggests that Trumm and Lehmann had left. The last that is recorded of Trumm is an application for arrears of salary and commission in November 1916. The application was rejected.

In the spring of 1916 the Warley factory was requisitioned by the Southern Army Signals Company at a rental of £5 per week. The plant was sold for £7000 later in the year and the boiler and other machinery for £1100 at the beginning of 1918. Thus ended the second Warley venture.

The factory was released by the Army in October 1918, but two months later a request was received from No. 4 Quartering Committee to allow the factory to be reoccupied, accompanied by an appeal for 'amicable possession to obviate the necessity of imposing competent military authority powers'. The factory was not finally vacated until June 1920 and steps were then taken to re-establish film production.

When the First World War broke out, it was anticipated that Ilford, Limited business would collapse due to reduced home demand and the difficulties of obtaining raw materials and exporting. A notice was issued to employees warning that it might be necessary to work half-time, but only if it was unavoidable, and that everything would be done to prevent suffering and loss by the employees. Nevertheless, 41 boys were discharged in September with one week's pay in lieu of notice and two weeks' half-pay for six months' service or four weeks' half-pay for over six months' service. All those employees wishing to join the armed services were assured that their jobs would be available to them at the end of the war. The company also formed a relief committee to look after the wives, children, and dependents of serving men.

Henry Charles Zerffi died, aged 63, in January 1915 and F. J. Jenks was appointed general manager in his place at £700 per annum. He was also made a director, without fees until the annual general meeting, and resigned his post of secretary, which was taken by B. L. Drake.

Ivor Philipps, who had been granted leave to take his command at the beginning of the war, and rose to the rank of Major General in 1915, resigned as managing director in the same year, but retained his position as chairman. Jenks was appointed managing director in his place at £1000 per annum in November 1915.

Payment of rewards to employees ceased from 1 December 1914 on the grounds of the heavy losses due to the war, increased prices of raw materials, and the reduction in the hours of work while full wages were still being paid. But with war came inflation, and, after an appeal from a deputation of workers, a war bonus was introduced in 1915. The board agreed to pay a bonus of 3s per week to men and 1s per week to boys for the duration of the war. Salaried clerks earning less than £200 per annum also received 3s per week.

Twelve months later a deputation of girls appealed

for two days' holiday in place of the Whit Monday and August Bank Holidays, suspended because of the war, and a bonus of 2s 6d per week. The men supported them for an increased bonus. As the amount of work in hand prevented the granting of holidays, two days' full pay was given instead and the bonus was increased to 5s per week per man and 2s 6d per week for girls and boys.

Further increases in the bonuses were made in April and December 1917 and again in January and July 1918, by which time men were receiving 20s per week, women 7s 6d, boys 7s 6d and girls 6s.

In October 1918, the National Union of General Workers intervened and negotiated a bonus of 20s per week plus $12\frac{1}{2}$ per cent on total earnings for men over 18 and $12\frac{1}{2}$ per cent on wages plus 10s per week for boys under 18. Under union pressure girls under 16 were given 2s 6d extra and between 16 to 18 1s 6d extra four months later.

The staff did not receive a bonus until October 1918, when a 20 per cent bonus was granted, backdated to November of the previous year.

At the beginning of the war, the supply of sensitizing dyes, which came from Germany, was cut off, so Professor Pope at Cambridge University was engaged in 1916 to devise methods for synthesizing suitable dyes. For this work he was given an initial grant of £500 plus a retainer of £100 per annum later increased to £250 per annum. Two years later an assistant, J. E. G. Harris, was employed by Pope to make the dyes, also for £250 per annum. The culmination of this work was the manufacture of Pinaverdol and Pinacyanol dyes, which were used to sensitize Ilford plates and which were also sold under the names of 'Sensitol Green' and 'Sensitol Red'.

The British Photographic Manufacturers Association, originally formed in 1897 but re-established in 1916, suggested the formation of the British Photographic Research Association. Ilford, Limited applied for membership in 1918 and Renwick was appointed the firm's representative. The company agreed to 100 guineas per annum for a period of five years towards its running costs; this payment was increased to 200 guineas for three years in 1920.

The pessimism expressed at the outbreak of the war was, in the circumstances, not justified, since there was new and increased demand for photographic materials, in particular for plates for radiography and aerial photography. Business was also given a boost by a suggestion of Kodak's in 1915: soldiers serving abroad were to be supplied with snapshots of wives and families. This scheme operated through the YMCA who organized amateur photographers, through professional dealers, to take pictures. Members of the photographic industry paid for the advertising costs; Ilford, Limited contributed £450 over a period of two years.

The profits of the company which had slowly declined from their peak of £54 000 in 1901 to their nadir of £14 000 in 1907, climbed to £33 000 in 1913, dropped sharply to £23 000 in 1914, reached £48 000 in 1916, and at the end of the war in November 1918 stood at £35 000.

6. Amalgamation and consolidation (1918-1939)

Acquisitions

As the First World War drew to a close, the company began to consider the possibilities of uniting the major British manufacturers. It first approached the Imperial Dry Plate Company which had acquired the Gem Dry Plate Company in 1912. J. J. Acworth, Imperial's founder and managing director, had just retired and it was felt to be the right time to make an approach.

The company's first two proposals were rejected, but, finally, a company was formed called the British Photographic Plates and Papers Limited (BPPP) to hold all Imperial and Gem shares, with Ilford directors on the board and B. L. Drake as secretary. Ilford and Imperial would maintain their individualities and independence in finance and manufacture, but would 'indulge in friendly mutual working'. This scheme was in operation until 1928, the two firms leading an almost independent existence apart from liaison at board level. After eight years, liaison committees were formed to coordinate work in different departments.

By 1924, Ilford had purchased 85 000 ten per cent preference shares in BPPP and from time to time lent Imperial and Gem substantial sums of money.

While negotiations with Imperial were in progress, Jenks suggested amalgamation with Illingworth and Austin Edwards. An approach was made to Illingworth. Thomas Illingworth was prepared to sell the ordinary shares for £250 000 (less commission due to Illingworth himself of £10 000), £100 000 in cash, the balance in the form of £120 000 of Ilford ordinary shares at 25s each. Ilford increased its capital to £500 000 by the issue of 120 000 £1 ordinary shares and concluded an agreement in December 1919. Developers Limited was formed to hold the Illingworth shares. Ilford applied for 200 000 £1 shares in Developers in January 1920 and, at the same time, lent them £50 000 at 6 per cent. Thomas Midgley Illingworth, Thomas's son, joined the Ilford board that year.

Ten months later Thomas Illingworth was asked to forego his right to a director's commission of £11 500 for 1919 because of the small amount of working capital of the Illingworth company and because of a continuing requirement to pay Excess Profits Duty (£8600 in 1920). Illingworth agreed.

To assist the Illingworth company, Ilford advanced loans of the order of £10 000 from time to time at interest rates which varied between 6 to 10 per cent. In April 1922, it was agreed that Illingworth should increase their capital by the issue of £1 six per cent preference shares and pay off their loans from Ilford. By 1928, Ilford had purchased 27 000 of these shares, but still found it necessary to lend money to Illingworth.

In September 1921, Ilford agreed to supply plates to Illingworth, to be sold under the latter's own label, at a 50 per cent plus 5 per cent discount. Previously, Illingworth had made papers, never plates. Two months later, copies of the formulae for Ilford Bromide and Gaslight papers were handed to Illingworth.

Another postwar venture, was a company to manufacture film, jointly owned by an association of plate manufacturers, Ilford, Imperial, Gem, and Amalgamated Photographic Manufacturers (APM); of these, only APM was independent of Ilford control. The new company, called Selo Limited, came into existence at the beginning of 1920 and was based at the old Warley factory. Ilford advanced £1000, later increased to £10 000 to the new company.

The Warley factory was let to Selo, from 1 July 1920 at £1000 per annum with an option to purchase for £17 000 after five years. The option was taken up in June 1922; Ilford received 17 500 £1 ten per cent preference shares in Selo of which 8750 were sold at par to APM, 3500 to Imperial, and 1750 to Gem.

The next few years saw some complex financial exchanges. During 1923, Ilford financed Selo by loans and by the purchase of 5 per cent debentures. In May of that year Illingworth joined the association and Gem transferred 875 ten per cent Selo preference shares to Illingworth. Six months before, Illingworth had purchased 10 000 Selo £1 ordinary shares with money borrowed from Ilford at 10 per cent interest.

In February 1924, APM decided to withdraw from the association and offered 25 000 £1 Selo ordinary

Figure 17   T. Midgley Illingworth, 1892–1961, joined the board of Ilford in 1920, when his father's company was taken over by Ilford, Limited. He later became a joint managing director, retiring in 1957.

Figure 18   The Illingworth factory quality control office, Park Royal, Middlesex, in 1920, just after the merger with Ilford.

shares and £7000 debentures to Ilford. Ilford bought 10 000 ordinary shares at £1 2s 5d each and £2800 debentures at par. The rest were purchased by the other companies, with money lent by Ilford at 5 per cent, redeemable at three months' notice against the shares as security. APM were paid £3000 as interest, since to that date they had had no return on their money.

The debentures were repaid in June 1924 with Selo ordinary shares. At this date, Ilford held 23 400 Selo shares, in addition to its own, as security for £21 000 lent to Gem, Illingworth, and Imperial. Two years later Selo increased its capital to £200 000 by the issue of 100 000 £1 ordinary shares.

During these financial exchanges, the main advantage of amalgamation—the opportunity to rationalize production between the various factories—was not taken. With the exception of Selo, the companies continued to enjoy a separate existence. The Ilford board had passed a resolution in favour of mutual cooperation, but the traditional

secrecy of the industry made this difficult to realize at that time.

In July 1927, a committee was formed to try to improve matters. It comprised:

F. F. Renwick (research director, Ilford)
T. Thorne-Baker (chemist, Imperial)
B. V. Storr (chemist, Ilford)
H. T. Gaseltine (works manager and engineer, Imperial)
W. C. Shepherd (works manager, Ilford)
W. Mann (works manager and chemist, Illingworth)
W. H. Smith (engineer, Selo)
H. W. Horton (engineer, Ilford)

Only two of the committee's recommendations were adopted. One recommended the exchange of confidential information between laboratory heads, works managers, and chief engineers of the associated companies. The other recommended the establishment of a department at Selo for testing their

Figure 19   A group of senior Ilford employees in 1922. Left to right: back row: A. Agnew, W. C. Shepherd, B. V. Storr, O. Bloch; front row: ?, W. J. Glasscock, F. J. Jenks, B. L. Drake, H. W. Horton.

products; previously the tests were done by the associated companies.

To carry out the first resolution, a number of standing committees was set up to cover various aspects of the companies' activities.

They were:

Research (monthly)
Ilford: Renwick, Storr, W. C. Shepherd, Agnew (testing) and Bloch (chemist)
Imperial: Thorne-Baker and Gaseltine
Illingworth: Mann
Selo: G. S. Whitfield, P. Whitfield, Davidson and F. Shepherd
Laboratory Heads (quarterly)
Renwick, Storr, Thorne-Baker, and Mann
Marketing and Advertising (quarterly)
Glasscock, Kraushaar, Withers, and Fuller
Interchange of Products (quarterly)
Renwick, Storr, Thorne-Baker, Mann, W. C. Shepherd, and Gaseltine

Evatt chaired all the committees and an advisory committee comprising: Mein, Jenks, Hill, Illingworth, Whitfield, Renwick, and Drake. This committee's function was to advise the boards of the associated companies of the action to be taken arising from the various committees' recommendations.

In September 1927, Drake was instructed to carry out an evaluation of the Imperial and Gem companies. He assessed the fixed and floating assets of Imperial at £162 000 and of Gem at £50 000 but considered that the true value was probably nearer £266 000. The goodwill, based on three years' purchase of average profits over seven years, came to £101 000, but as the profits for 1921 to 1923 were abnormally high, he settled for a value of £59 000, making a total of £325 000.

Imperial and Gem between them owned a large number of Selo shares and nearly 34 000 Ilford shares. The authorized issued share capital of Imperial was 500 000 £1 shares, of which 400 000 were only 10 per cent paid, and of Gem was 100 000 £1 shares, of which

60 000 were only 20 per cent paid, giving a paid up value of £192 000.

Ivor Philipps believed it would be possible to purchase the whole for £100 000 in cash and 150 000 Ilford shares. An announcement was made in October 1927, that 'the opportunity had occurred to acquire two valuable photographic manufacturers'. Ilford's share capital was increased by 160 000 £1 ordinary shares to enable the project to be carried out and BPPP sold to Ilford the entire issued share capital of Imperial and Gem in December 1927 at the price suggested by Philipps. In the following year Ilford lent Imperial nearly £60 000.

In July 1928, negotiations were opened with APM to purchase the Watford (Paget), Mobberley (Rajar) and Southgate (APM) factories. A new company, Apem Limited, was formed for this purpose with a capital of £200 000. Ilford bought 150 000 of these £1 shares at par in October 1928 and the stock of goods for £60 000.

During 1929, Ilford lent Apem £136 000 and purchased the remaining 50 000 shares, by transfer from the loan account. Marion and Company Limited, and Rajar Limited, were re-registered.

All Apem's formulae were handed to Renwick and, after inspection by Illingworth, Mann, and Bishop, Apem was advised to spend £16 000 on improving the Rajar factory at Mobberley.

The last of the major British photographic manufacturers to be acquired was Wellington and Ward Limited. Negotiations began in November 1929 and BPPP obtained a controlling interest in Wellington and Ward by purchasing 136 713 shares (out of a total of 141 795) for £189 997 two months later. These were sold to Ilford by BPPP in March 1930 at the price they had paid plus expenses.

To meet this expense and other commitments, Ilford's share capital was increased from £800 000 to £1.4 million by the issue of 500 000 six and a half per cent cumulative 'A' preference shares at £1 each.

A valuation of the assets of Ilford and its subsidiaries was made at the same time and is shown in Table 5.

Assets	Ilford	Subsidiary companies
Land and buildings	£72 251	£365 145
Plant and machinery	40 544	236 827
Stock, debtors, cash and investments	374 130	611 262
	486 925	1 213 234
GRAND TOTAL		£1 700 159

Table 5

After deducting liabilities and the share of assets owned by outside interests, the total assets amounted to £1 359 769.

The subsidiaries then owned either directly or indirectly by Ilford were:

Imperial Dry Plate
Thomas Illingworth
Selo
Apem (which included Marion, Paget, and Rajar)
Wellington and Ward
Gem Dry Plate
Fluorescent Materials

Selo Limited

The first meeting of the management committee of Selo Ltd was held on 10 June 1920. Those present were G. S. Whitfield (Paget), C. F. S. Rothwell (Rajar) J. Hill (Imperial). C. R. Finch (Paget) acted as secretary and H. W. Horton (Ilford) attended as consulting engineer. G. M. Bishop (Marion), F. J. Jenks, Ivor Phillips and F. W. Evatt (all Ilford) attended later meetings.

The committee had to start from scratch; all the plant of the Warley factory had been sold, transferred to Ilford, or scrapped. All that remained were the land and the buildings, which had suffered during wartime occupation by the Army.

The first step taken was to order the power plant. A 30 ft × 8 ft boiler for 120 lb/in² steam pressure was ordered from Thompsons for £2153: it was installed and working by the end of the year. To provide electricity at 220 V d.c. a 125 hp Bellis and Morcom steam generator set was purchased at £1050 with two 50 kW generators in tandem which could either be used separately or in parallel. In addition, a 30 kW gas-driven standby generator and a small petrol-electric generator for temporary lighting were acquired. These were on site and working by early 1921.

Two old festoon paper-coating machines were transferred from the Rajar factory at Mobberley in November 1920; new parts to adapt them for film coating were designed by Whitfield and Horton and made at Ilford. These machines were installed in suitable rooms in the old factory. At the same time, plans were made for two new coating rooms. The length of the rooms was restricted to 330 ft in order to leave a roadway between the end of the building and Britannia Road at the rear of the works. The designers were obviously not too concerned about dust, as the interior walls were cement rendered, and air-washing plant, such as that used at Ilford, was rejected in favour of gauze filters.

The two new machines were constructed mainly by Dixon and Company and were of festoon type, designed to coat film 41 in wide at 20 ft/min. The film was conveyed through the drying chamber draped over poles 2 ft apart, in loops of 12 ft. When the chamber was full there were roughly 300 poles and about 3500 ft of film in it. As the drying chamber was only 300 ft long, the track was bent back on itself at the far end by means of a turntable; 560 lb of water were removed by 14 000 ft³ of air per minute, heated to 90 °F.

As the work of re-equipping the Warley factory proceeded, experimental work on the production of film was started in September 1920 at the Paget works at Watford. Samples of film base were obtained from Guiterman and black duplex paper, for interleaving with the film on spools, from Schoeller and from Guiterman. Both Temple and Son and Kershaw of Leeds supplied specimen spools with both metal and wooden cores. Within six months, Whitfield was able to produce specimen roll films and, by December 1921, Whitfield and Rothwell produced film which, it was agreed, was as good as that of the competitors. The associated companies were invited to make emulsions to be used in further tests; any material suitable for roll films was to be sold by Rajar.

Each company was asked to state its requirements for roll films and to design labels for sealing the spools. The initial monthly output was estimated to be worth £10 000 gross. Spools for the various firms were sealed with the firm's label and then packed in shallow trays and sent to the appropriate factory to be inserted into individually-designed cartons. The films were supplied to subscribing companies at half the retail price and sold under the names of Ilford, Imperial, Gem, Apem, Paget, and Rajar.

The whole operation had taken less than two years despite difficulties in obtaining carpenters and cement in the initial stages and the lack of coal for two months in the middle of 1921 due to a miners' strike.

One of the earliest Selo employees was Savill, who had been the factory caretaker during the First World War. He was engaged as assistant engineer at £3 10s per week in October 1921. Many of the other workers at this time had been lent by the associated companies. Nelson, of Paget, came to supervise the first experimental coatings, but he could not be spared and was replaced by A. N. Creighton, also of Paget, in February 1922. He was paid £5 per week. H. H. Chapman was engaged as emulsion maker and Mrs. Chapman (no relation) as forewoman. The first chemist at Selo was T. Turner who received £25 per

month. At about the same time G. S. Whitfield was appointed resident managing director and general manager and W. H. Smith, works manager. C. R. Finch became assistant works manager and H. J. Grayson joined the firm as an emulsion chemist, responsible to Whitfield, in May 1923.

The works manager, William Henry Smith was a remarkable man. Born in 1862, he left school at 12 for a job with Joynson's Paper Mills, a five mile walk from home. Three years later he joined William Willis, a wealthy chemist who had perfected the Platinotype process, as a laboratory assistant. In 1879 at 17, he was sent to France to promote the Platinotype process for Poulenc, the French agent. The French company failed a year later. After trying other jobs in France he returned home in 1882, assisted by the British Consul, when he was still only 20 years old.

On his return he secured work with the Humber Cycle Company in London making gear wheels for cyclometers. A few years later, he accidentally met Willis again who invited him to rejoin Platinotype as manager to set up a factory and mechanize the process. There he devised a system of universal machine fittings, a kind of large-scale Meccano for constructing experimental machines, and he later used this system at Warley for constructing coating machines. In 1916 he designed a miniature camera which used 35 mm film, with a frame size of $1\frac{1}{2}$ in × 1 in and an interlocking frame advance and shutter mechanism to prevent double exposure. This is now in the Science Museum, London.

After the war, he accepted a proposal from Imperial to set up a POP factory at Grenoble, France. The coating machine he constructed used his universal fittings and metric ball races. The project, however, was unsuccessful and the machine was returned to England to be stored at the Imperial factory. Smith was then employed by Imperial as a technical promoter of X-ray materials for radiography. After his appointment as manager at Selo the French coating machine was transferred from Imperial to Warley and parts of it were used to improve the existing machines.

In 1923, Smith designed and constructed the first spider coating machine. Instead of the film being draped on poles to dry, it was led around rollers arranged in an open spiral. The film could be reeled up at the centre of the spiral when dry. In its construction, Smith used his universal parts system taken from the old Grenoble machine; this is why from the beginning Selo film coating machines used metric bearings. This machine proved very successful and a full-scale model was made for coating 21 in wide film (no. 3 machine) with a spiral capable of holding 600 ft

Figure 20   Frank Forster Renwick, 1877–1943, was a brilliant chemist. Born in Mile End, London, he attended the City of London School and later studied at the Central Technical College, South Kensington, where he worked with H. E. Armstrong, F. S. Kipping, and W. J. Pope. His friendship with Pope proved valuable later when the Pope carried out pioneer work on sensitizing dyes at Cambridge University during the First World War. Renwick joined Ilford in 1898; he concentrated on the scientific testing of photographic materials. A densitometer he designed was made by Adam Hilger and exhibited in London in 1906. In 1919, he was active in the formation of the Scientific and Technical Group of the Royal Photographic Society; in 1921, he helped the Group establish Photographic Abstracts, *with B. V. Storr as its first editor.*

He moved to Du Pont-Pathé Film Manufacturing Corporation, USA, in 1922 and served there as research and development director until 1925, when he returned to Ilford. He became research director in 1930. Renwick received the Royal Photographic Society Progress Medal in 1921 and was elected president of the society in 1927–29.

of film. The machine was completed in 1924 and had a coating speed of 15 ft/min. A second spider machine was completed soon after and used for coating double-sided X-ray film in 1926 at 5 ft/min. A third was completed probably during 1928. Both of these machines coated double-width film (40 in).

Despite the success of the spider machines, two more festoon machines were built between 1925 and 1933. Thereafter, all the new coating machines were of the spider type. H. W. Horton retired in 1934 and G. H. Farrington replaced him as chief engineer. Farrington was responsible for the larger and improved spider machines and for the introduction of pneumatic controls: no. 7 machine was completed before the Second World War and no. 8 in 1941.

As soon as the problems associated with roll films had been solved, attention was turned to the production of cine film. A 35 mm cine film slitting machine was obtained from Dixon in 1922 and a Williamson-type perforator from Cinechrome Instruments. Film was imported from the American Celluloid Company through Guiterman. The first cine film was ready for the market in 1923. As business increased, five Bell & Howell perforators were obtained during 1924; they were more accurate than the Cinechrome machine.

The first double-sided X-ray film was produced in 1923. This consisted of film coated on both sides with emulsion so that it could be used sandwiched between a pair of fluorescent screens, thus increasing the speed and reducing the exposure of the patient to X-rays.

At about this time L. H. Davidson was transferred from Imperial to Selo to become chief chemist. When Smith retired, in about 1931, L. H. Davidson was made manager and G. Hudson assistant manager. Smith and Whitfield, who had also retired, were allowed the use of a room at the factory to experiment in colour photography.

Ilford, Limited

Meanwhile, at Ilford, the parent company continued to expand. In 1922, a property known as 'Rodenside', in a lane south of Roden Street, between the factory and Ilford Lane, was acquired for £2000. Two years later, the company bought the Loxford Social Club in Roden Street adjacent to 'Rodenside'.

When Renwick returned from the United States in 1925, he was made head of research, without a seat on the board. He was given temporary accommodation in 'Rodenside' to direct basic research into the photographic process. Rodenside was demolished in 1927 and a new laboratory built on the site. Although still under Renwick's control, the laboratory was leased to BPPP, a holding company for Imperial.

The Loxford Club was demolished and a new office block costing £10 000 was erected in 1928 (Figure 21). The Ilford laboratory had been extended in 1919 and again in 1925. During this period it was equipped with its own plate-coating machine and drying room for experimental work. When the new offices were complete, it expanded into the old 1895 offices, adjacent to the laboratory building.

When the British Photographic Research Association was dissolved in 1930 for lack of support, Dr G. B. Harrison, Dr S. O. Rawling, J. Mitchell, and C. S. Hall joined Ilford. Harrison took charge of the Rodenside laboratory; the other three became assistants to Olaf Bloch, chief chemist of the expanded Ilford Laboratory.

In the period of expansion which followed the First World War, Ilford, having in the past relied on wholesale dealers to handle their products, for the first time employed its own sales representatives—M. H. Stark and A. Webb who were appointed in 1923.

X-ray films became freely available in 1926, so in 1927 A. Sefton Wilson was engaged as X-ray representative, followed a year later by H. Abbot. W. Marshall, who was employed as representative for Scotland at the same time, became an X-ray man in 1936. Bruno Wittegrefe, taken on as continental X-ray representative in 1933, became a well-known figure at X-ray sales meeting. By 1936 there were 17 representatives; by 1938 at least 35.

The rapid expansion of the 1920s was halted by the world slump of the following decade. Profits, which had climbed from £44 000, with an 8 per cent dividend, in 1920 to £133 000, with a 15 per cent dividend, in 1930, declined to £95 000 and a 6 per cent dividend by 1933.

This decline produced a decision to tackle a problem which had hitherto been shirked—rationalization of the structure of the parent company and its associates. The first step, taken in 1930, was to centralize the sales departments. Plans were drawn up to build a central sales office at Ilford for £40 000, but as an interim measure part of the Ilford Skating Rink was rented for £800 per annum.

The Apem sales staff were transferred to Ilford and space thus freed at Watford was occupied by a central advertising department under G. A. Peck (Apem). The European export sales departments were concentrated at the country house in Elstree which had served Wellington and Ward as offices, under C. S. Downing, a director of that company. Half the European markets were given to W. S. Withers (Imperial) with H. S. Clark (Illingworth) as an

Figure 21   Head offices, Ilford, built in 1928 on the site previously occupied by the Loxford Club.

assistant and the other half to A. J. Catford (Wellington and Ward) with L. Verhulsen (Apem), and T. K. Bower (Ilford). The overseas markets outside Europe were under W. J. Glasscock of Ilford and the home sales under H. J. Kraushaar of Illingworth. Later in the same year C. S. Downing resigned and A. J. Catford became the head of export sales.

The idea of a new sales office was abandoned in 1931 and the new despatch building was converted to offices, fronted by a lawn and gardens. No bonus was paid to the staff in that year and this garden was always referred to as 'Bonus Garden' on the assumption that the money spent on it might have provided a bonus payment. The various sales divisions, home and export, were installed in the new offices by the end of the year.

Another decision was that all roll films should be sold under the name 'Selo' and that different company names for plates and papers should be phased out and the name Ilford used instead.

The Southgate (Apem) and Edgware (Wellington and Ward) factories were put up for sale in 1931 but proved difficult to dispose of: Southgate was finally sold in 1934 for £7250 and Edgware in 1937 for £9500. The Imperial factory was closed in 1933 and sold for £6000 in 1937, except that part of it which was occupied by the central specimens department under K. Gaseltine, the son of H. T. Gaseltine, factory manager of Imperial. This department was formed in 1930 to prepare prints and enlargements for display and advertising purposes.

The Elstree factory was closed in 1934 and compensation paid to redundant staff: three to ten years' service, two weeks' wages; ten to twelve years', four weeks' wages, and over twelve years', £1 per year of service. This factory was later sold to Dufay-Chromex.

Selo, Developers, Gem, and Fluorescent Materials went into voluntary liquidation in 1932, Illingworth in 1933, and BPPP in 1934. Selo, Developers, Gem, and Fluorescent Materials were reformed with a nominal capital of £100 and BPPP with £100 000.

This left the company with five main factories, Ilford (plates), Selo (films), and Park Royal, Watford, and Mobberley (paper). In principle, it was decided that paper coating should be concentrated at Mobberley, but it was not for some years that this

Figure 22   Olaf Frederick Bloch, 1872–1944, was an unusual personality: a chemist, a wit, a practical joker and an exponent of publicity in science. After attending Finsbury Technical College and Birkbeck Scientific and Literary Institute, he became a research assistant at the Royal Institution, London. He joined Ilford in 1910, working under Renwick on emulsion chemistry and dye sensitization; he became chief chemist in 1931. Bloch was associated particularly with the development of special plates of value in scientific work: 'Q' plates, for F. W. Aston's mass spectrometer; the first nuclear plates, R1 and R2; plates for astronomy; and infra-red sensitive plates.

Not content with normal activities in middle age, he took up mountaineering at the age of 51, surviving a slide of several hundred feet in the Pyrénées when escaping from the Spanish Civil War in 1936. For his services to science, he was made an Hon. LLD of Aberdeen University and awarded the Royal Photographic Society's Progress Medal.

was achieved. In the meantime, expenditure at Watford and Park Royal on paper coating was restricted, Watford concentrating more and more on the manufacture of X-ray screens and chemical packing and Park Royal on paper finishing and packing. The Cassio Photographic Paper Company Limited, acquired through Wellington and Ward, was solely concerned with the coating of paper with baryta in preparation for emulsion coating.

The administrative organization was overhauled. Committees set up in 1927 were abolished three years later and replaced by three 'boards': executive, sales, and production. The first was concerned with all company matters, the sanctioning of expenditure, and the recommendations of the other two. It comprised Blundell Mein (chairman), V. B. Ramsden (vice chairman), F. F. Renwick, T. M. Illingworth, and B. L. Drake. The sales board supervised all sales and marketing and was made up of Illingworth (chairman), G. M. Bishop (vice chairman), Ramsden, C. S. Downing, W. Glasscock, and J. Hill. The production board covered manufacture, research, and development and consisted of Renwick (chairman), Ramsden (vice chairman), W. C. Shepherd, W. C. Mann, B. V. Storr, and A. J. Child. Philipps (president) and Evatt (vice president) were *ex officio* members of all the boards.

In 1931, a fourth board was set up to monitor financial, legal, and domestic affairs and relieve pressure on the executive board. Its members were Philipps, Evatt, Mein, and Drake.

This structure was revised at the end of 1933, when the sales and production boards were abolished and replaced by committees, each responsible to one of the directors on the executive board—finance (Drake), production (Ramsden), sales (Illingworth), and research (Renwick). In addition, controllers were introduced for plates (Ramsden), papers (Mann), films (Balmain), home sales (Kraushaar), continental sales (Catford), overseas sales (Dimsdale), and advertising (Peck). A 'jury' committee was also formed to monitor the introduction of new products and a Rodenside committee, comprised of heads of laboratories, to discuss research projects.

In January 1934, the executive board was abolished and each of the executive directors was given special responsibilities.

F. Evatt (deputy chairman and supervisor of factories and laboratories).

D. Blundell Mein (finance director and assistant to the managing director).

V. B. Ramsden (production director).

T. M. Illingworth (sales director).

F. F. Renwick (research director).

B. L. Drake (finance director and company secretary).

The Rodenside laboratory was still under Renwick but the factory laboratories were controlled by the production director, although the laboratory heads were responsible for telling Renwick of their research requirements.

The company's fortunes began to improve in 1935; profits rose steadily from the low of £95 000 in 1934 to £131 000 in 1939.

An X-ray sales department had been formed in 1930 with E. W. G. Wesson of Wellington and Ward as its head. He had always been keen to have a centre for radiography, rather like the Holborn Galleries centre for photography. His hope was realized in 1935 when a medical radiographic department was set up under Kathleen C. Clark in the British Medical Association's building, Tavistock House. Its object was to obtain practical experience in the use of X-ray materials with a view to their improvement; it was not a sales department but a demonstration and teaching unit. It was thus similar to the process department established under F. J. Tritton in 1932 to assist the printing industry and the company to develop plates suitable for making printing blocks. Within a year Kathleen Clark had embarked, with F. Melville, on the task of producing what was to become a world-famous textbook—*Positioning in Radiography*. It was published in 1938, with 500 pages and 1400 illustrations and diagrams, and sold at 3 guineas. By 1942 it had achieved a sale of some 6500 copies.

Despite the recession, Ilford continued to introduce new products in the 1930s. The wartime association with Sir William Pope at Cambridge had lasted until 1924, when Ilford decided to make dyes themselves and the agreement was terminated. Pope recommended Dr Frances M. Hamer to Ilford and she joined the firm in October 1924. Frances Hamer had worked with Mills and they had published a paper on the structure of Pinacyanol in 1920. At Ilford she produced new sensitizing dyes and, in 1927 and 1928, published a number of papers on the subject in the *Photographic Journal*. These were seen by workers in the laboratories of rival photographic firms and led to an upsurge of activity in this field. After a disagreement with Renwick, Frances Hamer resigned in 1930 and joined Kodak. She was replaced at Ilford by Dr J. D. Kendall.

Nevertheless, as a result of her work, Ilford by 1930 were the leaders in the field of dye sensitization.

Building upon the foundation she had laid, Kendall, Bloch, and Waller enabled the firm, in the early 1930s, to introduce the Hypersensitive Panchromatic plate (H & D 2000) which was three times faster than the previous fastest plate. Also marketed at about the same time was the Infrared plate (1932) which enabled pictures to be taken without visible light and through haze. *The Times* featured large pictures taken with these plates. The year 1935 saw the production, by O. Bloch and R. C. M. Smith, in cooperation with M. Blau, of plates R_1 and R_2 for recording nuclear particles. Improved versions of these plates were, after the Second World War, to play an important part in research in nuclear physics and cosmic rays.

In the same year Chambon demonstrated a printing machine developed by Armelin, based on the use of a hardened gelatin image as the ink-carrying vehicle. Ilford joined Chambon in the formation of a new company called Kemitype Limited, to exploit this invention. Associated with the development of the process was R. J. P. Bayley, who later became manager of the Bexford base-making plant. Arrangements were made with Lumière SA to supply the French market on a royalty basis. When the Second World War came, Ilford bought the stock of Kemitype and operated the process during the years that followed. The process was particularly suited for short printing runs.

Another innovation of 1935 was the establishment of an X-ray laboratory under H. S. Tasker in the Rodenside laboratory for research on films and intensifying screens for medical radiography. It was also equipped with a high voltage X-ray set for work in industrial radiography. This unit was transferred to Watford in 1938 where Tasker and Snoxall produced a new fluorescent powder for screens, based on an old idea of Renwick's—barium lead sulphate. This material was used for Kryptoscreen paper and Brytex leaves during the war and for HV screens after the war.

Intensifying screens for radiography had been made at Imperial in the early days from barium platinocyanide and from calcium tungstate in the same way that plates were made. The fluorescent powder was suspended in gelatin and coated on a plate-coating machine. In 1931, an agreement was made with L. Levy and D. Willoughby to supply a zinc sulphide phosphor which was used to make Fluorazure screens. These emitted yellow-green light and were suitable for visual observation. In 1934, the manufacture of calcium tungstate screens was transferred from Cricklewood to Watford. Improvements were also made in the method of manufacture.

Plastic materials were substituted for gelatin and the screens were coated in long lengths, as were film and paper.

During the 1930s, there was a frantic search by all photographic manufacturers for a viable colour process. Finlay and Whitfield of Paget had collaborated in the production of the Finlay Process and Ilford for a time had a financial interest in the English Finlay company, which went into liquidation in 1933.

In the 1920s, Ilford had been interested in the Dufay colour process, a mosaic screen process similar to the Finlay process, but had decided that the claims for it could not be substantiated, However, in 1932, Ilford entered into negotiations with Colortone, to assist in the development of the Spicer-Dufay colour process, as it was now called, and a new company called Spicer-Dufay (British) Limited, was formed. Ramsden was the chairman of the new board; Drake, Illingworth, and Renwick were members of it; Blundell Mein represented other parties to the deal. By the end of 1935 Ilford had control of the new company.

Difficulty was experienced in obtaining selling and manufacturing licences as this depended on the formation of two American companies, the Dufaycolor Corporation and Dufaycolor Incorporated, which was delayed. The licences were finally granted in March 1935. A licence was also granted to Spicer-Dufay (British), to sell the réseau base to Kodak for 16 mm and double 8 mm cine films.

The réseau base consisted of film on which had been printed a network, or réseau, of tiny patches of red, green, and blue colour in a regular pattern. This base was printed at Sawston in the Spicer-Dufay factory and coated with sensitive emulsion at the Selo works by Ilford. It was exposed through the back of the film so that the coloured patches acted as filters and recorded the red, green, and blue content of the picture on the film. The first films were reversal processed; this yielded a positive picture which, in conjunction with the réseau, yielded a colour transparency.

A difficulty of this process was that, if any attempt was made to take a copy from an original, moiré patterns were obtained due to the interference between the réseaus of the original and of the copying material. This was overcome by G. B. Harrison and his staff (R. G. Horner, E. T. Purslow, and S. D. Threadgold).

Material was ready for sale at the beginning of 1935 in roll films and film packs. A processing station was set up in the old Elstree factory and another at Brentwood. A 35 mm cine film was made of the King

George V Silver Jubilee celebration in 1935 and copies exhibited in cinemas. Work was also proceeding on a negative-positive process for Dufaycolor and this was used to film the coronation of King George VI in 1937.

To obtain a better understanding of the requirements of the cinematographic industry, a cine laboratory was completed at Warley in 1935 and Harrison and his staff were transferred there from Ilford. Part of the laboratory included a large cine studio fully equipped for making sound films and a projection theatre. Although intended mainly for work with Dufaycolor film, it was also used for work with black and white films.

J. Mitchell was appointed service technician for Dufaycolor materials in the cine sales centre at National House, Wardour Street, London, in the same year.

The disadvantages of Dufaycolor, especially for cinematographic work, were that it was slow and, because of the density of the réseau, much more powerful light sources were required for projection than for black and white films. Also, when projected on a large cinema screen, the individual elements of the réseau became visible.

In 1936 Dufaycolor and Chromex merged to form Dufay-Chromex Limited. Ilford exchanged its shares in Spicer-Dufay (British), for those of Dufay-Chromex in 1937. At the beginning of 1938, Dufay-Chromex needed to raise £60 000 and asked Ilford to contribute £20 000, but they declined. The Ilford board by now were becoming disillusioned with the process and had probably lost a lot of money. Spicer-Dufay (British) had made a loss of £40 000 in 1934, £32 000 in 1935, and £19 000 in 1936. Ilford began selling its shares in Dufay-Chromex in 1938 and at the end of the year Drake and J. Philipps resigned their seats on the board of Dufay-Chromex. The agreement with Dufay-Chromex was terminated in September 1939, although an undertaking was made to coat réseau for Dufay-Chromex and to do research at cost. The manufacture of the réseau material was tranferred from the Sawston factory to the old Elstree factory which Ilford sold to Dufay-Chromex in 1937.

Dufaycolor was not the only venture into the field of colour. Some money was spent investigating the possibilities of the Nordman lenticular-film colour process in 1934 and an investment was made in 1937 in the Veracol Film Syndicate for which consultants Murray, Bull, and Spencer were doing research. Ilford also subscribed to shares in the Linked Engraving Company, formed to exploit Dr D. A. Spencer's method of making blocks for colour printing. Both of these companies were dissolved at the beginning of the war.

During these 20 years, many changes took place among the Ilford staff. When the First World War ended in 1918, Sir Ivor Philipps had been chairman, F. J. Jenks managing director and W. Ashmole, F. W. Evatt, J. Kemp-Welch and R. D. Lewis members of the board, with B. L. Drake as company secretary.

Thomas Midgley Illingworth, the son of Thomas Illingworth, had joined the board in 1920. W. Ashmole had died of pneumonia in 1924 and been replaced by Debrisay Blundell Mein who had been Philipps' adjutant during the war. F. J. Jenks had died in 1930 and severed one of the last links with Harman whom he had assisted as bookkeeper in the earliest days. He had been replaced by V. B. Ramsden, Philipps' son-in-law.

Both Ramsden and Kemp-Welch died in 1936, the latter having been a director since 1903. They were followed by Blundell Mein who died in 1937. W. H. Dimsdale (Philipps' nephew) replaced Ramsden and James P. Philipps replaced Blundell Mein. On the death of Ivor Philipps in 1940, B. L. Drake became chairman and W. E. H. Metcalfe took Drake's place as secretary. Drake had risen from bottom to top in 47 years, having joined the Britannia Works company under Harman in 1893. The Rt. Hon. Laurence Richard Philipps (Lord Milford) replaced Ivor Philipps. In the same year R. D. Lewis retired to be replaced by Sir Philip Haldin in the following year. Thus, at the end of 1940, only one of the directors of 20 years before remained—F. W. Evatt.

During this period many of the first employees either retired or died. There was no fixed age for retirement and many worked until prevented by ill-health. Thomas Hughes, factory manager, who had joined Harman only three years after he started his venture, retired in 1919 aged 72; he died three years later. Two more old-timers retired in 1920: G. Lindsell, aged 78, because of ill-health after 32 years, and J. Farley, aged 72, crippled with rheumatism, after 29 years. Others to go were: W. Clarke, 36 years' service, 1920; W. Hay, assistant emulsion maker, 35 years, 1921; J. Hallows who died after 40 years' service in 1923. J. Field Dodgson, who had joined Harman in 1891 and been factory manager of both the Ilford and the prewar Warley factory, retired in 1928 and died in 1932.

In 1930, the practice was started of making presentations to those who had been with the firm for 50 years. Clocks were given to J. P. Coyle, senior foreman, in 1930 and E. J. Lewis, plate-coating foreman, in 1931. In 1932, gold watches were introduced in recognition of the same length of service, the first recipient being A. Linsell. Others included W. J. Withers, chief engineer Watford, 1939. Withers had joined the Woodburytype company in 1888 and then the Paget Prize Plate Company when it was formed. When he retired in 1945 he had served the company for 57 years. Long-service certificates, to be issued for 30 years' employment, with a border decorated with views of the various factories, were introduced in 1932.

Until the introduction of the contributory Group Life and Pension Scheme 1932, on retirement employees received a 'voluntary' pension which was usually renewed from year to year but not invariably so. For some reasons not stated, a few pensions were stopped after two or three years. In 1939 retirement was fixed at 65, unless the directors decreed otherwise.

A. J. Agnew, who had joined Harman in 1889, was retired in 1934 but had his retirement postponed three times and finally retired at the end of 1937, aged 71. W. Maclaren Smith, the veteran emulsion maker, was retired at 62 but kept on as a consultant until he reached 65 and was then eligible for his pension. Others, such as A. W. Linsell and W. Cooper, on reaching retirement were retained as nightwatchmen for as long as they were capable of doing the job.

The amalgamation of so many companies and the subsequent rationalization brought many changes of staff and interchanges between factories. The latter, on the whole, was probably beneficial as it reduced rivalry between the factories and helped to weld the new Ilford Limited into one.

When T. Hughes retired in 1919, W. C. Shepherd became factory manager at Ilford in his place. C. N. Potter was transferred from Imperial to Ilford to become his assistant in 1930, becoming factory manager a year later when Shepherd became a member of the production board until his death in 1935. In 1934, Potter, as well as being factory manager, was made plate production controller in place of Ramsden, with L. F. Davidson as film production controller. In January 1935, Potter was made both film and plate controller. A fortnight later, G. Hudson was appointed Selo factory manager in place of Davidson who was made assistant to Potter; Davidson resigned. At the same time, W. B. S. Donovan was made assistant factory manager at Ilford and became manager at the end of the year.

By the middle of 1936, Hudson was taken ill and Potter became Selo factory manager, as well as controller, with Hudson as his assistant when he returned. To relieve the pressure on Potter, Evatt became plate controller as well as production director. With the coming of the Second World War, to increase efficiency Potter was transferred to Ilford as factory manager to replace Donovan who had joined the RAF, Hudson became factory manager at Selo, and Mitchell was transferred to Warley as assistant to the production director.

On the scientific side, B. V. Storr replaced Renwick as chief chemist when he left for the United States in 1923. Storr remained in this post until 1930 when he became assistant controller of production and, in turn, was replaced by Olaf Bloch. J. Mitchell became head of the Ilford laboratory for a brief period when Bloch retired in 1939, after which Cecil Waller took over and R. B. Collins was transferred from the organic laboratory as his assistant, to work on dye sensitization and the newly discovered gold sensitization.

At Selo the chief chemist was L. F. Davidson, who had been transferred from Imperial. On W. H. Smith's retirement (1931) he became factory manager and was replaced by Dr Henry Baines, also of Imperial. Baines resigned in 1937 to take an appointment with Nuro, a new firm making films. D. P. Woosley was made chief chemist in his place.

When Harrison was transferred to Selo to take charge of the cine laboratory in 1935, L. V. Chilton was moved from Park Royal to take over the Rodenside laboratory and undertake research into colour processes. S. O. Rawling, who had been Bloch's assistant for many years, took charge of routine control at Selo in 1937 with administrative responsibility for the laboratories. A year later A. G. Jenkinson became head of sensitometry, a post which he held for many years, replacing D. Chilton who had become an assistant curator at the Science Museum, London.

As the consolidation of the various factories into one unit progressed, engineering research and development was concentrated more and more at Ilford under H. W. Horton. G. H. Farrington was engaged as his assistant in 1932 and became chief engineer in 1934 when Horton retired. A. Horton, H. W. Horton's son, was put in charge of all new constructional work in 1935. A new central engineering department building at Ilford was completed in 1937.

The process of reorganization was halted by the Second World War, but the firm was in a much better condition to meet the difficulties ahead.

7. The Second World War and after (1939-1959)

Ilford Limited celebrated its Diamond Jubilee on 28 January 1939 with a dinner at the Trocadero Restaurant in London. Almost all the senior staff were present, about 250 in all. The occasion, including a private room, cocktails, dinner, and wines, cost £340—roughly £1 5s per head.

The celebration was presided over by Major General Sir Ivor Philipps, who had led the company out of a perilous situation into a position of considerable influence over a period of 34 years. He was supported by many who had helped to achieve that position: Colonel F. W. Evatt, the deputy chairman and his chief aide; F. F. Renwick who had led the outstanding progress in research and development; Olaf Bloch, another brilliant chemist with a roguish sense of humour, wit, and charm; B. L. Drake, company secretary and a penetrating judge of human nature; Andrew Agnew, the tough, Scottish quality controller, and probably the only person at the celebration who had worked with Alfred Harman in one of the Clyde cottages.

Those present must have felt they had reached a peak of endeavour. The company, though not as profitable as in Harman's days, was paying a dividend of eight per cent and had survived both the crises of amalgamation and of the slump. Above all, it had achieved a worldwide reputation for fair dealing; good, reliable products and bright technical ideas. The technical personnel assembled, at least, knew that further great advances lay immediately ahead. Few can have realized, however, that, within ten years, the world they knew would be changed, with their company under new leaders and operating under totally different philosophies of marketing and scientific development.

Within a month of that dinner, the company was preparing for the coming war. Three air raid shelters were under construction at the Brentwood site. Under Air Ministry instructions, all factories were 'blacked out'.

Before war came, all the factories had shelters, extra concrete protection had been applied to the roof of the Brentwood coating block, and buildings were covered in camouflage paint, and even the 'Bonus Garden' at Ilford had been undermined with shelters. All important documents were microfilmed and buried. (There seems no trace in the records of their later retrieval.) The work of each employee was recorded, with formulations and other facts, so that, if necessary, a stranger could, in theory at least, carry on the job with a minimum of dislocation. At that time, almost everyone was certain that intense bombing would start as soon as war was declared and that dead men's shoes would have to be filled promptly, effectively, and quite frequently!

In many other ways, life continued normally. Two more of the original Clyde cottages at Ilford were vacated by their tenants in favour of factory departments; the company donated £45 to promote the annual staff photographic competition; a new boiler was installed at the Mobberley factory; foundations were laid for a new coating block at Brentwood; advertising and the production of publications continued unabated and discussions continued with Dufay-Chromex and Veracol on improved colour films. Film prices were raised to cover a new tax in the 1939 budget of 4½d per square foot on all materials, including paper negative, but excluding X-ray film and papers. Sales abroad were picking up and S. W. C. Hale was appointed to assist A. P. Downie in building up the business in Australia.

But the country was now obviously on the verge of war. The company paid £8990 to the National Defence Fund: notices warning employees of the danger of loose talk were posted, and employees in the Territorial Army were given four weeks' extra leave with pay to attend training camp. Some reservists had been recalled already and the company agreed to make up their service pay to their current Ilford rate. A war bonus of 10 per cent of pay was awarded to remaining employees to counter a swift increase in the cost of living.

When war was declared in September 1939, the photographic industry was scheduled as 'Munitions Work—Scientific Instrument Making (Photographic Materials)' and an Air Photographic Research Council was in operation to coordinate photographic effort. Apart from the development of better aerial

68

Figure 23   The Diamond Jubilee staff dinner, held at the Trocadero, London, 28 January 1939.

films and new printing papers, the laboratories worked on problems of resolution in aerial pictures, transmission of camera lenses, the use of flash-bombs dropped from aircraft and other projects. Dr G. B. Harrison, later research director, led a team of physicists which included R. J. Hercock, R. G. Horner, and E. T. Purslow.

A 'Farnborough Committee' was set up by the Department of Scientific and Industrial Research to study the photographic problems of aerial reconnaissance. Harrison and G. S. Moore joined it to represent Ilford; the latter was seconded almost immediately to the Royal Aircraft Establishment at Farnborough to run its section on photographic aerial research.

Most people's lives were jerked into a new orbit. Key men had been on the reserved list for some time but others were directed to jobs in other industries or called up. Both James Philipps, a nephew of Sir Ivor who had just been appointed to the board, and the group accountant, W. E. H. Metcalfe, were re-called to the Army. Metcalfe had served in the First World

War and was on the Regular Army Reserve of Officers; Philipps was an officer in the Territorial Army. Metcalfe was released within a few months. Sir Ivor was by now in failing health and B. L. Drake was appointed managing director to assist him. Sir Ivor died in August 1940 and Drake became chairman. The death of Sir Ivor was reported to the board on August 15 by Colonel Evatt who said that: 'he had acted since 3 January 1906 with . . . untiring energy, wise guidance and zealous and faithful service to the company.' A board resolution was needed to close the office and factories on the following day, a Saturday, for the funeral.

To fill the board vacancy arising, and as James Philipps was on active service, his father Lord Milford was appointed a non-executive director.

Although the demands of war reduced staff in the offices and, for a short time, the factories and laboratories, work was carried on even more effectively than before. While working hours increased, nights were spent on duty as air raid wardens or fire watchers. Soon the Local Defence Volunteer

Figure 24   Bertram Lansdowne Drake, 1876–1945, joined Harman as a junior clerk in 1893. He soon opted to work in the factory. Although hours were then 6 am to 6 pm, six days a week, he used his spare time to study business methods, law, and accountancy, and obtained professional qualifications. In 1915, he was elected a Fellow of the Chartered Institute of Secretaries and became secretary and chief accountant of Ilford. He was deeply involved in the negotiations for the companies purchased between then and 1930, when he was appointed to the board, becoming managing director in 1936 and chairman in 1940, on the death of Sir Ivor Philipps.

Figure 25 'Dad's Army': a Home Guard group during the Second World War. Among those present are L. H. Drake (the son of B. L. Drake and later company purchasing officer), E. H. Willison (later chief architect), H. Y. Bubbers, F. P. Doyle, D. J. Fry, and H. Seabrook.

Force (later the Home Guard) was formed; a series of spears and other weapons made by the Ilford Home Guard, are on exhibition in the Imperial War Museum, London. Those on air raid duty were allowed by the company to use any available darkrooms if they wished; many interesting discoveries were made, including the ability of cold tea to develop photographic materials—after a fashion!

The government regarded photography as an essential weapon of war; civilian home consumption was curtailed until, by 1942, sales were limited to 25 per cent by value of those in 1938–39. Price rises made this an even larger cut to home market supplies than it appeared.

On the other hand, exports were encouraged, to obtain foreign currency to pay for war supplies. The general sales manager, A. J. Catford, and the export representative, Oscar Phillips, travelled abroad to find new business. Phillips was almost caught when the Germans overran France but escaped in a shipload of refugees. The sales companies, most of which were in Europe, experienced difficulties.

The Danish company, Ilford Foto Akts, had been set up in 1929 with Knut Jenson, former Ilford sales representative for Denmark and Sweden, as managing director. He was an excellent salesman and had a good technical knowledge but, above all, he never lost his faith in the Allies' capability to win the war. When

Germany invaded Denmark in 1940 he kept the company running by selling any photographic goods he could acquire. As a result, business was resumed in 1945 with minimum dislocation.

The Dutch company, Ilford-Selo NV was run by H. C. N. Becker and his son: the German invasion greatly reduced their business. However, the Rolleiflex agency was maintained, despite requests from the German authorities to cancel the agreement with the makers, Franke and Heidecke, and give the agency to Agfa. Eventually, a 50–50 split had to be agreed but this was to be rescinded after the war, when Agfa had re-established their own range of cameras and Ilford-Selo NV resumed the full agency.

The manager of Ilford-Selo SA in Belgium, set up to compete with Gevaert in their home territory, escaped to England and was sent to South Africa to improve export sales there. He returned through Lisbon, where he was met by German agents; he disappeared until 1945. He afterwards said that pressure was brought to bear upon him to reveal Ilford business and technical secrets by threatening the lives of his wife and family. He therefore worked in Brussels, selling German goods and utilizing Ilford capital and resources. Later, when the Allies liberated Belgium, he was imprisoned for seven years and apologized to Ilford for disclosing documents and for disposing of the parent company's assets in Belgium. The manager's father had also

71

collaborated with the Germans during the First World War; he had been rewarded with considerable estates but had also subsequently been punished by the Allies. Meanwhile, in England, Ilford was supplying Gevaert with films, plates, and papers to enable them to continue business.

The French company, Wellington and Ward SA, had been running, somewhat unsuccessfully, for many years. After the war it was revitalized under Raymond Bernas, who had been an X-ray representative, and his brother Robert, an engineer interested in X-rays and nuclear physics. As Jews, they had decided to go to the USA in 1939. The Germans expropriated the company when France fell and ran it very effeciently. In 1945, when Ilford people returned, all was found in perfect order, with well-kept accounts, except that many share certificates were missing. They were bearer shares, which gave rise to grave suspicions until they were found hidden in a cellar. The name was changed to Ilford SA, which ran until Lumière SA took over the business in 1969, both companies by then being owned by CIBA AG.

In the United Kingdom, the company changed its structure to meet new needs. The product range was streamlined. Seltona and POP, the backbone of the paper business for many years, were discontinued and plate production was reduced by closing one of the four machines. This, coupled with the introduction of night shifts, enabled film and bromide paper production to be increased greatly and run at higher efficiency with a much smaller staff.

On the marketing side, the sales committee gave place to an 'allocation committee', needed to ensure that the armed forces, industry, and government departments obtained priority of supply and that export needs, rather than those of the residual home market, were met from the remaining output. The few remaining sales representatives spent most of their time explaining to professional photographers and dealers that they would gain reward with superb new products after the war.

They were not exaggerating, the research department was, in fact, at work developing some striking new products. Largely as a result of brilliant work started before the war by R. B. Collins, working under Dr Cecil Waller, new methods were evolved for controlling the emulsion-making process during the digestion stage and for increasing sensitivity by the addition of various new agents, principally small traces of gold salts.

Agfa had achieved some prewar success with gold sensitizing but had not obtained the full effect through failing to find the optimum stage and conditions for the addition of the gold. The Ilford 'Tetragam' patents were not released for publication, by order of the Ministry of Aircraft Production.

Ilford's discoveries resulted in a series of film emulsions with greatly improved sensitivity to light, lower graininess, and other attractive attributes. This led to a particular call for film from the RAF for aerial reconnaissance in general and night film in particular, as Kodak were unable to match the film quality.

The demand by the RAF for better materials of other types led to the introduction of 'Multigrade' paper, which F. F. Renwick had been developing before the war and which was to be the last major product he introduced as director of research, before his death in 1943. This paper dispensed with the need to use a range of contrast grades, the negative being matched by varying the colour of the printing light. One area in which Ilford was not allowed to work by the government was that of colour photography. This had catastrophic results on the postwar success of the company. Ilford was unable to apply its research expertise, at a time of peak achievement, to the special problems of subtractive tri-pack colour materials or to silver dye-bleach techniques. The old additive process, Dufaycolor, was discontinued in 1940, although Dufay-Chromex continued it alone for a few years; Ilford was supplying them with some material until 1942.

One of the uses of the new high-speed emulsions was to improve X-ray materials. 'Red Seal' film, made by the new technique, had finer definition and the speed enabled a lower X-ray dosage to be given to the patient.

Because film supplies were short, F. J. Shepherd, G. E. Whitfield, and H. S. Tasker evolved an X-ray material coated on paper called 'Kryptoscreen'. As the use of paper base precluded the use of a pair of intensifying screens, one on either side, as with film, a layer of fluorescent material was coated between the paper and the emulsion layer. In use, a screen coated on paper (called a 'Brytex' leaf) was held against the emulsion surface during exposure to X-rays. Although these materials produced radiographs inferior to those on film, they were adequate for checking assemblies such as shell fuzes and were cheaper than film. They were used from 1941 until film base became more readily available.

The high wartime demand for X-ray materials led to the expansion of the department of radiography and medical photography in Tavistock House, the London Headquarters building of the British Medical Association. This department, opened in February 1935, employed a very remarkable woman, Kathleen

Figure 26   Miss Kathleen C. Clark, radiographer, head of Tavistock House X-ray Centre and author of Positioning in Radiography.

Clark, as a radiographer. She had joined Ilford in October 1935 after working with the chief radiologist of the RAMC to try to perfect methods of locating accurately the position of bullets and shell splinters in the human body. The techniques evolved led to the preparation and publication of the textbook *Positioning in Radiography* mentioned earlier. Instruction courses were set up which led to the creation of a full-scale School of Radiography within the department.

Shortage of film also led to experiments with mass miniature radiography for the early detection of pulmonary tuberculosis, then rife and growing as a result of poor wartime living conditions. Instead of using a full 14 in × 17 in film for a chest radiograph, the image on a fluorescent screen was recorded on a small piece of film. Ilford promoted a miniature camera of special design, using the recently popularized 35 mm film. This was designed by W. Watson of Miss Clark's team and made by Schall & Son Ltd. By this means, thousands of patients could be screened quickly and those with suspected lesions re-examined on full-size film.

When the Germans invaded Norway, the Norwegian Medical Service found a home in another section of Tavistock House. As close neighbours, Ilford offered them radiographic facilities and this led to an experiment in which 23 000 Norwegian service men were screened by Kathleen Clark's department. This proved the value of the technique and 40 teams to run mobile units were trained for the Ministry of Health, other staff being trained for the British Red Cross. This led to the early detection and control of tuberculosis before drugs were available to eliminate it. In December 1942, the Norwegian government presented Kathleen Clark with a silver tea set and sent £100 for distribution to her staff as a token of their gratitude. The department steadily grew under Kathleen Clark and Herbert Flower. Diploma courses for the Society of Radiographers were set up; they continued until 1975. Kathleen Clark later assisted UNRRA and the International Refugee Organization to organize similar teams in Europe. She was awarded the MBE and the King Haakon Liberty Cross.

In April 1941, discussions were held, at the request of the Post Office, on the microcopying of letters for transmission by air, an extension of an idea used at siege of Paris in 1871. Ilford decided it had not the resources to tackle the job. It was eventually put into operation as the 'Airgraph letter service', run by Kodak alone, and was used both for civilian and Forces mail overseas.

The company did not escape enemy bombing. The Ilford Gallery in High Holborn was surrounded by burning buildings on 10 September 1940, and again on 25 September 1940. It suffered only minor damage, apart from the flooding of the basement with sewage.

At about the same time, the Ilford factory also suffered damage from incendiary bombs. Three plate factory sections were put out of action. However, the Kodak factory at Harrow, which had taken up plate manufacture for the first time only a few years before, now helped by packing some of their plates under the Ilford label until production was resumed completely.

No further damage was caused until July 1944, when a V1 (flying bomb) hit the Park Royal factory: little damage was caused. The Ilford factory was not hit again until 12 January 1945, when a V1 caused damage, to be followed on 20 February by a real disaster. A V2 (rocket) hit the plate factory, killing 3 people and seriously injuring 12 others. Plate production was impossible for about six weeks and restricted thereafter for some time. The Brentwood and Mobberley factories escaped unscathed—apart from a small hole in the roof of one building at Brentwood caused by a British anti-aircraft shell! Tavistock House was hit next, on 17 April 1941, but Miss Clark carried on after rapid repair work.

On 4 July 1945, L. V. Chilton and E. W. Lee left with a government mission to see the captured Agfa base-casting and paper-sensitizing plants at Leverkusen in Germany. The Ministry of Supply also requested the services of Dr S. O. Rawling as a chief technical officer in the Control Commission in Germany.

When, finally, V-E Day came, the whole company closed from Saturday, August 4, to the morning of Wednesday, 8 August 1945.

Almost at once negotiations with BX Plastics Limited, over the creation of a joint company to produce triacetate film base, came to fruition. Bexford Limited was formed, a liaison name derived from the two names of the parent companies. Its creation had been helped by the Ministry of Supply when base was very difficult to obtain from the USA. Production started in 1946.

As the world began to readjust to peace, the company took stock of its position and prepared to meet the new conditions. F. F. Renwick had died in 1943 and W. H. Dimsdale, who had been production director since 1937, had taken over temporarily as director of research and development. In 1945, Harrison and Mitchell had been appointed to the board; Harrison took over as research director and Mitchell as sales director. Mitchell had been in charge of Technical Service, had been involved in the

Figure 27   Wilfrid H. Dimsdale. From King's College, Cambridge, Dimsdale joined Ilford in 1926, at the age of 20. Although he was the nephew of the chairman, Sir Ivor Philipps, he was put to work under Renwick as a chemist at £3 a week—chemists with first class degrees were then normally paid £4. He then applied to become a management trainee and was sent for short periods to the various departments of the company and its subsidiaries, including Thos. Illingworth, where he met E. Roy Davies, later to be director of research for Kodak Ltd, Harrow. Later, he managed the sales department of Imperial, touring the world and establishing connections which were to be of great use to the company in Australasia, India, Canada, and the USA. Finally, he was appointed production director, a position he held until he became managing director on the retirement of T. M. Illingworth.

Dimsdale was impressed by the complete empiricism of the photographic process and the relative crudeness of the plant. He set himself to improve the research and engineering in the company, aided by an excellent memory and vast knowledge of photographic patents and technology. He retired in 1973.

Figure 28   The Bower House, Havering-atte-Bower, used by Ilford as an engineering research centre.

development of Dufaycolor for the cine industry and had edited the *Ilford Manual* and other technical publications. Drake relinquished his appointment as managing director to become chairman; Dimsdale became a joint managing director with T. Midgley Illingworth, who had been sales director since he joined Ilford at the time his company was purchased in 1920.

Drake soon relinquished the chairmanship in favour of James Philipps, but remained on the board until 1950. Colonel F. W. Evatt, his deputy chairman, who had served on the board since 1908, also retired from the company. Illingworth was elected deputy chairman in addition to his post as joint managing director. William E. H. Metcalfe, an accountant from Price, Waterhouse & Co. who had been chief accountant and company secretary of Wellington and Ward and subsequently accountant to the Ilford Group since 1931 and secretary since 1940, joined the board in 1946.

The new team worked hard to modernize the company. A fresh directors' executive committee was set up, consisting of Illingworth, Dimsdale, Harrison, Mitchell and Metcalfe, with James Philipps in the chair, and the sales and production committees were reconstituted. The latter consisted of James Mitchell (as a technical link with sales), W. A. Berry (paper controller), G. H. Farrington (chief development engineer), A. G. Horton (chief engineer), George Hudson (film factory manager) and Cecil N. Potter (plate factory manager), under the chairmanship of W. H. Dimsdale.

Dimsdale, a world expert on photographic technology, studied the economics of manufacture and encouraged the research department to follow on the successful pioneering work of a few years earlier. He was determined to improve the efficiency of production, especially of the coating and drying processes for film and, later, for paper. To this end, the central engineering department was reorganized. The maintenance and redesign of existing plant was established under the new chief engineer, A. G. Horton (son of a former chief engineer) at the Ilford site; experimental engineering and design of new buildings were moved

Figure 29   A fireplace, typical of the interior of the Bower House, much of which had to be covered during its use as a research centre.

to a new location under Farrington as consultant engineer and C. W. Sully as chief architect. The new premises, opened in May 1948, were at the Bower House, Havering-atte-Bower, between Ilford and Brentwood (Figure 28). This beautiful and historic mansion, in nine acres of parkland, provided the peace and quiet necessary for inventive work but the lovely panelled walls and moulded plaster work needed careful protection (Figure 29). Workshops were constructed in the yard and outbuildings. In these surroundings, attention was turned to new and untried engineering techniques. Dip-coating of film and paper, running at about 12ft/min, clearly had to be replaced. Various means of reverse-roll and air-knife coating were examined, together with application by slots. The higher speeds of operation inherent in these techniques required parallel work on high-speed drying.

The spider drying system, unique to Ilford, which had been used since 1924 was, for its time, efficient and highly economic of power. However, it was unsuitable for higher speeds and it could now be seen that coating in the future might well be carried out, not at 12–15 ft/min but at up to 1000 ft/min, hence the idea of flat-bed impingement drying, with close control of temperature and humidity along the web of film, was investigated.

High-speed machines were evolved for the cutting, notching, and collating of professional cut-sheet film and for the automatic spooling of roll, miniature, and cine films.

Other aspects of the economics of production were also studied, one important achievement being a plant to recover virtually all silver in the wash-waters and other effluent.

While this overhaul of production activities was taking place, the sales division was not idle. The sales committee, revived in February 1946, consisted at first of A. J. Catford, G. Dorman, S. T. Ferris, L. W. Fuller, R. S. Liddle, and F. J. Tritton, with T. M. Illingworth in the chair; in 1947 Catford, who had been general sales manager for over 20 years, retired and was replaced by two men. R. S. Liddle, who had been in charge of sales to the cinema industry, became homes sales manager, while Sydney T. Ferris took over export sales. Ferris had started with Imperial in 1912 and had moved to Ilford on the merger in 1920. He was later to become export director on the board of Ilford, at a time when the company was greatly increasing its overseas sales. The X-ray film business was organized by Herbert Flower.

After much heart searching, the paddle-steamer trademark, well known since 1886, was dropped in 1945, although it has been retained in the company seal. At the time, it felt almost like abolishing the Union Jack but it was seen to be outmoded. Steps were taken in 1945 to employ design consultants, Design Research unit run by Milner Gray, to produce a new, bold logo applicable to all goods, and to modernize the colour scheme, labelling, letterhead and advertising, and to redesign the Ilford Galleries. New advertising agents were employed and the slogan *Ilford Films for Faces and Places* was coined. This led to a highly successful campaign of advertising in periodicals, on posters and the sides of buses. The time had come to start dropping the old brandnames, Imperial, Gem, Illingworth, Selo, and so forth; from now on Ilford was the brandname, apart from the residual use of Selo in Selochrome.

Many other new ideas flourished in the peacetime atmosphere. Photography was encouraged in the Butlins holiday camps by two joint companies Butlins Photographic Services Limited and Golden Memories Limited. Kodak were supplied with X-ray intensifying screens under their own brand label, an arrangement which continued for some years.

The company also decided to make serious entry into the camera market. Contact was made with a number of possible manufacturers. The first design to emerge was the Witness, a sophisticated precision 35 mm camera designed by D. A. Rothschild, who had worked in the German camera industry in the 1930s, and manufactured by Peto Scott Electrical instruments (Figure 30). A cheaper 35 mm camera, the Penguin, was bought for resale and a roll-film box camera, later to be called the Craftsman, was also designed by Rothschild. By 1947 agreement had been reached with David Kennedy (Engineers) Limited (later Kennedy Instruments Limited) to develop another, simpler 35 mm miniature camera to be called the Advocate. This proved successful over a period of years and a special model costing £340 10s was presented to the Princess (now Queen) Elizabeth by the Borough of Ilford in March 1948. This was subsequently stolen but came to light again when received by Ilford for repairs.

While the Bower House grappled with the technical shape of the future, steps were being taken to improve productivity. In 1948 a firm of consultants, AIC Limited, was brought in. They recommended the introduction of bonus incentive schemes. At that time, before totally enclosed automatic machines, photographic production was carried on in almost total darkness: the problems of work study were considerable. Methods in the factories were not much changed by the investigation but other departments were much

Figure 30   The Witness camera, marketed by Ilford in 1946.

improved. Incentive payments, which had not previously been employed, increased productivity significantly.

Development of colour photography, held up by the wartime government, was actively resumed. It was decided to follow the lead of Agfa and Kodak by introducing a colour reversal (transparency) 35 mm film and to innovate by introducing a colour printing system from such transparencies, using the little-known silver dye-bleach system.

Although production of Dufaycolor had not been easy before the war, a single-coated film of that type was easier to produce than either of the new materials chosen. The available processes were complex compared with monochrome photography, and called for methods of coating extremely thin uniform multiple layers of emulsion.

It was decided not to use the postwar information gleaned about Agfa products, although this was available from government reports. Ilford decided that it lacked the expertise to make the complex organic chemicals needed. It had no difficulty in making or buying the rather simpler materials used in non-substantive processes similar to Kodachrome. With non-substantive materials, the dye-forming

substances (couplers) are placed in the processing solutions instead of in the emulsion layers. In addition, the latter gave finer-grained images and could be used for 8 mm amateur cine film, which appeared then to be a fast-growing and lucrative market. To obtain good results, while avoiding infringement of Kodak patents, Ilford introduced a new concept—a 'barrier layer' of silver sulphide between the green- and red-sensitive emulsion layers. This enabled a different processing procedure to be used and led to the marketing of Ilford Colour 'D' film in 1948. This could be processed only under very tightly controlled conditions, which restricted the processing to Ilford's own laboratories and, for about ten years, films returned by customers were processed in the research laboratories at Brentwood.

Ilford felt that the customer would want prints, transparencies being difficult to reproduce well and needing projection to view them properly. A print material to produce direct prints from transparencies seemed a better answer than the alternative of a colour negative film with a colour print paper, as in the Kodacolor process. Attention was therefore turned to silver dye-bleach printing.

Pioneer work had been carried out in the 1930s

by Bela Gaspar in the USA and suggestions for collaboration were received from him during 1946 and 1947, following his invitation in September 1945 to cooperate in the production of a colour cine film. These suggestions did not lead to definite results and Ilford worked on its own process, largely as a result of work by Dr G. B. Harrison and R. B. Collins in 1948, the dye chemistry being supervised by Dr J. D. Kendall and the dyes produced specially by Geigy in Manchester.

The prints produced by this process in 1949 were the first acceptable direct prints to be made by any manufacturer in a single step from a transparency, though excellent prints had been made laboriously by three-colour separation methods before the war. The following year, Gasparcolor prints were introduced in the USA by Du Pont.

The silver dye-bleach process necessitated very accurate coating on an opaque white cellulose base of high quality. This base was made by Bexford, which had by that time been built up by Ilford and BX Plastics to produce a variety of types of film base of excellent quality.

A print production station was eventually set up at Richmond in 1953 under J. H. Coote, who had been engaged in the intricacies of colour photography for some years.

Meanwhile, a number of new moves had been considered, only to be discarded. A possible move of production to a new area was examined, as labour was difficult to find in Brentwood. Sites in Wales, at Bridgend, Wrexham, and Treforest, were examined; one at Bridgend was almost purchased but the idea eventually lapsed.

Another important policy decision was to investigate diversification into wholesale photofinishing, photographic publishing, retail trading, manufacturing in European countries and participation in fine chemical manufacture in the United Kingdom.

The decision had wide ranging results. The Britannia Works Company, which had been registered (but inoperative) for nearly 50 years, was revived as a vehicle for the entry of Ilford into wholesale photofinishing—the developing and printing of amateur snapshots. The Rosedale Works at Richmond, later to house the silver dye-bleach printing plant, was bought in 1946 and to this were added businesses in Swindon, Margate, and, later, Liskeard.

Other results of the new policy were: an arrangement with Miles Aircraft to enter the document-copying field with the Copycat reflex machine; agreement with the Ocean Trading, to sell Ilford

goods on passenger ships; discussions with Ceaverken, a Swedish company, on a possible merger; the setting up of film spool production at Edmonton, London under R. E. Pinder after purchase of the plant from Watford Metal Pressings; and the purchase of Dysart Works, Leyton, London for use as a warehouse for cameras and accessories under A. R. Holliman.

In 1952, a world shortage of sulphur developed and Dimsdale decided to safeguard the company's supplies of sulphur chemicals, including sulphites, bisulphites, and thiosulphate, by purchasing the J. S. Hanson Company of Low Moor, Bradford, who had a dilapidated plant on the site of a munitions factory which had exploded in the First World War. The ground was still strewn with debris, but the company had had the foresight to stockpile sulphur. This carried Ilford through a period of shortage. The plant was sold again after about 20 years.

Geigy, who were making dyes for Ilford colour paper, also produced Phenidone, a completely new type of developing agent invented by Ilford chemists, which, though its potential was not at first fully realized, was later to revolutionize photographic printing papers. In 1952, Ilford set up a joint company with Geigy called Gyl Chemicals to manufacture hydroquinone, an essential developing agent then in short supply.

For ten years after the war there had been a strong sellers' market and Ilford prospered. Dividends of 25 per cent were paid until 1950 followed by 15 per cent until 1957, apart from 20 per cent in 1953. Its black and white, X-ray and graphic arts products were of the highest quality. It had a large proportion of the British market—at one time over 60 per cent of the X-ray business and about 80 per cent of the graphic arts plate trade with printing houses and newspapers. Its export business was good. But signs of difficulty were appearing. It could not produce enough of the best goods to satisfy all potential customers. Moreover, new products were not being evolved as quickly as during the war years; the attempt to enter the colour market was draining the company of capital, and scientific effort was being spread over an area almost as big as that of its large competitors, Kodak and Agfa, both of whom had greater resources and a long, valuable start in colour materials.

None of this was apparent when the 75th anniversary celebrations were held in May 1954. Although the price of silver had risen by 85 per cent over the past five years, business was booming, and a licensing agreement had been concluded with van der Grinten NV of Holland to manufacture diazo papers under licence. W. H. Dimsdale and J. W. W. Smith

Figure 31   A group of senior marketing employees, 1957. Left to right: Sydney T. Ferris, export manager and later a director; James Mitchell, sales director; A. J. Hill, assistant export manager; Richard S. Liddle, home sales manager.

had visited them in Venlo in March 1949 to examine their 'Retocee' copying process but their papers for office and plan copying proved of even greater interest. Diazo materials contain no silver and, coupled with Ilford's knowledge of paper-coating techniques, seemed a good hedge against a shortage of the element essential to other photographic materials.

In 1954, exports rose by 20 per cent and profits by 38 per cent over the previous year, though a dividend of 15 per cent was maintained. The authorized capital was increased to £3.5 million by the issue of 4 million ordinary 5s shares and reserves of £1 133 333 were capitalized. The business was growing rapidly; sales turnover had increased 3½-fold since the war ended and £4 167 000 capital had been injected, £2 814 000 from profits.

The Australian company, formed in 1951, was being expanded and a decision was taken to cut and pack films and papers there. Two years later a new site was purchased at Notting Hill, Melbourne.

The fast films invented during the war were still selling well, with minor improvements. A new plate of extreme speed, named HPS, had been introduced for press work during the coronation year of 1953. The main success was in the new field of atomic research, where photographic materials produced by Ilford were proving pre-eminent. A block of emulsion sensitive to cosmic rays was sent by balloon to a height of 20 miles. It measured $14\frac{1}{2}$ in $\times$ $10\frac{1}{2}$ in $\times$ 6 in, weighed over 1 cwt and contained silver worth over £300. This paved the way for later studies in space, putting Ilford materials on the moon in the next 20 years.

But by 1955 the company had begun to feel the effect of stiffer competition. Although the Advocate camera was selling well, the others were not as successful as had been hoped. Azoflex, the dyeline range of materials made under licence from van der Grinten, was proving more difficult to make and less profitable to sell than had been predicted. Gyl Chemicals and J. S. Hanson were not profitable. To counter these trends, the extension of manufacturing and laboratory facilities continued at the Brentwood and Ilford sites and a new multistorey office block was started at Ilford. The BBC television monopoly had just been terminated and among the first advertisements on the commercial channel were ones for Ilford products.

By the next year net profit had dropped, despite a

record sales turnover. Times were difficult, with food and petrol still rationed and oil for the factory boilers scarce. The company acquired a new factory site, at Basildon, Essex, feeling that concentration of the smaller, scattered sites on to one near Brentwood would enable overheads to be reduced and would provide more scope for expansion.

The American market was attacked by the creation of Ilford Incorporated, in New York, to replace several agents who had previously handled the company's goods in the USA.

The 1957 profit was up again and the dividend, held at 15 per cent since 1953, was increased to 16 per cent. Illingworth retired as joint managing director, after nearly 50 years' service, leaving Dimsdale as sole managing director. He was watching production economics and since 1955 had employed G. A. Jones, who had worked for Kodak and PA Consultants, to improve efficiency in the factories following the incentive bonus introductions in 1948, which had been only partially successful.

Bexford was keeping down the cost of film base by efficient running. The Pembroke Carton and Printing Company was acquired to enable Ilford to cut packaging costs by producing its own cartons. The Duke of Edinburgh opened extensive new research laboratories at Brentwood, named after Colonel Ramsden, who had been managing director of Selo from 1933 to 1936.

However, although it was clear that profit would be difficult to increase in the coming years, the reasons were hard to analyse. The company relied mainly on a system of historical accounting, which was slow in operation. Standard costs were produced for stock evaluation and product pricing but factory controls were based primarily on time rather than money and there was no financial budgetary control system, only rudimentary planning and no systematic factory scheduling. A classical business situation had arisen; turnover was increasing but profit was not and nobody knew why.

A careful study persuaded the board that it would be difficult to raise more capital on the market but that colour photography, which was possibly the key to the future, could not be developed without further massive injections of cash.

At this point, Imperial Chemical Industries, who had made a previous tentative approach to Ilford in 1947–48, made new overtures. ICI had been attracted by colour photography in 1947, mainly as a new venture for their dyestuffs division at Blackley, Manchester, following information published after the war in the British intelligence reports about German industry. With some help from scientists brought from Germany, they had created a plant at Fleetwood, Lancashire, to make colour negative film and printing paper but had experienced technical and economic problems. They now offered Ilford £6.4 million for additional shares in the company, thus becoming holder of 32 per cent of the issued share capital, and gave Ilford access to ICI research results in the negative-positive colour film field and exclusive licences on a royalty basis, to enable Ilford to manufacture and market material based on ICI research.

This appealed to the board and the shareholders were informed on 23 September 1958. An extraordinary general meeting on October 23 accepted the proposal and, for the first time, Ilford had a substantial industrial company supporting it, with two ICI directors on its board. Once again, the future looked rosy and Ilford shares reached an all-time high on the London stock market.

8. New ownership (1959-1979)

From the beginning of 1959, Ilford was therefore for the first time associated with a large industrial organization. Although Imperial Chemical Industries negotiated for only 32 per cent of the new and enlarged equity, it effectively gained control; no other shareholder held nearly such a large proportion.

The two ICI representatives appointed to the Ilford board were Leslie H. Williams, a deputy chairman of ICI, and Dr John Avery, chairman of their dyestuffs division. Albert E. Frost, treasurer of ICI and Rowland S. Wright, later a chairman of ICI, were appointed alternates.

Both Williams and Avery had helped to initiate and had strongly supported the ICI entry into the colour photography market; they had now determined to make Ilford the vehicle for a stronger attack on the world photographic market, based upon Ilford's already strong position in black and white products. Their strategy, apart from the injection of capital, was to let the company direct its own affairs, but to provide support in three ways: in research, especially on dyes; in modern management techniques; and by throwing open ICI central facilities to Ilford.

The entry of ICI was taken calmly by most Ilford employees: the directors had explained the benefit of ICI support and everyone was convinced of the excellence of Ilford products. Practically nobody felt threatened by the virtual takeover of the company. The shareholders, too, were generally confident of the value of ICI backing.

There had been no surprise, except possibly on the part of ICI, when Ilford technicians recommended closure of the ICI plant at Burn Hall, near Fleetwood, Lancashire, on the grounds that it could not be run economically.

Both the ICI directors and Sir Frederic Hooper (managing director of Schweppes and a non-executive director of Ilford) felt that top management should be strengthened, especially as Wilfrid Dimsdale had been ill for two months at the end of 1958.

James Philipps remained as non-executive chairman, but a new appointment, executive deputy chairman was filled by Rupert Withers, who was also, from April 1959, a joint managing director with Dimsdale. The last-named had been sole managing director since Illingworth retired two years before, while Withers had been a senior partner in Urwick Orr & Partners, management consultants, and had previously held senior positions in financial management, with particular emphasis on business overseas, but never within the photographic industry.

At the end of 1959, William Metcalfe retired from the board. He had ceased to be company secretary in 1953, that position being filled by Francis W. Hutchinson, assistant secretary since 1950. Metcalfe had since been financial director and Hutchinson now joined the board in that capacity as well as remaining secretary. George A. Jones, production manager since 1957, joined the board at the same time.

A new, young chief accountant, W. R. M. Ross, was appointed in November 1958; budgetary control and a standard costing system were introduced soon afterwards by C. F. Howell, an experienced newcomer, who had been a financial management consultant.

The new arrangements made little difference to the normal routine of company business, mainly because considerable activity was already evident on a variety of new ventures. The building of a factory on a fresh site at Basildon had been proceeding well since 1958 despite exceptionally bad winter weather. In preparation for the move, plans were being laid for the closure of the factories at Watford and Edmonton and of the warehouse at Leyton. Key personnel were offered posts at Basildon; the advertising department, under George Dorman, moved to Ilford.

It was also decided to close the Park Royal factory and to move the paper cutting and packing operations carried out there to Mobberley, where the papers were coated.

This redevelopment was carried out with great skill by W. J. Kemp, who joined the company as head of work study in 1961 and was later to become managing director of Ilford Australia Pty. He worked out a simplified layout on material-movement principles and achieved a very large increase in productivity. This resulted in 127 redundancies (half the Park Royal labour force) but was accomplished without disruption as a result partly of the disinclination of most of the employees to move so far and because of the (for that time) good compensation terms offered. Stanley Saville, factory manager at Park Royal, became distribution manager for the company and the new combined plant at Mobberley was managed very successfully by the existing factory manager, Tom Mitchell, who further improved the efficiency of the combined operation.

Edgar Willison, staff architect, received an award from the RIBA for the design of the new Mobberley finishing building.

The Bower House was sold; the engineering development activities were transferred back to the Ilford site under the chief engineer, Archie Horton. Farringdon had retired in February 1957 as a result of ill health and John Thornton was now chief development engineer. The chief architect, Edgar Willison, had become responsible directly to Dimsdale, managing director.

The factory at Warwick, purchased from Austin Edwards in 1952, had by now ceased manufacture except for the spooling of roll films. However, the spider coating machines were still available there and they were prepared for film coating again, the demand on Brentwood having begun to exceed the capacity despite improved manufacturing methods. Mobberley was also investigating new methods of producing emulsions and coating paper products.

The sales department continued much as before apart from the closure of the Ilford Galleries in High Holborn, originally inherited from Wellington and Ward for use as a demonstration centre and picture gallery. The manager, A. F. Braithwaite, who had taken over in September 1956 from E. Scott Job, had to close the galleries, to make way for a new one-way road system. The company was unable to find other suitable London premises until the opening of Ilford House in Oxford Street, in August 1960, although the trade counter and London stockrooms were installed at Alan House in Saffron Hill. The Oxford Street premises was opened by the Duke of Bedford and was used as a show-place for new products and as a centre in which amateur photographers could discuss problems.

Meanwhile, Collins, by now chief chemist at the colour research laboratories, was examining, with the help of the engineering staff, the ICI colour know-how to supplement Ilford's own research and trying to make up for time lost during the Second World War. It was a disappointment to the board to find how difficult the ICI techniques were to merge with Ilford formulae and manufacturing systems.

An overriding benefit was the ICI patent for 'integral masking' of colour negative film, which avoided the Kodacolor patents. This led to the introduction in 1960 of Ilford's first colour negative film. At first it was available in roll-film format only and was named Ilfacolor.

A printing paper, based upon ICI work, was made to match the film but, for a time, developing and printing of the products was restricted to Ilford's own plant. This was mainly to gain experience and make any necessary adjustments in specification without having to persuade large numbers of photofinishers to alter their processing techniques. However, to avoid a monopoly situation, photofinishers were free to make prints on competitive printing papers from negatives processed by Ilford.

The introduction of the Ilfacolor negative made necessary a decision on the Ilford Colour 'D' transparency film and on the silver dye-bleach print service, since Ilford research and production were unable to continue to handle such a wide range of totally different colour systems, in addition to all the work needed to progress monochrome camera films, papers, X-ray, graphic arts and motion picture films, and a range of glass plates.

In 1960, after much heart-searching, the decision was taken to concentrate resources upon Ilfacolor, the improvement of Colour 'D' under the new name Ilfachrome, and to extend the latter to double-8 cine format. All these materials were to be processed at the new Basildon factory; Jack Coote was transferred from Richmond to manage the unit.

Almost at once, Agfa protested against the use of trademarks using the prefix 'Ilfa' and, after some negotiation, the materials were renamed Ilfocolor and Ilfochrome; the small change from 'a' to 'o' was sufficient to settle the dispute.

The silver dye-bleach print system was dropped as, although very successful, it could be perfected only by a large amount of long-term research.

By this time, the postwar sellers' market was on the wane: profits started to fluctuate. Between 1948 and 1954 they had risen by nearly 70 per cent but since 1955 they had dropped steadily. The board decided to examine the reasons. Entry into the USA had been much more difficult than forecast and Ilford USA were still running at a considerable loss. The capital injected by ICI, much as it was needed, had to be serviced: Ilford were simply not generating the profit needed to pay ICI and the other shareholders a good dividend while carrying out a massive research programme and expanding their business overseas. Turnover was rising steadily but costs were rising faster.

This was the time of the United Kingdom's original decision not to join the European Economic Community, which had then just been formed. Ilford felt that they would have benefited from UK entry and that exporting would now be more difficult. They responded by formulating a new approach to export markets.

A minority interest was secured in the equity of the Spanish company Valca SA to obtain access to that market and, it was hoped, indirectly to those in South America. Ilford obtained this in return for know-how and technical assistance—its first attempt to sell its knowledge as opposed to products. Additionally, a selling company was formed in West Germany; the Australian company was strengthened by the appointment to its board of Group Captain W. R. (later Sir Raymond) Garrett and was encouraged to manufacture a wider range of products; finally, steps were taken to reorganize the export sales department, now housed in Clements Road, near the main offices at Ilford.

A number of new products was introduced during 1960. A call from the hospitals for materials allowing patients to receive lower dosages of X-rays resulted in Gold Seal X-ray film. A growing demand for higher productivity among professional and industrial photographers produced Ilfoprint paper and its associated processing machines. Apart from Azoflex, Ilfoprint was the first deliberate 'systems' approach—a material linked with special equipment without which it could not easily be handled. Ilfoprint enabled prints to be produced quickly in a small roller machine which also stabilized them to light by chemical means, thus eliminating lengthy fixation and washing unless an unusually permanent print was needed.

A new range of cameras was introduced, the Sportsman, an inexpensive 35 mm camera made in Germany by Dangelmaier, which later proliferated into a large number of models, some of which incorporated refinements such as coupled range-finders and automatic exposure control.

The home sales department was reorganized in December 1960 on a regional basis. The United Kingdom was split into eight regions. Five were under the management of existing staff (Leslie Miller, Terry Hinchcliffe, Willie Gordon, Norman Giles, and Tom Holmes) and three under newcomers, Stanley Boxall, J. R. Gooch and Brian Hopley, all picked for their ability to introduce a new style of marketing. The company was determined to change its rather old fashioned image and utilize different methods of promotion, especially in the area of retail sales in general and of colour film in particular. There was a determined drive on the professional cine market and on the X-ray business with new films. A decision was taken to develop and manufacture magnetic tape, which was seen as a possible challenge in the motion picture field. Azoflex materials were extended from drawing office application to the duplicating of commercial office material.

In 1961, Sydney Ferris was appointed to the board, continuing in his control of export marketing. George Jones was transferred from production to be sales director under James Mitchell, now joint managing director with Dimsdale.

This was a period of intense activity. Sales of X-ray film had picked up and the Brentwood factory was unable to meet the orders pouring in for films of all types. The cause was partly the long time taken to coat colour films, which therefore occupied an undue proportion of manufacturing capacity. However, very great hopes were placed on these materials, especially as Ilford emulsion expertise had enabled the research laboratories to produce films of higher speed (ASA 32) than Kodak's (Kodachrome was still only one-quarter of that speed). Enormous efforts were therefore made to market the new materials quickly, although new technical difficulties were constantly encountered.

Several attempts were made to find an electrographic copying system to widen the company's activities in the office document field, but without success. The magnetic tape investigation was backed by the commissioning of a report on this market from the Economist Intelligence Unit and a research programme on the technology of striping from Planer. Discussions were held with EMI on a possible joint manufacture project.

Very large numbers of amateur cameras were being sold and, although not a very profitable business, this programme was felt to encourage the sales of films. However, the Advocate camera had proved a disappointment; its design was not to the public taste and the cost of the lens made the retail price of the camera too high. Kennedy Instruments ceased production in October 1960.

The professional motion picture market was also attacked. L. J. Wheeler from the BBC joined in June 1960 as head of motion picture technical service. A number of popular films was made on Ilford stock.

One of the difficulties at this time was the situation in the graphic arts market. Ilford glass plates had been pre-eminent in the printing industry and their films had also been widely used. However, competitors had introduced films on base materials more stable than the triacetate produced by Bexford, in spite of the

85

surface coating of Saran resin which they used to reduce water absorption. Ilford was therefore disturbed by a considerable loss of lucrative business and looked actively for improved base materials.

ICI had produced polyethylene terephthalate (polyester) sheet under the trade name Melinex and Ilford had hoped in 1958 that ICI would improve the specification of a proportion of it to meet photographic standards, as Du Pont had done with Cronar base. However, ICI considered the project financially unattractive and Ilford was precluded by licences from obtaining supplies from elsewhere. It turned to two other materials, polystyrene and polycarbonate, but neither was satisfactory.

As a result, Ilford lost a large volume of profitable business and was unable to justify continued research on any scale into the special emulsions required. It is arguable that if at this stage Ilford had obtained polyester base and, instead of working to introduce colour films, had concentrated on materials for the graphic arts and for radiography the company might have regained a high level of profitablility quite quickly.

In the event, it was decided to push ahead with colour materials and equipment for the amateur market and for wholesaler photofinishers. In spite of very considerable teething troubles with the colour materials, sales were climbing.

The policy on cameras and associated equipment was to support the sale of films by selling three ranges: a roll-film camera to sell at not more than £2, inclusive of purchase tax; a range of 35 mm precision cameras carrying the Ilford name but imported from Germany; and an 8 mm cine camera from Japan to take the expected 8 mm colour film.

Hopes of a spectacular success in colour were dashed when, in April 1961, Kodachrome II was introduced. This had the same speed as the materials Ilford had been struggling hard for nearly two years to introduce. At this stage, a decision was reached to drop efforts to modify the Ilford materials in such a way that photofinishers could process them in the same baths as the Kodak films. Instead, a new 32 ASA 35 mm Ilfochrome film and a 25 ASA double-8 Ilfochrome cine film were to be introduced as soon as possible, together with a free 'contact' strip print from Ilfocolor negative film, which would allow amateurs to select the negatives from which they required larger prints made. The 'contact' strip was, in fact, printed by projection on an elaborate machine which made allowance for variations in printing times of the negatives on each strip.

New advertising agents were used for the amateur market. Everett Advertising, who had been so successful with the Ilford Films for Faces and Places campaign were replaced in 1961 by Foote, Cone and Belding, who introduced a new approach to the advertising of colour film and advised on packaging and retail marketing aids. Samson Clark (later Davidson, Pearce, Berry and Spottiswoode), who had handled the advertising of other goods since 1930, continued to do so until 1971.

The new material came on the market early in 1962 and was well liked by the customers. By 1963, Ilford had gained 60 per cent of the UK double-8 cine market; Ilfocolor, helped by the strip print, was selling well. Steps were taken to expand the export market. As processing laboratories are expensive, methods were devised of returning exposed films by air from dealers in Europe to Basildon for processing. A very fast handling time was achieved by the use of special transit boxes handled through an arranged customs channel at Southend airport.

Although demand was high, availability of the films was restricted, partly because of the relatively slow manufacturing methods and partly because there was a high level of waste while the company learned the very complex technology. Unforeseen complications arose, such as a tendency for the colour of the picture to be dependent upon the time between exposure and processing. The materials were also found to be sensitive to temperature; a processing laboratory established in Melbourne had eventually to be closed because of the inability of the films to withstand the Australian summer conditions, in spite of confidence based upon prolonged prior testing in the UK in incubators.

During this period the company kept its profit fairly level, despite the difficulties. However, the return on capital employed was dropping. When the budget for 1963 was compiled in August 1962, a decision was taken to curtail overhead expenditure. After much discussion, the board agreed to study the effects of a reduction in the numbers employed in a range of departments by 10 per cent and other areas of overhead expenditure were examined. This study continued to the end of the year, when the customary salary increases were greatly reduced and no annual bonus was paid for the first time for many years. At the same time, Withers combined the duties of managing director with those of deputy chairman and chief executive; J. Mitchell and Dr G. B. Harrison left the company; Dimsdale relinquished the post of joint managing director but remained on the board as a consultant director; Dr C. Waller was appointed research manager.

A managing director's committee was set up attended by the four remaining executive directors and by the research and production managers (the last being W. J. Kemp, who had been appointed in November 1961).

The year 1963 showed a slightly better financial result than 1962; the gross margin fell but by less than the increase in the cost of silver, which rose 27 per cent. Net profit was up, though not in proportion to the 17 per cent increase in turnover.

That year, two events occurred which were to have powerful effects upon the future of the company.

The first was an approach from CIBA AG of Basle, Switzerland. Like ICI, CIBA had been attracted by colour photography as a diversification for their dyestuffs business and had developed silver dye-bleach printing materials. They had acquired for this purpose two small companies: Tellko and Lumière SA. They now sought from Ilford an exchange of research information and technical aid in building a new factory for Lumière in France and for their subsidiary, CIBA Photochemie, in Switzerland.

To speed progress, they now wished to work with an established photographic manufacturer and this wish coincided with Ilford's own desires, since its research effort would be effectively greatly increased by the collaboration and since its ambitions to exploit the European market more vigorously would be facilitated by the formation and operation of joint selling companies with CIBA. Dimsdale was given particular responsibility for technical relations with CIBA.

So Ilford re-entered the silver dye-bleach print market, which they had so recently left, with a new product, 'Cibachrome'. At the same time, Sir Arthur Vere Harvey (later Lord Harvey of Prestbury), a member of the CIBA board in Switzerland and also chairman of CIBA (UK), became a non-executive Ilford director.

The second important event in 1963 was a Board of Trade decision to refer the supply and processing of colour film to the Monopolies Commission following a complaint from wholesale photofinishers that they were being deprived of potential business in processing colour film as a result of manufacturers' selling film 'process paid'. Their report was not published until 1966. Whatever the intention may have been, it eventually succeeded in eliminating Ilford as a serious competitor in the amateur snapshot business.

However, Ilford continued to expand. In 1964, a range of 8 mm equipment made in Japan by Elmo was marketed under a joint name; an agreement was reached with the Polychrome Corporation to market their presensitized lithographic plates; the motion picture business was strengthened both by the introduction of a new camera stock Mark V Cine Negative and, even more, by the acquisition of Zonal Magnetic Coatings. Ilford, having failed to develop its own magnetic recording tapes, saw the threat to photographic film posed by video-tape and stepped in when it heard Zonal was for sale. That company's production of magnetic sound-recording and computer tapes was also of interest, as both fields had attractive business features.

Ilford's marketing department was studying customer reaction and, with minor improvements to Ilfochrome and Ilfocolor, renamed them Colorslide and Colorprint respectively, as being more descriptive of their use. They also had to consider whether to sell film in the new type of easy loading cartridge introduced by Kodak as 126 (Instamatic). Partly because of the manufacturing complexity of the Kodak product, a decision was reached to market materials in the Agfa Rapid cassette, a simpler, easy-loading system developed from the older Agfa Karat cassette. In the event, this proved an abortive decision: the weight of demand forced Ilford to offer the 126 cassette within a couple of years.

Also in 1964, the company installed a new-generation computer, a Honeywell 200, to replace the Leo in handling the mounting volume of invoices and statistics.

In 1965, John L. Porter was seconded from ICI to act as joint managing director (technical). James Philipps resigned after 28 years on the board, 18 as chairman; this marked the end of the company's association with the name of Philipps stretching from 1905, but not with the family, as Dimsdale was related and remained on the board until August 1971. He retired as a consultant to the company in 1973.

The year 1965 was one of mixed fortunes. Net profit exceeded £1 million for the first time since 1957; colour was continuing to do fairly well, although only five per cent of the UK market had been obtained; a new fast black and white film, HP4, was introduced and *Zorba the Greek*, shot on Ilford Mark V stock, was awarded an Oscar. Zonal was showing a good profit. The Cassio company, baryta-coating paper for Mobberley, was modernized. A new 'sunburst symbol' was introduced, the first company identification since the old paddle steamer symbol. And a new style for packaging was adopted, abolishing the old yellow-and-red livery and using a dead-white glazed board for all cartons and boxes.

However, the company was beset by problems. Costs were still rising faster than turnover. The Britannia Works were making losses both in their wholesale photofinishing activities and at the hypo works at Low Moor.

Total wage costs throughout the company were rising fast, partly as a result of a low level of improvement in machine productivity and partly as a result of the end of the Ilford wages plan introduced by T. P. Lyons, chief personnel officer, in 1963. This plan had been evolved to allow shopfloor workers to receive regular wage increments and thus to cool inflationary demands. It had been greeted by the press as a startling innovation and had been intended to run a minimum of four years.

However, by the end of 1965 inflation had overtaken the increments built into the plan. Lyons feared the deteriorating situation would lead to unofficial strikes, a practice which was just then spreading rapidly through the UK. He therefore negotiated an agreement with the General and Municipal Workers Union which would allow a gradual move to 100 per cent trade unionism among process workers, provided all the employees involved signed statements that they would unreservedly agree to abide by union rules.

This agreement again attracted a great deal of attention in the press, as it appeared to be a way of avoiding the growing unofficial disputes in industry. It eventually collapsed as, although Ilford never experienced any serious stoppages, official or unofficial, a proportion of the 2000 employees involved refused to sign the undertaking. Nevertheless, the company was saved from a wages explosion.

The next year brought the Monopolies Commission's report, which found that Kodak's monopoly was not against the public interest. The Commission recommended a reduction in prices and the abolition of the practice of selling reversal films with the cost of processing included in the price. These recommendations were upheld by the Board of Trade but a further recommendation, that import duties on colour films be abolished, was not. Ilford submitted that it was not a monopolist and would be adversely affected by the Commission's report. However, the Board of Trade rejected the company's submission. The consequent price reductions and elimination of certain services, killed the budding Ilford colour business. It was unable to compete profitably at reduced prices while still in the stages of expensive technical and market development.

A flurry of activity followed. Marketing methods were examined, with the intention of reducing the enormous advertising and retail distribution costs, while still providing ways of achieving large-volume sales with a reasonable proportion of film returning to Ilford for processing. Eventually, it was decided that the only effective answer was to offer the film to other distributors to market under their own label. Of them Boots and Film Corporation of America proved, for a few years at least, to be the most effective.

The subsequent agreements with the Film Corporation of America resulted in sales of colour film to America in far larger quantities than those lost within the UK. The Film Corporation of America had developed new methods of marketing through supermarkets, to provide very large quantities of film to feed their photofinishing houses. They offered the snapshot photographer a low-cost alternative to the conventional processing services and soon built up a very large volume of business. Although Ilford sold them the film at relatively low prices, Ilford gained overall because it was able to ship the millions of films in bulk direct to the USA, and later other countries, and it also saved all advertising and distribution costs, which had been very considerable.

In 1966, ICI and CIBA made an offer for all outstanding Ilford shares; the offer was accepted in 1967 by over 90 per cent of shareholders.

The AGM saw the retirement of Leslie Williams who, in his capacity as a deputy chairman of ICI had played a large part in guiding Ilford policy for the preceding eight years. He was succeeded by John D. Rose, the other ICI director on the board being Albert E. Frost, ICI treasurer. Dr P. Erni, chairman of CIBA Photochemie also joined the Ilford board. Rose became chairman in place of Withers, who remained chief executive and joint managing director with John L. Porter. Sir Arthur Vere Harvey became deputy chairman.

The next two years were disappointing. Profitability dropped steadily although sales increased, especially in export markets. Raw material prices increased; silver rose rapidly in price and later reached a peak of 259d per ounce in June 1968, after having been less than one-third of that figure at the beginning of the decade.

In spite of increased business in the USA and the opening of new selling companies in Sweden and Ireland, the only part of the business showing adequate profitability was the magnetic tape operation of Zonal at Redhill, Surrey.

In June 1967, Sir Paul Chambers, chairman of ICI, wrote a critical letter to Withers saying that both ICI and CIBA were disturbed at the low profitability of the Ilford business and were jointly instructing Messrs. Cooper Bros. to make an investigation into the business before any major new investments were undertaken.

This decision was prompted partly by the decision of the Ilford board to try methods of marketing of colour films which were highly unorthodox at that time, though they became commonplace later. The marketing proposal was kept highly secret under the title 'Project X'. It involved marketing Ilford products through unconventional UK outlets, somewhat on the lines of FCA in America. It was disliked by some members of the Ilford board but was shown to be essentially viable by the work of a young accountant, Arthur J. Irwin-Hunt. However, the scheme was eventually voted down and the managers concerned, Jack Britton and Brian Hopley, left Ilford.

Meanwhile, urgent investigations continued to determine ways in which savings could be made. Rationalization was thought to be the answer. The Ilford interest in Bexford was sold to ICI, the owner of the balance of the equity. The Azoflex business was sold to NIG Halden, who were almost immediately bought by Ozalid, Ilford's most formidable competitor in the dyeline business; the hypo works at Low Moor was sold to William Blythe & Co.; shortly afterwards, the Ilford holding in Polychrome GmbH was sold to the company in the USA. Ideas were considered, but discarded, for cutting out other operations such as the production of cassettes and spools, the mixing of compounded chemicals, the manufacture of X-ray screens, and the design of equipment for resale.

In November 1968, Rupert Withers left the company after nine difficult years, John Porter took over as chief executive and joint managing director, Dr Anthony J. O. Axford being the other joint managing director. Axford had originally worked in the Ilford organic chemical research laboratories under Kendall and had been largely responsible for the use of Phenidone in developer formulations shortly after its discovery. He had left to join Ozalid as director of research and development. He had rejoined Ilford in 1966 as research director.

During the year, a new engineering centre was built at Warley, near the Brentwood factory, largely as a result of ideas put forward by Norman R. Wynn, the research leader concerned with the development of coating and drying techniques, who realized that no small part of Ilford's economic difficulties lay in the relatively low productivity of the film-coating department, in spite of major improvements to the spider machines. The last of these, no. 12, had by then been running for nearly 14 years.

In November 1969, ICI decided to sell their share of Ilford to CIBA; the latter company thus became the sole owner of Ilford Limited.

This led to another board reconstruction. John Porter returned to ICI; the other ICI directors resigned, their places being taken by Joseph E. Duffy and Allan S. Rae, both of CIBA. Sir Arthur Vere Harvey became chairman with Axford as chief executive and sole managing director.

At the same time, Cooper Bros (afterwards Coopers & Lybrand), the CIBA auditors, took over the Ilford audit from Turquand Young (later Turquand, Barton and Mayhew & Co.) who had been continuously associated with Ilford since the formation of the company was discussed in 1898.

One consequence of the ICI withdrawal was the new 'arms-length' position occupied by Bexford who were then Ilford's only supplier of film base. When Bexford had been formed, the intention had been to incorporate it within Ilford in due course. Now Ilford was left as the only major photographic company in the world without its own captive source of film base. The consequences of this were to be unfortunate, both financially and technologically.

New plans were now coming to fruition. Although CIBA had a new factory in Marly, Switzerland, and a new coating machine designed by Ilford at Lumière SA, Lyon, France, agreement had also been reached to build a new film-coating machine at Brentwood. This was being designed by the Warley Engineering Centre to produce exceptionally clean and high-quality material at higher speeds and to be capable of applying the very thin multiple layers needed for modern colour films.

Coupled with this project was a new automatic film emulsion-making plant and a new warehouse at Basildon to house the increasing volume of production. Overseas sales were again buoyant.

Despite these investments, morale of Ilford employees was low. When ICI had become a shareholder, the mood had been generally one of satisfaction at obtaining the backing of a large British concern. When CIBA had bought out the remaining shareholders, there had been some disquiet among staff but no serious anxiety. Now, however, there was a fear that the UK operation might be closed in favour of the Swiss and French factories, which were of much newer design. This fear was not allayed when CIBA, following government refusal to allow further major expansion in Essex, actively sought a new site in South Wales on which to build a factory to replace Brentwood, Ilford, Basildon, and Mobberley: as far as most employees were concerned, Llantrisant was as far from home as Marly or Lyon. Moreover, CIBA were seen to be sending technical and financial men to Ilford to assess the capabilities of many who felt themselves to be fully experienced in the industry.

In 1969, an agreement was reached with the Polish government to provide designs, know-how, and plant for paper- and film-manufacturing plants in the Warsaw area. The aim was twofold: to bring a larger return on the company's research effort than could be achieved with the relatively small turnover available to Ilford itself, and to open up business in territories not otherwise available for the sale of the company's products. Formulae and instruction books were provided to cover the production of up-to-date papers, X-ray film, and high-speed camera films. A similar deal had been concluded with Valca SA, in Spain, in 1960 but that had involved acquisition of Valca equity, while this Polish contract was on a cash payment basis and therefore somewhat more attractive in the short term. Both contracts led to protracted internal arguments on the adequacy of Ilford's resources for such activities.

Profits improved continuously from 1969 to 1972, as a result of the steps taken to revitalize the business. Ilford gained its first Queen's Award to Industry in 1970 for its export achievements and a long-term agreement was reached with Film Corporation of America for the sale of a large part of the negative colour film which Ilford had the capacity to make. A new type of Ilfoprint paper was also introduced.

In 1970, CIBA merged with J. R. Geigy Ltd. Geigy were not strangers to Ilford, as many executives had made contact ten or fifteen years before. They had supplied dyes for the Ilford silver dye-bleach process, had collaborated in the production of hydroquinone at Gyl Chemicals and had helped produce Phenidone and other organic chemicals.

The immediate appointment by Ciba-Geigy of Henri Schramek to the Ilford board was therefore popular, particularly as it was known that he had worked for Geigy in Manchester and knew the British industrial scene intimately.

Some important decisions were taken at once, the largest being to sell the Ilford site, occupied for 93 years, while the property market was booming. Agreement was reached with the purchaser to continue to use the site for three years, while a new head office was built at Basildon, new research laboratories at Warley and a new glass plate manufacturing plant at Mobberley for the production of nuclear and scientific plates.

The Zonal magnetic film company was sold to Racal as Ilford no longer felt either involved in the motion picture business or as interested as at an earlier stage in video-tape recording. The Britannia Works business of developing and printing amateur snap-shots was also sold, though with some misgivings, as the possession of photofinishing houses was realized to be a good way of testing new products and keeping in touch with a market which Ilford might wish to re-enter. The name, Britannia Works, was, of course, retained.

In 1972, as a result of the Ciba-Geigy decision to operate Ilford as part of their photographic group, the Ilford board was reorganized again: Hans-Ruedi Hug from Geigy joined George Jones as joint managing directors and John C. Cooper joined the board as finance director. Lord Harvey who was retiring from business, handed over the chair to Allan Rae.

Meanwhile, steps had been taken to improve morale. Undertakings were given that moves of the major sites, apart from that at Ilford, would be avoided, so that employees could be assured of reasonable stability. Provided the company remained adequately profitable, capital would be provided for the modernization and expansion of existing plants.

More important to British employees, however, Ilford Limited was declared not merely to be part of the photographic division of Ciba-Geigy but rather of a newly formed Ilford Group, which would be responsible for the worldwide operation of the parent company's interest through its own factories and independent selling companies. The Ilford Group would include *inter alia* Ciba-Geigy Photochemie AG at Fribourg and Lumière SA at Lyon.

The formation of the Ilford Group was a unique step on the part of Ciba-Geigy, as no other division's management was located outside Switzerland.

In August 1973, Dr Axford took up an appointment with American Can Corporation, and relinquished his position as deputy chairman, though he remained on the board until 1975. Thomas W Parton was appointed to the board in August 1973.

Parton, who had worked for Geigy at Manchester and latterly been head of the Ciba-Geigy organization in Canada, had joined the board to follow Axford and became chief executive and managing director of the Ilford Group from January 1974.

In that year, the company gained its second Queen's Award to Industry, again for export sales, which had increased by over 50 per cent between 1972 and 1974. Shortly afterwards a clever new system called Ilfospeed was introduced; this enabled enlargements to be processed extremely quickly and proved popular with professional, industrial, commercial, and press photographers.

However, the new group had decided not to concentrate entirely upon those markets and had

Figure 32   Ilford House, Group head office, opened in 1977 at Basildon.

realized that, although the amateur colour snapshot market had largely been removed from its grasp by the Monopolies Commission, the amateur hobbyist, who carried out his own developing and printing, provided an interesting market. Consequently, Cibachrome A was introduced, which enabled excellent colour prints to be made relatively easily from colour transparencies of any make. This proved popular in the United States and later in Europe.

The board was strengthened in 1975 by the appointment of John S. Fraser as marketing director and Dr Franz Trautweiler as research director. Fraser had graduated from the Ilford company in Australia, where he had demonstrated that he could handle larger projects; Trautweiler had been applying his lively mind to research at Marly for some years, after having worked for Eastman Kodak in the USA.

In 1976 Ilford left the Ilford site, after 97 years; the last glass plates were coated there on 11 November 1975. While there were many regrets, the move was seen to be necessary. The rebuilding of the old site would have been expensive and difficult.

When it had been decided in 1973 to sell the site, a relocation project team had been set up under Keith J. Williams, with representation from all levels within

the company. The architects, Farmer and Dark, for the new head offices at Basildon, were briefed to design a landscaped internal layout to accommodate 400 staff but without separate offices even for the most senior executives, in order to provide good air-conditioned facilities and a flexible layout (Figure 32). The building was also to house the technical service department with its darkrooms and experimental equipment and a 100-seat lecture theatre. A new research block was also built at Warley alongside the engineering centre.

This last was welcomed, though the open office plan at head office was received with mixed feelings; some of those who had good personal offices before found the open plan distracting while others, less fortunate previously, welcomed the bright comfortable new surroundings.

A very similar relocation was carried out by Lumière SA in France, which moved from le Rue de 1me Film, Lyon, where the Lumière brothers had pioneered cinematography, to a new site at St Priest some miles outside the city. Other changes took place that year. The association with Valca SA in Spain was ended; the shares being sold; the Ilford holding in Pembroke Carton and Printing was also sold; Norman

R. Wynn, who had been responsible for production improvements for some years, joined the board as production director.

The company was still introducing interesting new products: a range of microfilm had been launched; HP5 film replaced HP4 as the group's ultra-high-speed film for professionals among whom it attracted considerable interest; a new version of Multigrade paper was introduced, similar to Ilfospeed but with printing contrast controlled by the colour of the light source; and a new combination of X-ray film and screens (activated by rare earth salts) was introduced to enable radiographers to give still lower dosage of rays while achieving better diagnosis.

So, by 1979, Alfred Harman's company, having passed through 100 years of sunshine and storms and now an autonomous part of a worldwide commercial organization was preparing itself to take an even more effective position in a rapidly-changing industry. Of the many manufacturing companies operating in 1879, very few stayed the course. Many, including Tellko and Lumière, had merged with Ilford or formed part of the Ilford Group. Four or five others had, however, risen to challenge their position.

Where did Ilford now see its future? Tom Parton had taken over as chief executive at a time of growing world financial crisis. Possibly this had merely spurred him into revitalizing the company by the introduction of profit centres and new financial control systems, ably assisted by John Cooper who had spent the previous two years reorganizing the procedures in the finance department and improving management control through new information systems. John Fraser moved from marketing to be chief executive when Parton was promoted to other duties in Ciba-Geigy in November 1978.

The Ilford Group of Ciba-Geigy was now a structure based upon five main profit centres, four manufacturing and one comprising the selling activities, which in turn were broken down into the individual profit centres of the selling companies around the world.

The group employed nearly 6000 people, the majority being in the UK but 650 being employed in Switzerland and 550 in France. As a result of improvements in efficiency during the relocation exercise, the total of employees had been reduced by 900 since 1975.

The group turnover represented only 2 per cent of the world photographic market. However, this market was dominated by the Kodak organization which held about half the business. Agfa-Gevaert, Polaroid, Fuji, and Du Pont had a somewhat bigger proportion than Ilford, while 3M, GAF and Konishiroku enjoyed a similar amount; about 7 per cent of the market was split between another 15 or 20 smaller manufacturers, including those in eastern Europe, and South America.

These figures, however, have to be read in the knowledge that Ilford operated in limited sectors of the market, while many of the others included a variety of products in their ranges, such as cameras, colour films, instant snapshot materials, diazo papers, and other goods not offered by Ilford.

The problem for Ilford at the end of its first century was to know how far to change its policies. The withdrawal from a large part of the colour market, from the amateur snapshot market, from wholesale photofinishing, from magnetic tapes, and from the manufacture of film base, had placed the group in a relatively low-growth and low-profit sector of the market. However, the Ilford Group retained great technical strengths. The long experience of Ilford Limited, with its continuing tradition of active research, the newer contribution of Ciba-Geigy Photochemie in Switzerland and the long experience of Lumière SA in France provided a formidable combination poised to introduce new facets of photographic technology. With the increase in the price of silver, moving steadily towards £3 per ounce, film products in smaller formats, coupled with materials using little or no unrecoverable silver, were of increasing importance. These Ilford was singularly well adapted to exploit. With even more sophisticated products, and more economic methods of manufacture, profit margins seemed likely to rise.

Ilford entered its second century with confidence and keen expectation.

9. Members of the family-1

Thos. Illingworth & Co. Ltd

In the decades following Harman's start in business, many others entered the field. Some soon faded; some were absorbed by the more successful companies; very few have survived. Ilford, Limited took over many of those that did.

One of the first companies to join Ilford was Thos. Illingworth & Co. Ltd; its well-equipped works at Park Royal, London, became a major manufacturing site of the group. Moreover, it was one of the few companies whose top management came to hold a similar position after amalgamation; Thomas Midgley Illingworth, son of the founder, became a joint managing director of Ilford, Limited.

Illingworth's was a family business and the family had had a long association with photography. The head of the family, Thomas Illingworth, was born in Oldham, Lancashire, in 1838 and served his apprenticeship in photography under J. Eastham of Manchester in the pioneering days of the 1850s. At 24 he set up as a photographer in Halifax and, at various premises, practised there all his life. His cousin, William Illingworth, was also a portrait photographer with a considerable reputation at Northampton. Thomas's son, another Thomas, was born in Halifax in 1869. He went to London and at 19 set up a business as photographic printer and dealer at 38, Sheriff Road, West Hampstead; a note in the *British Journal of Photography* (1890) refers to the receipt of a price list from Thos. Illingworth & Co. who 'besides printing in a variety of ways also engages to refill roll holders and to keep some Scovill goods'.

The business prospered for, after only two years, Illingworth took over bigger premises at Ruckledge Avenue, Willesden, the *BJP* reporting that: 'the growth of Messrs Illingworth's business is a testimonial to the excellence of their work'. In 1896 the company opened showrooms at 5 Soho Square, London, to display enlargements and photographic goods—including the popular Seavey backgrounds in the fashionable romantic style of the portrait painters of the eighteenth century.

At first, the works were used primarily for the production of prints and enlargements by the carbon and bromide printing processes, but from 1900, manufacture of photographic materials was gradually undertaken and expanded. The improved carbon process (by Swan) required 'tissues' coated with gelatin containing carbon black or coloured pigments. After sensitizing with a dichromate solution the tissue was exposed through the negative to daylight, the action of light hardening the gelatin, imagewise. By washing in warm water a relief image was formed which, on transfer to paper, formed the final print.

Because of the long exposure required, large pictures were made by printing from enlarged negatives made by the wet collodion process: the enlargers used for this stage, and for the bromide enlargement, employed daylight as the illuminant and the exposures were timed by counting seconds. Mounting and framing were undertaken and artists were employed to colour bromide prints and to retouch. Artists were a very important section of the factory and in the period from 1895 to 1898 the monthly wage bill for artists was about half the total, which varied from £40 to £80. Artists were better paid, the top ones earning £4 per week compared with the top wage of £3 10s in other departments.

Illingworth started selling photographic equipment but by 1903 this line was dropped as the company increased its manufacturing processes. Starting with the manufacture of tissues for the carbon process in 1902, two years later Illingworth was marketing Zigo, a self-toning printing paper, and bromide papers; both were launched by competitions. By 1908 the range was further increased, an advertisement depicting 'the Famous Factory from whence flows daily to all parts of the world an endless stream of the Popular Printing Papers "Zigo", "Zigas" the King of Gaslight papers, "Zelvo" the bromide paper with a carbon surface, "Ivory Matt Bromide", the very latest success in bromide papers and POP—the best in the World'.

The picture of the works showed three main buildings: a photo works of four storeys, studios with two storeys and expansive glass roof, and a three-storey office block. The original site at Ruckledge Avenue was described as a double-fronted house with room for expansion. In 1907, over 60 people were employed. The largest department, the manufacturing department, employed 18, the gross profits of this section having grown from £93 in 1903 to £10 144 in 1912. This expansion had been brought about by increasing the capital. In 1902, the nominal capital was £20 000 of which £9370 had been issued, by 1905 the issued capital had been increased to £14 000. In the same period, assets had increased from £14 000 to £35 000 and net profits from £1018 to £8526.

In July 1909, there is an account of Illingworth's annual outing. A group photograph shows about a hundred people, the ladies in flowing white dresses and large-brimmed ornate hats and the men mostly in dark suits wearing stiff-brimmed boaters with an occasional bowler. The party started at 7.00 am, travelling by train to Richmond, and thence by steam launch to Chertsey. The day was favoured by steady sunshine and the afternoon was devoted to sports of various kinds including 'some races of a novel character'. Judging from the dress of the ladies and the formality of the men's attire one wonders how strenuous the games were or how far stripping was allowed. They arrived home, the report said, shortly before midnight 'for the firm of Illingworth plays with the same amount of zest and energy with which it works'.

In the Japan-British Exhibition in London, 1910, Illingworth won gold medals for its self toning papers and for its enlargements, but the main feature of an advertisement announcing these awards was the introduction of Slogas, hailed as 'a new epoch in photographic development papers'. The name, implying a paper suitable for exposure to gaslight and slow enough not to need a proper darkroom, lasted over 20 years.

With a go-ahead management and business booming, the company was ready to expand and on 4 September 1912, the foundation stone for a new factory in Cumberland Avenue, Park Royal (not far from the Willesden site) was laid by Illingworth's mother, recently widowed.

The ceremony was semi-private, attended by members of the family, co-directors, and heads of departments, but the publicity value was not overlooked and a photograph appeared in the *BJP* with a short report of the event. Later in the year another note appeared saying that Willesden UDC had passed plans for the erection of additions to the works in Cumberland Avenue. A full account, illustrated by six photographs, appeared in the *BJP* for 19 September 1913, of a visit to the new factory. The front view showed buildings which were basically

unchanged up to the time Ilford Limited left the site in the late 1950s. The view within the factory, looking at the front office block from the other side, showed that the factory yard was still under development: other photographs showed the showroom, the showcard-mounting department, the laboratory office, and the trimming and cutting machines.

At the time, the site was described as being on 'high ground commanding a view of the rural district which stretches from Alperton in the direction of Harrow and Uxbridge' and was 'in the clear air of the country'. Nevertheless, the observation was made that air admitted to the factory was filtered and either heated or cooled according to the needs of the particular factory operation. The total floor space was said to be in excess of 40 000 ft², 'this being taken up in administrative offices and showrooms, the photo manufacturing unit of emulsion making, coating and finishing, the work rooms for enlarging and printing and dining and tea rooms for the numerous staff'. The factory equipment was judged to represent the most modern practice, the emulsion plant, for example, 'removing the emulsion from chance contamination by handling in mixing and washing': there was emulsion storage facility for 3000 gal of emulsion.

The coating machine was of the festoon type, the track being some 270 ft long and the loops 12 ft high. This one machine was capable of turning out 3 miles of paper a day and in 1912 the production of postcards was said to have been 15 million. Comment was made on the well-arranged flow of materials through the processes and low light traps enabled such movement from dark rooms to light rooms 'without the possibility of fogging'. The testing of the coated paper was briefly mentioned, the quality being tested 'both as regards good black prints and sulphide toning'. Carbon tissues were made in another factory block, 50 different tissues and 30 different transfer papers being marketed.

Pigments for the tissues were ground, mixed, and coated on the premises. The enlarging and specimen departments were also visited and in contrast to the 'fluted mirrors' reflecting daylight for the enlargers at the old Willesden works, the new equipment used mercury-vapour lighting. The largest enlargements were up to 54 in wide, Illingworth believing this to be the widest material coated in the country (Rajar made the same claim at about the same time). Wet collodion plates were still being used for making enlarged negatives for printing by the carbon process in sizes up to 50 in × 40 in,

With the starting up of the new factory, business

continued to flourish and agents were appointed worldwide: the old site at Ruckledge Avenue remained on the books of the company until 1919 but how much of it was used is not known. Illingworth, very publicity-minded, encouraged visits to the factory and in the May before the outbreak of the First World War a party of over 250 members of the Photographic Congress visited the factory. They were conducted round the works in small parties by well-informed guides and, on leaving, were given souvenir albums containing photographs of the factory. The report of the visit made a special point of noting that before being sent out every sheet of paper was examined by 'gloved girls'. This thorough inspection was a feature of the company's subsequent advertisements.

Soon after the war started, Illingworth went to the Continent to buy and arrange the transport of baryta-coating machinery and managed to get it to the UK having, the report said, to avoid a U-boat on the way. Prior to the setting up of this department within the factory, supplies of baryta-coated paper had been obtained from Germany. The old ledgers of the company quote the value of the baryta department in 1914 at £832 and an entry for 1915 quotes as additions to plant 'a coating machine for B' (assumed baryta) at £443. All photographic manufacturers seemed to do well during the war and Illingworth was no exception, net profits increasing steadily from £7918 in 1914 to £41687 in 1918. An advertisement in the latter year claimed the largest photograph in the world—a picture of tanks advancing into battle, shown at the official Naval Exhibition at Princes' Galleries, London, and also at an exhibition at Brighton, opened by Lord Beaverbrook, Minister of Information.

During the war the department doing trade enlarging and printing (including carbon prints) was gradually run down, closing completely in 1917, so that Illingworth had then divested the company of the lines with which he had first started business and was now entirely a manufacturer of photographic papers. At the end of the war, still seeking publicity, demobilization of one of the company's representatives was reported and so was the reorganization which followed the war. Among those demobilized was Thomas's eldest son Captain T. Midgley Illingworth, who was to play an increasingly active part in the company's affairs.

In the next few years a number of new products were introduced and the Illingworth trademark, a horse shoe, appeared. The advertisements said this was, 'itself a guarantee of quality'. Two new products were Zona a warm-tone development paper and Salona a slow-speed paper intended for the portrait photographer. Around this period, too, indicative of the connection now being formed with Ilford, Limited, 14 varieties of plates were marketed, Studio Fast, Studio Extra Fast, Studio Ortho Fast and Fleet being among them. The last was a rapid plate for press photography and other high-speed outdoor work: they were made at Ilford.

In October 1922, it was announced that Thomas Illingworth had resigned as managing director and was being succeeded by his son. The founder, however, remained on the board as a consultant director. Illingworth's retirement was short, for he died on 13 May 1923, after an operation for peritonitis. The family had only two years earlier suffered the loss of their second son, Captain Guy Russel, in a motor accident in Poona. Apart from the vigorous pursuit of his business Thomas Illingworth had taken a prominent share in local affairs. He was a JP for the county of Middlesex, vice chairman and a governor of the Willesden General Hospital and president of the West Willesden National Unionist Association. He was also vice president of the Society of Yorkshiremen in London. He had served on the council of the British Photographic Manufacturers' Association and the council of the Royal Photographic Society, of which he had been a member since 1898.

As a result of collaboration with Ilford, Limited and the formation of Selo Ltd, Illingworth in 1923 started to market roll films in what was to become the familiar bright blue carton. At the same time, completing the full range of papers, a collodion self-toning printing-out paper was introduced.

During the 1920s the policy of encouraging visits to the factory was very much in evidence. An advertisement during the British Empire Exhibition of 1924 invited overseas visitors to the exhibition to visit the factory—only 10 minutes run by car from the exhibition grounds. In May 1927, some 300 members attending the Photographic Congress were shown around the works and a group photograph was taken at the start on 'staging erected for that purpose'. A 10 ft long enlargement of the photograph was on display by the time the party had completed their tour. In the following year there were visits from the North London Professional Photographers Association and several parties from the International Congress on Photography held in London that year.

From this period on, the Illingworth company was progressively absorbed into the Ilford organization. The site at Park Royal was fully used for paper production until the mid-1930s when the emulsion-making and coating operations were transferred to Mobberley, Cheshire, the factory of the old Rajar company. The baryta-coating department, started up in the early years of the war, was closed about 1932 when Cassio Ltd, an Ilford-owned subsidiary, became fully equipped to undertake the whole of the baryta-coating requirements. The finishing operations which had been carried out on the paper coated at Mobberley were finally transferred to Mobberley in the mid-1960s, making this the complete and only paper manufacturing plant of Ilford Limited.

Midgley Illingworth, who had assumed control of the company on the death of his father in 1923, became joint managing director of Ilford Limited and sales director in the years following the amalgamation.

The Imperial Dry Plate Co. Ltd

Imperial Dry Plate was started by Dr J. J. Acworth at Cricklewood, in north west London. He set up laboratories at Cricklewood primarily for research purposes but, sensing a growing market for photographic materials, he expanded his laboratories into a plate-making factory. These were first advertised in 1892.

The works at Cricklewood were visited by the editor of the *BJP* and reported upon in that journal. The factory was:

> . . . pleasantly situated on the outskirts of Cricklewood and facing the pretty open country of Dollis Hill and Edgware . . . the erection itself is a neat structure in harmony with its surroundings and should the meadows in its vicinity be one day covered, as seems possible, with villa residences, the inhabitants will have no cause to complain of that unsightliness or other drawbacks usually associated with manufacturing premises.

Particularly interesting is the concern shown for the local inhabitants—an aspect over which Ilford Limited took great care when rebuilding the frontage of their main factory in Woodman Road, Brentwood, in 1975.

The main products of the Imperial factory were plates coated on a Cadett machine and albumen paper for which, some 40 years after its introduction, there was still a demand. This process occupied a considerable amount of space, as the paper was prepared by hand dipping single sheets, which were then dried. Although the plate-coating machine was conventional, the plate-drying arrangements were unusual in that the drying was done in small 'chambers'—too small to be entered by personnel and thus, it was claimed, the risk of contamination could

be avoided. It was noted that Acworth 'had provided himself with a handsome and well-appointed private laboratory for experimental purposes'.

The factory was revisited seven years later and considerable expansion had taken place: the frontage had been extended to 170 ft which was also the depth of the site: the original building used for dry-plate manufacture had been added to on three sides making departments for POP and bromide papers. Not only had the factory grown but so had Cricklewood which had become 'a very large and prosperous suburb'. The factory was now lit by electricity, generated on the premises, and the visitor commented that all the building work and the installations had been personally supervised by Dr J. J. Acworth 'whose success has been thoroughly well deserved'.

Imperial was indeed a flourishing concern, Acworth showing great business acumen in all aspects of manufacture and marketing. He still had not lost his purely scientific interests and had presented a number of papers to the Royal Photographic Society. In these papers, and in the technical side of the business, he was much helped by his wife Marion (*née* Stevenson) whom he married in 1893 and who was the first woman to receive the Diploma of the Royal College of Science. A ledger of the company for this period includes among entries on salaries, payments to 'M.S.' varying from £25 monthly in 1898, £41 in 1903 and £30 in 1911. The 1899 annual outing was shown as: 'Beanfeast £10'. Among more serious matters there were payments of a royalty to Paget Prize Plate of £100, probably for plate-washing machinery and of £25 to Cadett, probably a royalty on the plate-coating machine.

The company specialized in plates, seven types being marketed in 1898; they included Flashlight, Special Rapid, and Fine Grain Ordinary. Orthochromatic plates were introduced in 1908 together with an Orthochrome Non-Filter plate which matched competitors' products. Panchromatic plates came in 1919 with a speed of H & D 275 and X-ray plates were introduced at about the same time. An interesting novelty was DS Backing plates with an antihalation backing containing desensitizer which enabled the plate to be developed in a relative bright light once the backing had dissolved.

In 1902, there were 'reports from both amateurs and professional sources that the Imperial Dry Plate Company is to be Americanized'. Imperial issued a firm denial. Eastman made two bids for Harman's company, one in 1897 when, as the Britannia Works Company, it was still in Harman's hands and another in 1902, when, as Ilford, Limited, the offer was thrown out by the action of a group of shareholders. Did Eastman make an offer for Imperial as well?

By 1918 Acworth had acquired two other small companies, the Gem Dry Plate Co. and, with it, Fluorescent Materials Ltd, but his health was failing. Suffering badly from asthma, he decided to retire from business and this was an additional reason for the amalgamation with Ilford. Acworth died in 1927 leaving £562 000.

Although after Acworth's resignation the company came fully under the control of Ilford, this was not made generally known and a very full range of products continued to be marketed under Imperial's name. Since 1898, the company had issued an annual publication that became well known to photographers all over the world—the *Imperial Handbook* which ran until 1927; a complete set is held in Ilford's research library. The handbook listed materials marketed by the company and contained articles on interesting photographic topics and techniques. Eclipse and Eclipse Ortho plates were introduced in 1922 and at the same time, as with the other companies joining in with Selo, roll films. Imperial's cartons were green whereas Illingworth chose blue but the film within was the same. Flat films called Excelsis appeared in 1925 together with film packs which were popular at that time, enabling users of plate cameras to have the advantage of a dozen exposures on light-weight film without having to handle bulky dark slides.

In the twenties also, Imperial specialized in X-ray materials not only in plates and films for recording the exposures, but also in the fluorescent intensifying screens (see page 98). Before the introduction of these screens, and of plates and films specially formulated for X-ray exposures, Imperial issued a booklet *Radiography with Imperial Plates and Papers* in which the normal lines of plates, the Special Rapid and Ortho Special Rapid, were advocated for X-ray work. Typical exposure times of a number of radiographs shown were 12 sec (dislocated thumb) to 90 sec (shoulder or knee joint). It was recommended that prints should be made on POP unless wanted urgently, when Gaslight paper was advised.

Special plates for X-rays were first marketed in 1919 and in 1921 a very special plate, the Impex, was introduced, the novelty of which was that the fluorescent material, calcium tungstate, was coated on top of the emulsion thus ensuring optimum contact and hence definition: the tungstate layer was washed off before processing. This was clearly a very wasteful way of employing the expensive fluorescent material. Another booklet on the same topic was *Radiometallography*—a very brief account of the application of X-rays to the non-destructive testing of metallic structures; welding, and reinforced concrete were the examples cited. Two types of screens were made, the Platinocyanide and the screen based on calcium tungstate known as the BV (Brilliant Visual) screen. The former containing a platinum salt was twice the price of latter as was the reclaim value of the screens when their useful life was finished. Later on (1926) a double-coated (i.e., emulsion on both sides of the film) Duoplex M was marketed—the forerunner of all current X-ray films. Imperial also marketed the processing chemicals for their X-ray films.

As a result of the reorganization which took place after full amalgamation the Imperial site was used as the company's central specimen department and the manufacturing facilities transferred elsewhere, intensifying screens, packed chemicals, and film packs going to the Watford factory. The works were finally vacated in 1967 and the activities transferred to Ilford.

The Gem Dry Plate Co. Ltd

The Gem Dry Plate Co. Ltd was first registered in January 1895 with a capital of £2000 in £1 shares. Founder shareholders were R. G. Modera, of Brighton; his wife Helen; the family governess, Annie S. Turnbull; Conrad H. Modera, of Manchester; two clerks; and a traveller.

The interest of the Moderas in photography is not known, but they very soon took on T. E. H. Bullen, described as a merchant of Cricklewood, as managing director to supply technical know-how. Bullen's knowledge of photography and photographic manufacture had been acquired first in the 1880s when he was partner to Leon Warnerke, a well-known pioneer inventor and consultant on photographic matters, and later with Imperial, in what could have been only a short stay. Gem started as a small family business and never achieved any great success.

The factory at Villiers Road, Willesden Green, consisted of two-storeyed buildings surrounding an open yard 150 ft × 50 ft at the end of which was a three-storey building. The plate-coating machine was an Edwards and, after drying, the plates were cut and packed by the same operator, indicating the small scale of the operation. The plates sold in this period were the Meteor, claimed to be the 'quickest' plate on the market. These plates were followed in 1903 by orthochromatic and panchromatic plates (some years earlier than Imperial) these latter, aimed at the photomechanical trade, were the Gem Tricol: 'the finest plate made for three colour work; it has three maxima of sensitiveness, being very sensitive to bluish-violet, greenish-yellow and red'. Another introduction was the Salon, the advertisements warning the user 'Remember the Great Speed of the Gem Salon Plate. DON'T OVEREXPOSE.'

The year 1904 was one of upheaval: T. E. H. Bullen resigned from the company and became managing director of Messrs Bell's Photo Company Ltd of Leigh-on-Sea, Essex: the Moderas resigned as directors but remained shareholders: H. J. Cook took over as chairman, Bullen's position was filled by J. B. Harkness of the Birmingham Photographic Co. and T. Thorne-Baker, who was later to form Fluorescent Materials Ltd, became a director. In the following years the company slumped badly, gross profits falling year by year from £3421 in 1906 to £372 for a half-year in 1912: the paper side having started in this period with a gross profit of £631 showed losses of £23 to £135 in subsequent years.

At the thirteenth AGM held in April 1912 it was reported that 'the work was unsatisfactory and Cook proposed that the company should go into voluntary liquidation at the end of the year'. Later, Cook was empowered to sell the business, including freehold, goodwill, and name, for a sum above £4000. Acworth offered £5250 and this was accepted at the next meeting. From this date until 1918 the sole shareholders and directors of the company were Acworth and his wife Marion. Throughout the war, Gem continued to advertise and market; the accounts showed much improved gross profits fluctuating with a general upward trend from £2367 in 1914 to £14 009 in 1918. It must be assumed that Gem and Imperial worked as one company although advertising and marketing under their own names and keeping separate accounts. In 1918 Acworth resigned from the company and Major General Ivor Philipps and G. H. Fookes, FCA became directors. From this time on it would appear that Gem was continued as an extra holding company for the eventual transfer of it and Imperial to Ilford, Limited, although British Photographic Plates and Papers was the main company for this purpose. The Gem works at Willesden Green were sold in 1919 for £2650 but products under the name of Gem were marketed throughout the 1920s.

Fluorescent Materials Ltd

Fluorescent Materials Ltd formed in 1915 by T. Thorne-Baker, was a very small company. It was formed to manufacture X-ray intensifying screens for radiography with premises at 4 Marlborough Road, South Croydon; not more than three or four people were employed. It supplied screens to Watson and Sons who retailed them to the War Office as was made clear from a record of a complaint that a delivery had been unsatisfactory. At the end of 1918, Thorne-Baker, a well-known figure in scientific photographic circles, and his co-director H. C. Merrett who was a chartered accountant, resigned and the company was taken over by Imperial; the registered address of the company became 14 Ashford Road, Cricklewood. Colonel F. W. Evatt, a director of Ilford, Limited, became managing director and W. S. Withers, secretary of Gem, took over the secretaryship.

Fluorescent Materials continued to hand-coat screens, although Imperial screens were machine coated. Separate books and accounts of the former were maintained although early in 1927 the plant and stores were disposed of to Imperial. The ledger of the company for 1923–32 shows profits starting at £323 and falling to £62 for 1931 with losses in 1924 and 1926 averaging £60. In 1932, the company went into voluntary liquidation. The hand coating of screens was obviously uneconomic compared with machine coating and it is probable that after 1927 this method was no longer used.

10. Members of the family - 2

A number of companies coming into the Ilford organization around 1930 had already banded together as the Amalgamated Photographic Manufacturers Ltd (APM 1921). This amalgamation, of seven companies, regrouped itself in 1928 as Apem Ltd. This regrouping contained only three of the original seven—those that made sensitized materials, leaving out the suppliers of equipment: it was these three that joined with Ilford.

Marion and Co. Ltd

The earliest of these companies was Marion and Co., through which Harman first marketed his plates. Marions were established in 1850 as an off-shoot of the Parisian firm of A Marion & Cie and was set up in England to exploit the *carte-de-visite* and *carte*, photographic novelties which, first introduced in France, soon gained worldwide popularity. The company was described in 1875 as manufacturers, publishers, and dealers in photographic materials of all kinds, advertising 'photographs, plain and coloured—portraits, views, and from pictures, Portrait Albums and albums for unmounted photographs, leather and fancy goods and French Stationery'.

They were also the sole agents in the UK for the 'celebrated Rives papers' used for the albumen process current at the time. The paper had to be sensitized by the user and was sold by the ream: the best grade was 'Extra Superfine Rives, Extra Albumenised' (£10 per ream), each sheet stamped 'Extra Super, Marion & Company'.

Their headquarters were in Soho Square at numbers 22 and 23; they celebrated their half century there by moving to more commodious premises at number 3. When dry plates began to be manufactured by Harman and others Marions became agents for these materials—Britannia Dry Plates, 'Britannia Solution' for developing the plates, Britannia Gelatine Bromide Paper and, among their usual range of albumenised papers, 'The Britannia—a new brand'. Cameras were also sold and Marions are credited with the first real pocket camera (but non-folding) hardly bigger than a hand, introduced in 1884.

After the disagreement with Harman, Marions set up their own dry plate factory at Southgate, north London, and, in 1887, announced that the Britannia plates would now be manufactured there and would bear an intimation to that effect on the label. The advertisement said the factory was under the management of Alexander Cowan and 'is probably the largest and best appointed Dry Plate Factory in England'.

These works were visited in 1896 by the editor of the *BJP* and among the usual run of descriptions of such premises two items are of particular interest. To quote the original words of the report:

> . . . celluloid in strips not more than a yard long and little wider than the finished film is laid down upon glass plates coated with a composition which holds the film firmly and quite flat but allows it to be separated easily by pulling . . .

—the early method of coating film. The second description refers to the coating of paper by what appears to be the slab-coating method:

> . . . the paper is not passed round a roller through a trough of emulsion but the latter is fed up against the surface of the paper in a smooth stream. As it travels vertically upwards the paper picks up as much of the emulsion as it will carry and the surplus flows back again into the receptable from which it is pumped up again for use.

The company was reconstituted in the 1890s, the application for the Certificate of Incorporation being signed by A. L. Marion, G. Bishop, Frank B. Bishop, Gerald M. Bishop, B. F. Bishop, all of the Soho address, and Henri Louis Gaibout and L. Michelet, both of 14 Cité Bergère, Paris. They were the directors and shareholders of the company. Gerald Bishop became one of the joint managing directors of APM Ltd when this amalgamation took place.

Although Marions made a comprehensive range of materials, the company was probably better known for its cameras, particularly the Soho focal plane reflex and the Dainty Soho, a semi-folding reflex camera.

There were two firms closely associated with Marions in this. They were A. Kershaw & Son Ltd, with works at Leeds which made reflex cameras, cinematograph projectors, binoculars, and scientific apparatus, and an off-shoot of this firm, the Kershaw Optical Company Ltd, formed in 1917 to handle contracts for optical instruments for the Ministry of Munitions and which doubtless supplied the lenses for Kershaw's equipment.

A company with a longer connection with Marions was Marion and Foulger which made photographic mounts, frames and mouldings at Magna Works in Bedford. These companies together with Paget and Rajar (and with it Rotary) formed APM Ltd in 1921. After the final link-up with Ilford, Marions' works and premises were not used. The Soho premises became the headquarters of Soho Ltd, formed from the two Kershaw companies and Marion and Foulger.

Paget Prize Plate Co. Ltd

The next of the trio in chronological order of founding was the Paget Prize Plate Co. Ltd. This company played a larger part than Marions in the link-up with Ilford, for its premises were used for miscellaneous manufacturing processes until 1961.

The start of Paget Prize Plate, and its name, resulted from a prize offered in 1879 by Captain (later Sir) Joseph Paget of Staffynwood Hall, Mansfield, Notts. The competition, with a prize of £50 for the best formula for a dry plate emulsion, was organized through the (later Royal) Photographic Society. The winner was W. J. Wilson of Hammersmith. The emulsion was a pure silver bromide washed emulsion and full details of the process were published shortly after the competition.

Wilson decided to go into business and found backing from George C. Whitfield, managing director of the Woodbury Permanent Photographic Printing Co. with the trade mark 'Woodburytype' and works at Castle Bar, Ealing, West London. The new enterprise was set up in the premises of the Woodbury company. From 1882 onwards Paget Prize Plates were listed in the catalogues of Jonathan Fallowfield, the biggest dealers in London, and in the same year the *British Journal Photographic Almanac* had, as the frontispiece, a 'Woodburytype' print from a negative on a Paget Prize plate, thus showing the close linkage between the two companies. At an exhibition of photographs and photographic apparatus held at the Crystal Palace, Paget's display of transparencies from exposures on their plates, particularly some fine yacht studies made by West and Son, attracted much attention.

In 1889, there was a serious fire at the works at Ealing and Whitfield and Wilson decided to build new works in St Albans Road, Watford, on the Callowland estate close to the LNW railway and station. Whitfield relinquished his interest in Woodbury, and that company continued under the proprietorship of Eyre and Spottiswoode.

The new Paget Prize Plate works were soon visited by the photographic press and reported on by both the *BJP* and *Photography*. The factory was run by Whitfield, Wilson, and Whitfield's two sons Sydney and Laurence: it was reported that the whole of the emulsion was prepared personally by Wilson and Sydney Whitfield.

Before coating, the glass was washed in a plate-washing machine patented by Whitfield and Wilson which was capable of dealing with 100 dozen whole-plates in an hour. The coating machine was a Cadett with a coating head made entirely of silver; initially this machine was rented from Cadetts at £100 per annum but was purchased in 1890 for £175, ancillary equipment having been purchased in the previous year for £150.

All the machinery was powered by a 12 hp Marshall engine and boiler (total purchase price £218) which also supplied the steam for 'boiling' and the heating for drying. There was a small gas engine, a Crossley 'Otto', used to keep the ventilation going at night and at other times when the steam engine was not running. The steam from the engine was used to prepare distilled water, 60 gal always being on hand. The general water, from an artesian well was softened before use. The article in *Photography* closed with these words 'we believe this to be one of the most complete and perfectly designed dry plate factories in the World'.

When first started, Paget produced only dry plates but by 1894 was advertising Paget Matt Printing-Out Paper and Paget Prize Collodiochloride Paper; a few years later (1899) a gaslight type paper Gravura, giving a range of tones by development, was introduced. The exposure required, according to an advertisement, was: 'about 2 minutes a few inches from a gas flame'. Plates and Lantern plates continued with new introductions and improvements from time to time.

The Paget company seemed fated to have fires and one on the night of 17 April 1902, completely gutted the block housing the plate manufacture. Within a year a new plate, the Swift H & D 270, was marketed; it was claimed to be twice as fast as the Paget XXXX Plate and competed with the Ilford Monarch introduced earlier in the year and advertised as the 'fastest plate in the world'.

At the annual exhibition of 1908 the Paget stand showed prints made on bromide papers, self-toning papers, POP, Platinoid (a POP giving 'platinum' tones), and Gravura. By 1910 yet more plates came on the market; the Extra Special Rapid (H & D 350 to 400), claimed to be most rapid plate in the world; Special Rapid (H & D 200 to 250) 'for special work requiring the highest quality', Ortho (H & D 200 to 250), and others including Lantern plates. The company was justifiably proud that its plates had been chosen by Herbert Ponting, photographer with Scott's South Pole Expedition of 1910, 'after the most extensive and severe tests' and that they were chosen for their 'superiority and reliability'; they were not, however, used exclusively on the expedition contrary to the claims of the advertisement. In the following year Panchromatic plates were marketed giving 'real colour values and doing away with the necessity for retouching for portraiture'.

Just before the First World War, Paget marketed a colour screen process known as the 'Paget' or 'Finlay' process, developed jointly by G. S. Whitfield and C. L. Finlay: it differed from other screen processes in that the réseau containing the colour elements was a separate entity. One was used for making the exposure and another was bound with the positive made from the camera exposed negative. This system enabled duplicates to be readily obtained.

Although the motto during the war was 'business as usual', the coming of the war must have militated against the marketing prospects of this colour process. Paget, living up to the motto, marketed bromide papers in nine different fancy surfaces. They were able to do this since they held large stocks of French papers. A 1918 price list showed, in addition, about 20 different types of plates including X-ray plates and process plates.

After the war, amalgamation was the order of the day; first there was the cooperative venture of Selo Ltd, enabling Pagets to market roll films and then, in 1921, the formation of APM Ltd followed by Apem Ltd in 1928 when the Paget works at Watford became the headquarters of the new company. Finally, the full merger of Apem with Ilford took place. During these periods Paget products continued to appear under their old names until rationalization of products in the early 1930s.

Pagets was a family business—that of the Whitfields—starting with the founder George, his two sons Laurence and George Sydney and his two grandsons, Geoffrey, works manager of the Watford factory during the Second World War and Philip, who served in the emulsion laboratories at the Brentwood works in the 1940s and 1950s. George Whitfield had a lifelong interest in photography. He died in 1918.

Rajar Ltd

The last of the trio of companies to be founded was Rajar Ltd. Its factory at Mobberley, Cheshire, became, and still is, the sole paper production factory of Ilford Limited.

Rajar appears to have derived from the Brooks-Watson Daylight Camera Company Ltd, formed in 1901, and had works in Great Homer Street, Liverpool. This company marketed the 'Rajar System of Photography'—a film pack adaptor for plate cameras covered by a number of patents taken out by A. A. Brooks and G. A. Watson in the years 1900 to 1902. The Rajar works at Mobberley were built in 1903, and in 1907 a company, Rajar (1907) Ltd, was formed with a capital of £25 000 in £1 shares: 'to adopt an agreement with Rajar Limited, H. T. Parke and others to carry on the business of manufacturers of and dealers in photographic films, plates, cameras, apparatus, materials, etc.' Rajar Limited had been formed by H. T. Parke and C. F. S. Rothwell FCS, the latter being well known in the Liverpool area for his interest in the science of photography. Rothwell later became managing director. Brooks and Watson appeared to have severed connection with Rajar for, although taking out more patents in the period from 1904 to 1908, these were not associated with the name of any company. The name 'Rajar' is of interest because of its unusual spelling—it may have been chosen because it was a palindrome.

The factory, built in the clean air of Mobberley, was enlarged in 1905 the buildings then covering about three-quarters of an acre on a site of two acres. The factory made its own gas to drive engines to generate electricity for lighting and power—all the machines being driven by 'electromotors'. At this time Rajar was marketing the Patent Film Slide for the Rajar System, several varieties of 'Cleron' film to use with the slides (in ten sizes ranging from $2\frac{1}{4}$ in square to 5 in × 4 in in either 6 or 12 exposure packs) and among other items the Rajar quarter-plate folding camera advertised as 'a folding camera that will really go into your pocket'. It looked, however, as if a really large pocket would be required. Although the original interest of the company was in the film changer cameras and the films to go with them, they were soon marketing sensitized paper and by 1907 were advertising that 'Rajar POP Postcards had the largest sale in the world—the natural result of quality':

bromide and gaslight postcards were said to be equally good, with the demand increasing daily. By 1911 a very full range of materials was made: POP and self-toning paper and postcards in glossy, matt, and semi-matt surfaces and a special Rajar enlarging paper in rough and smooth: Isochromatic roll films, the Cleron flat films now also in Iso-Special Rapid, three varieties of Rajar dry plates and Lantern plates: a collodio-chloride paper in matt and glossy for 'high class portraiture' were also in the range.

When the factory was visited by the editor of the *BJP*, a description of the paper coating was given but no mention was made of plate or film coating except to say that there were departments 'for the manufacture of roll film for cartridge cameras and of positive and negative cinematograph film'. The report of the visit ended with the comment that:

> the progress of the Rajar Company, though one of the youngest of the photomaterials firms, is undoubtedly conditioned by the unremitting personal attention which is given to the control of both manufacturing and sales by its managing director and chemist C. F. S. Rothwell.

During this period the fashionable taste in printing papers was for those giving warm tones obtained either from printing-out paper (either subsequently toned or the self-toning type), slow development chlorobromide papers or by sulphide toning prints made on bromide or gaslight papers. To meet this demand Rajar marketed Rajina, a paper giving 'by simple development the warm-black tones obtained with Collodio-Chloride paper when toned with the Gold and Platinum bath'. The self-toning paper brought out was called Autona, the advertisement blinding the reader with science by saying 'It tones automatically with fixing with the gold (Aurum) in the paper'.

At the start of the war new buildings and plant were completed, enabling a doubling of production, and a social event was held to celebrate this achievement. This was held at St John's School, Altrincham, Cheshire, in December 1914 and took the form of a tea followed by evening entertainment of dancing, music and whist. During the war Rajar's advertisements tended to reflect the war to a greater extent than those of other manufacturers. One in 1916 referred to the vital sea line of communications, illustrating it with a photograph of shipping taken and printed on Rajar materials; a later one under the banner of 'The Nation's Call' advertised National War Bonds.

In 1917 Rajar acquired another business—that of the Rotary Photographic Co. Ltd. This had been formed in 1898, with premises at West Drayton, west of London, as an off-shoot of a German firm the Neue Photographische Gesellschaft of Berlin. Both the German and British companies had been founded by Arthur Schwarz, a one-time traveller in the UK for photographic goods. The aim of these companies was the mass production of photographs 'by the mile' for postcards, cigarette cards, advertisements, and the like. The company also marketed Rotograph bromide and gaslight papers but it is not known whether these were made in Britain or—as seems more likely—imported from Germany.

The directors of the British company were all German and with the coming of the war Rotary was wound up and offered for sale by auction on 8 July 1917 at the Mart, Tokenhouse Yard, off Lothbury in the City of London. It was purchased by the directors of Rajar and a new company, Rotary Photographic Company (1917) Ltd, was formed. It is not known what the buying price was but the paid-up capital was quoted at £50 000 and when this (the 1917 company) was sold to APM Ltd in 1922, it realized £5 338. The company, although under the ownership of APM, continued in its own name and in 1929 was reported to have a staff of 400: with the formation of Apem Ltd in 1929 and the splitting up of the constituent companies, Rotary continued on its own and there is still a company of that name at West Drayton. From the time of buying Rotary, Rajar supplied them with the photographic paper for their automatic printing and processing machine. These machines required paper in 26 in widths and a coating machine was devised to coat paper 54 in wide to enable two rolls of 26 in width to be obtained.

The extra plant installed in 1914 enabled Rajar to claim in an advertisement in March 1919 that the Rajar record was that not one of the customers who dealt with Rajar in 1914 was let down in supplies throughout the whole period of the war and that, moreover, large quantities of sensitized materials were supplied to the allied forces. The advertisement also said that the Rajar had made all the baryta paper and card ('a new industry in this country') in their own factory—a story similar to that of Illingworths'. 'Difficulties were made to be overcome and they make business interesting', said the advertisement. The growth of radiography was evidenced by the introduction of Special X-ray Bromide Papers for printing from X-ray negatives giving perfect prints with excellent gradation and detail', made in two grades Normal and Contrasty. They were developed, it was said, in association with experts in this field of radiography.

At the end of 1919, the company was re-formed, a new company, Rajar Ltd (a private company), being registered on November 24 with a capital of £300 000 in £1 shares:

> . . . to take over the business of Rajar (1907) Ltd and to carry on the business of manufacturers of and dealers in photographic materials and apparatus, advertising specialities and novelties, showcards and almanacs, chemicals, etc.

The directors were those of the earlier Rajar Company, A. E. Parke (also a director of Wiggins· Teape and Co. (1919) Ltd and Rotary), T. L. Parke (also a director of Wiggins Teape) and C. F. S. Rothwell (managing director also of Rotary and a director of Lilywhite Ltd). This reorganization of the financial side of the company must have been made as a prelude to joining with APM in 1921.

In this period, Rajar often advertised to supply baryta-coated paper for sensitizing in small or large amounts and the offer was even made to baryta-coat customers' own paper to their requirements: they must have had baryta-coating facilities in excess of their own needs. These advertisements continued after the formation of APM. Rajar continued to market under its own name and had a full range of bromide, gaslight and POP papers and roll films, which by this time were being made by Selo. A new type of material introduced in 1923 was the Plan Copying Paper: 'Supplied in reels to fit Plan Copying Cameras—as used in all up-to-date Engineering Works, etc'.

The Rajar company of 1919, having served its purpose, was put into voluntary liquidation, a proceeding that although started on 28 January 1921, was not completed until 17 September 1929— a cause of the delay in settling the accounts was a dispute over the excess profits duty. The assets of the company were stated to be £304 796: for comparison, the capital of the 1907 company was £25 000 and that of the 1919 company £300 000. The principal shareholders were T. L. Parke, Miss A. M. Parke, H. T. Parke and C. F. S. Rothwell; among the minor shareholders were members of the staff.

Although Rajar as a company ceased to exist, the Rajar works at Mobberley have continued in full operation to the present day and it is only relatively recently that the name 'Rajar' on the front of the building was replaced by 'Ilford Limited'.

Wellington and Ward Ltd

The last company to join Ilford was Wellington and Ward who, shunning APM and Selo, maintained independence until finally amalgamating in 1930. Wellington's independence (and originality) was expressed in an advertisement of 1921 which, under the heading of 'The House of Wellington', was a drawing depicting a vast explosion with the wording: 'Another rumour exploded. Will our very many interested friends note that we are still absolutely independent, free and unfettered.' Shortly after this announcement, however, Wellington joined forces with Leto Photomaterials Co.

Wellington and Ward began as a partnership about 1895, the date of appearance of their first product Sylvio, a printing-out paper. The photographic know-how was provided by J. B. B. Wellington, who had just served a three year contract with Kodak as the first factory manager of their newly erected factory at Harrow. His partner H. H. Ward was an engineer and, unlike Wellington, did not seek the limelight. In 1906 they were joined by H. W. Hall, who was related by marriage to Wellington.

The works were established at Elstree, Hertfordshire, and were visited in 1896 by the editor of the *BJP* and reported on in an article *How Messrs Wellington and Ward make Bromide Paper*. The coating machine was of the festoon pattern, the track holding three-quarters of a mile of paper and when full the machine had to be stopped to allow the paper to dry. The drying system consisted of three large fans at the top of the room, hot water pipes along the floor, and, in the words of the report, 'cold air is admitted along the edges where the walls meet the floor'.

The dark rooms of the factory were illuminated by 'large wooden box-like structures containing a gas jet and having their sides enclosed with a golden fabric giving a safe and pleasant light'. The packing was done, not by girls but by lads who examined each sheet by the safelight to make sure it was blemish free and then packed the sheets in dozens.

Within a few years further additions were made to the factory and a full range of bromide papers on, mostly, special artistic surface were marketed. In 1901, Wellington brought out a stripping gelatin film (forerunners of coatings on celluloid) coated on paper which after exposure and processing was stripped from the base to give a clear, if delicate, negative. This film was marketed in a great variety of sizes in Daylight Cartridges 'for all Kodaks' and also as 'Roll Holders NOT for Daylight Loading'. This film and the cartridges and holders were covered by a number of patents taken out by Wellington.

In the following decade Wellington and Ward attracted attention by a series of full page advertisements which broke out of the tradition of factual statements about the products advertised and displayed pictorial themes given a photographic context. One series featured the signs of the Zodiac (changed in the appropriate month), another, also in 12 instalments, a competition, for the best picture, between a girl artist and a 'cameraman': another series featured 'Lame Lancelot' who explored the world with a camera and 'Ye Lady Belinda' and her adventures with her photographer boy friend 'Alphonso'.

The first appearance of these advertisements attracted the comment in the photographic press: 'as being attributable to Mr Wellington's fine artistic appreciation'. The introduction, in 1905, of a range of plates was made by Lady Belinda in these words:

> 'O my Alphonso! Fresh triumphs in store for you! The gods favour you, my own! Only think! Our great friends and allies are now manufacturing Plates! Speedy, Iso Speedy, Landscape—Nay more than my poor wit can hold in remembrance—Come! Come! my own. I burn for your further laurels!' Alphonso: 'Sweet Messenger of Joy! My Belinda!!'

From 1904 to the start of First World War, the business continued to be successful. Sales increased from around £80 000 to £130 000 and the gross profits doubled from £19 000 to £35 000. The net profits did not show such a regular increase, £6789 in 1904, £3555 in 1907, £8009 in 1913, and only £2556 in 1914. As with other companies, the war years were very profitable, the net profits rising rapidly to £17 078 in 1915 and reaching a peak of £112 070 in 1918. From the start the net profits were shared by the partners, Wellington receiving two-thirds and Ward one-third; although he joined the enterprise in 1906 Hall did not become a partner until 1912 when the three-way split was five-tenths (Wellington), three-tenths (Ward), and two-tenths (Hall).

In 1911 Wellington was elected to the presidency of the Photographic Convention of the UK and his presidential address was reported at length in the *BJP*. Having commented that photography 'had worked a marvellous revolution in the methods of investigating, recording, and distribution of information' he outlined some of the recent achievements of photography in those fields and went on to make sure predictions for the future. He visualized the next important development in photography as being in small plate cameras using lenses of two-inch focal length or even shorter, drawing the analogy from the Kinetograph of the great depth of field achieved by such lenses. (Having drawn this analogy it seems strange that Wellington should not have predicted the use of films for such cameras instead of plates.) He also suggested that standard-size enlargements would be made from these small negatives thus successfully predicting enprints. Being a good congressman he invited, in 1913, members of the Congress of the Professional Photographers Association to visit his factory and a group photograph of nearly 200 was taken outside his house 'The Leys', a house of considerable size. Advertisements of this period claimed that Wellington's plates, papers and films were used throughout the world and the company had offices in Paris, Berlin, Bombay, Calcutta, and Montreal. To further the business, showrooms known as the 'Wellington Gallery' were opened at 101 High Holborn, London: the ground floor was converted into 'an elegant salon' for the display of photographs and the basement was equipped for staging demonstrations. To facilitate the taking and execution of orders there was a direct telephone link to the factory at Elstree. These galleries were subsequently used by Ilford.

After the war, Wellington and Ward combined with Leto Photomaterials, forming Wellington and Ward Ltd. Leto had, in 1909, acquired the business of B. J. Edwards.

Edwards, a contemporary of Harman, typified the lone inventor and entrepreneur of the period. Like Harman he started as a photographer and then set up a dry plate factory, as an extension of his photographic business, at Hackney, North London. Edwards was primarily an inventor; his business activities were secondary to his inventiveness. He established his reputation with his patented plate-coating machine and over 20 of these machines were at one time in use in various parts of the world.

He was the first to introduce isochromatic plates into the UK (1887) having developed the use of the dye Eosin only to find that this substance had been patented in England by P. Attout from whom, however, he was able to obtain the sole licence for England. Among his other innovations was the focal plane shutter (not patented—'I made a present of it to photographers' he is quoted as saying) and among his patents were: a machine for casting film base from nitrocellulose (1890); a complete camera system—the camera of which had both a focal plane shutter and a blade shutter; an actinometer, and accessories such as tripods and dark slides; and, in 1895, a single-shot three-colour camera complete with a projector for recombining the three-colour records. In an interlude between his main photographic interests, he took over the Heliotype Co., and engaged in photomechanical printing by a modified collotype process. Darwin's book *The Expression of the Emotions in Man and Animals* (1872) was the first to be illustrated by prints made by this process.

Edwards gradually expanded his premises at The Grove, Hackney, marketing plates and emulsion for home coating from 1882 onwards and gradually increasing his range of materials with more varieties of plates, papers, chemicals, processing solutions, and accessories such as tripods, dark slides, and processing equipment, all made on his premises. The business was on a relatively small scale and in 1900 he converted it to a public limited company and moved the premises to Castle Bar, Ealing, possibly the same premises vacated earlier by Pagets.

In 1907 he severed connections with the firm which two years later was bought up by Leto Photo-materials. Edwards retired to 'Wistowe', Hayes, Middlesex, but even in retirement ran a small factory, marketing a special type of printing paper which he called 'Wisto'. He died in 1914.

The name 'Leto' first appears in advertisements around 1902 for a collodio-chloride paper marketed by the wholesale agents A & M Zimmermann of 9–10 St Mary-at-Hill, London. This material was made by a German company, Scherings, which primarily manufactured photographic chemicals, specializing in developers. In January 1904, Leto Photochemicals Co. Ltd. was formed with its registered office at 9 Rangoon Street, London, and a capital of £2000 in £1 shares. The principal shareholder was Ferdinand August Zimmermann with 1993 shares and the secretary was R. E. Zimmermann. The company was reformed as Leto Photomaterials Co. (1905) Ltd and in 1906 acquired a factory at Edgware, Middlesex,

north-west of London. A drawing of this factory shows a rather small building which does not appear long enough to house the conventional drying track of bromide or gaslight papers; yet these papers were marketed.

Leto's best product was Seltona, a self-toning collodio-chloride paper, and this continued to be marketed until the early years of the Second World War. The company favoured collodio-chloride papers and Seltona was joined by Valento, Leto-Juno and Tintona all papers of this type. In 1909 Edwards' business at Ealing was bought up and his full range of plates were marketed by Leto under Edwards' names. The Ealing factory was kept going until 1920 although its closure had been discussed several times earlier.

Although the company had strong German connections, the directors were British and they were thus able to carry on during the war. Unlike other photographic companies its profits did not soar during those years and this was most likely due to their specialization in collodio-chloride papers and the lack of demand for these papers compared with bromide and gaslight types. Its original directors were ageing and the death of first one and then another may well have prompted the merger with Wellington and Ward which started in 1920 as an arrangement whereby Leto supplied Seltona in exchange for bromide and gaslight papers and plates. In June 1922, a new company Wellington and Ward Ltd, was formed, Leto going into voluntary liquidation. The directors of the new Company were Wellington, Hall, Ward, and C. S. Downing from Wellington and Ward, and F. W. Krohn and S. Adamson from Leto, the joint managing directors being Downing (£1500 p.a.) and Krohn (£1650 p.a.).

11. Industrial relations

For his time, Harman appears to have been a good employer. He was evidently a quiet, kindly man who wanted to provide reasonable conditions for his employees. This cannot have been easy. Work was carried out in most factories at that time in unpleasant surroundings and photographic workrooms must have been even worse. The small amount of light was provided by carriage lamps fitted with deep ruby glass. Ventilation was unnecessarily poor and the candles in the lamp used up much of the oxygen in the air. The candles sometimes melted, sending out a stream of hot wax from the lamphouse and leaving the workplace in darkness. The atmosphere caused drowsiness and some employees fell asleep standing at the bench. Sometimes they retired to a corner for a nap. There are records of men fined or deprived of bonus for sleeping at work. Hours were from 6 am to 6 pm, the candles being renewed in the lunch break at noon. Moreover, employees in contact with silver solutions were liable to contract argyria, a form of silver poisoning which turned the eyes orange and the skin slate blue.

Harman's concern for the well-being of his employees, although more paternalistic than would now be tolerated, was certainly unusual for his time. In 1891, when he formed his first limited company, he also introduced a profit-sharing scheme which must have been one of the earliest in the world. This scheme was described in Chaptor 4. The restrictions introduced between Harman's first announcement to employees and the publication of the Articles of Association almost certainly resulted from the advice given to Harman by his associates who were rather more conventional and wanted to ensure that Harman's generosity in profit-sharing did not lead the company into difficulties, especially as the dividend was 20 per cent or more after tax. In 1897 it reached $27\frac{1}{2}$ per cent. Those not in the profit-sharing scheme received a special bonus of $2\frac{1}{2}$ per cent of wages with foremen receiving 5 per cent.

The profit-sharing system was replaced by a new bonus scheme soon after the public company was formed in 1898. This was paid on wages, but also based upon the dividend declared each year. Provided the latter was at least 6 per cent, employees were paid half the dividend percentage figure as an addition to wages.

Thus, for a 20 per cent dividend they received an extra 10 per cent of their annual wage as a bonus. To qualify, they had to have been with the company for at least six months, but no deduction was made for sickness unless it exceeded six months in the one year. However, the bonus could be withheld for negligence or wastefulness, or for other disciplinary reasons; the records give individual cases of conspiring to strike, bad timekeeping, playing games during working hours, hitting boys, falling asleep at work, and leaving without notice.

Knobel replaced this scheme in 1904, as he was in favour of alternative systems of reward for skill and careful work. More senior employees, however, were paid a fixed 5 per cent of monthly wages provided their work was considered satisfactory.

Before the public company was formed, Harman paid his employees on a curious basis of share-equivalents, even if they held not shares. For example, Mooney, a carpenter, was paid at 120 shares equivalent per annum, i.e., £120 per annum. However, in 1895 salary grading was introduced with the concept of annual increments rising to a grade maximum. Fansett and West, office clerks, were awarded annual increments of £10 and a maximum of £100 per annum. At that time junior clerks were engaged at £60 per annum. Culling, Norden, and Vivian, other clerks, were placed on the same scale in 1897. However, more junior men, Glasscock, Grigs, and Lofthouse, were still on share equivalents: annual increments of 10 shares and a maximum of 150. None of the employees was told of the existence of their maxima.

Awards were made on retirement and for special reasons. Lewis, an emulsion maker who retired at the end of 1895, received a gold watch which appears to have been paid for personally by Hughes, the factory manager. Smith who had worked extra hard during the commissioning of the new factory, was given a fortnight's holiday with pay and a bonus of £10; Hughes and Howson received £100 each and Jenks £50.

The directors were sympathetic to those who fell ill. Although there appears to have been no settled policy, they often paid employees' medical bills; during a smallpox epidemic in 1894, they paid for the whole staff to be vaccinated and by that time they were paying a Dr Shimeld a retainer to act as factory doctor. One employee, Newman, who was taken seriously ill, was given 3 months' leave of absence on full pay and then £1 a week and a house to live in rent free until he died.

However, the attitude to trades unions was tough, and, when the Carpenters' Union called for a strike unless the company raised wages from 9½d to 10d per hour, Hughes rejected the request out-of-hand and stated that 'any attempt by the unions to dictate terms upon which we engage our employees should be most strenuously resisted'.

It had been the custom to fine employees for lateness and other misdeeds, but in 1897 it was realized that that practice was illegal and that it was necessary to have a set of rules and a table of fines which should be read and signed by every employee. The new rules for lateness which were drawn up were:

1. It is very important that employees keep correct time in the morning and at meal times.
2. An absentee often occasions considerable inconvenience to the work of others and wastes their time by being unable to proceed with their work owing to the 'sets' of workers being incomplete.
3. Fines will be inflicted on those who do not keep proper time.
4. The undersigned do hereby agree with the above rules.

The table of fines laid down:

1. Up to 10 min late 2d.
2. Up to 20 min late 4d.
3. Up to 30 min late 1s.
4. Anyone being late or losing quarter-time without sufficient cause is liable to dismissal.
5. A fine of 1s was also imposed for the breakage of lamp glasses without a satisfactory explanation.

Previously, the fines collected had been donated to the London Hospital, but it was resolved that henceforth they should be made available to the Britannia Works Institute funds.

Harman's care for his employees' welfare is probably best illustrated by his gift of the Britannia Works Institute. He had been concerned by the lack of facilities for eating the meals employees brought with them to work. He therefore had built, at his own expense, a hall in Ilford Lane which remained in use as a clubroom until 1973. This not only provided a place to eat their breakfast and lunch but also facilities to make tea and for recreation in the evenings, including billiards and amateur dramatics. The Institute was opened on 18 December 1895 with a meat tea for shareholders followed by an entertainment to which all regular employees were invited.

By this time the workforce numbered over 100 and was further increased by the transfer of 7 extra women from the Tottenham factory of Austin Edwards. The forewoman received 30s a week and others 10s to 16s.

The company was also concerned to provide houses for its employees if needed. Accommodation was fairly easily available in Ilford, but when the Warley site was developed in 1903 it was realized that employees transferred from Ilford would need new houses. Land was purchased for £400 with a view to building 35 pairs of cottages and a new road (Britannia Road). Eventually, this had to be reduced to 19 houses for a price of £5225, the road costing £1026 and gates and fences £30. These houses, in two red-brick terraces still stand. They were completed in 1904 and let at 9s per week to employees and 10s 6d per week to others. Three of them were let at £25 per annum (ex rates) to the War Office for use by personnel at Warley Barracks.

Considerable changes took place during the period from 1900 to 1914. From the appointment of F. F. Renwick in 1898, a technical team was slowly built up, including engineers and chemists, and this had a direct influence on the company's attitude to its employees.

In the early days there was no standard policy on such matters as holidays, sickness benefits, and pensions. Whether the employees were entitled to regular holidays in addition to public ones is not recorded, but during the Christmases of 1894 and 1895 the opportunity was taken of closing both factories for alterations and paying the factory employees half-pay. In 1897, the whole factory was closed on June 21 and 22 with full-pay to celebrate Queen Victoria's Diamond Jubilee. In 1898, only the directors and the most senior employees received a regular four weeks' annual holiday. The rest had to be satisfied with the bank holidays, the 'bean feast', and periods when the factory was closed for modifications, usually during winter, when they received half-pay. The 'bean feast' was an annual holiday, taken on a Saturday in June, when the whole factory departed for a seaside resort such as Margate, Brighton, or Great Yarmouth and were given a three-course lunch. On these occasions the company granted £25—later £30—to meet expenses.

The first occasion on which a schedule (see Table 6) of holiday entitlement was issued was in 1912, and it is interesting to note the much more favourable treatment received by the clerks compared with the factory workers.

Years of Service	Holiday period with full pay
Factory employees	
Under five years	Nil
Five years	Three days
Ten years	One week
Foreman	One extra week
Clerks	
One year	One week
Five years	Two weeks
Fifteen years	Three weeks

Table 6. Holiday entitlement

In addition, members of the Territorial Army were allowed a week with full pay. For any time in excess of the allowed holiday period they received full pay less the dues received in the camp.

The hours of work introduced in 1911 were 8 am till 1 pm and 2 pm till 6 pm, with 8 am till 1 pm on Saturdays—a 50 hour week. This was reduced to 47 hours in 1919.

When W. Fell and W. C. Lindsell, who were in the reserves, were called up for service in South Africa in 1899, Fell's wife was paid 10s per week and Lindsell was given a grant of £3 6s 0d.

The company's policy on sickness, if somewhat erratic, was generous for the time. Underwood, the chief engineer, who underwent a serious operation in 1905 was granted two months' leave on half-pay. Bell, the foreman of the paper-coating department for 16 years, was granted £15 for treatment at Harrogate two years later. When G. Culling, who had been on the clerical staff for 24 years, had to go to a tuberculosis sanatorium in 1919, the firm paid the specialist's fee of five guineas and for four months' treatment. At the end of the four months, the payment was extended for a further six months.

Similarly, there was no pension scheme and the amounts paid depended upon the whim of the directors and the climate of the time. Eykelbosch, when he left in 1910, was given an honorarium of £100 for '20 years good service', whereas when Hughes, the factory manager and one-time director, retired in 1920, he received a lump sum of six months' pay and a pension of £400 per annum.

There was no fixed age for retirement. W. Theobald, who had been with the company 21 years, had a stroke at the age of 74, which prevented his working. He was awarded 10s per week in 1917. W. Farley, who had served 29 years and was incapacitated in 1920 at the age of 72 with rheumatism and varicose veins was awarded a pension of 25s per week. W. Clarke with 35 years' service, retired with a pension of 30s per week in the same year. He had been with the company for all but two years of its existence.

When Axtell died in 1912, his widow was given a cheque for £10 and her son's wage increased from 13s to 15s 6d per week. When he was called up in 1916 she was granted 5s per week. When H. D. Skinner died in 1920, his widow was paid £2 per week for four weeks, £1 for 18 weeks, 15s for 13 weeks, and 10s for 13 weeks.

It was customary at that time, in addition to the awards or bonus scheme, to give bonuses for specially meritorious achievements. For example, Renwick received £50 for the development of the Monarch plate in 1903, but it is obvious that the scientific staff, at least, did not favour this scheme. In 1907, Knobel offered a reward of £100 for an X-ray plate equal to Lumière's, but it was withdrawn after an interview between Ivor Philipps and Renwick, Potter, and Storr.

Potter received £30 for improvements to the Ilford exposure meter in 1905 and Brooker received £10, Agnew £10, and Kraushaar £2 for assistance at exhibitions in 1908.

An innovation launched in 1908 was a suggestion scheme whereby employees could be paid small sums (usually one or two guineas) for suggestions for improving the factory productivity or promoting Ilford products.

By 1914, the paternalistic attitude had markedly declined and labour relations were moving towards the unionized pattern familiar in more recent years.

From 1918 until 1940 there was little active trade union organization in Ilford itself or in the companies it acquired. This is somewhat surprising since the amalgamation led to situations which would not be tolerated today. It is recorded that soon after Ilford acquired Imperial Dry Plate in 1918, most of the senior managers were discharged without any substantial compensation and other employees received only one week's pay in lieu of notice. This was a common feature of industrial life in those days and, no doubt, somewhat similar situations arose with the other acquisitions, though the employees of Illingworth appear to have fared somewhat better as a result of the appointment of T. M. Illingworth, son of the founder, to a senior position on the Ilford board.

However, the company studied the interests of its regular employees and in 1932 introduced two Group

Life Insurance Pension Plans, one for monthly staff and the other for employees on the weekly wages payroll. Both schemes provided a pension for men, at the age of 65, which was related to annual earnings in each year of membership. Death benefits were also included, ranging from £100 to £1000 for monthly staff and between £100 and £200 for weekly paid. A minimum pension of £300 per annum or one-third of present salary, whichever was the smaller, was provided in the monthly scheme. The corresponding figure for the weekly scheme was £39 per annum.

This was quite a generous scheme for the time. These were also the days of facilities for recreation. The Institute at Ilford and the Clubroom at Brentwood were used for regular amateur dramatic performances, concerts, and Christmas parties. Facilities were provided for games, including tennis and bowls. Intersite athletics meetings, football, and cricket matches were held each year and found enthusiastic support.

In 1940, the National Union of General and Municipal Workers (later GMWU) started to organize process workers at the Brentwood factory and by 1941 were claiming 80 per cent membership. However, recruitment of members at the other factories was very small. From 1942, members of the union took a significant part in the running of the GMWU Brentwood branch and the shop steward and convenor system became firmly established. Up to about 1955, the Brentwood membership set the pace in negotiations, the company generally using the resulting conditions as a standard for the other factories. Industrial relations on the whole were very harmonious, mainly as a result of excellent personal relationships.

From 1950, the company embarked upon a large-scale programme of work study linked with incentive bonus working. The union attitude to this was critical, but the workers on short-cycle repetitive operations, who were nearly all women, accepted the schemes in order to achieve higher levels of pay.

This situation, coupled with a remnant of the old benevolent paternalism on the part of management, continued until 1956. A one-day work to rule by women operatives broke the industrial-action-free record of 42 years, the last incident having been a plate factory dispute in 1914. The 1956 incident resulted in a basic change in attitudes. The union was officially asked by the company to intervene, which it eventually did, calling a meeting of 400 workers.

Thereafter, union/management relations improved. A senior shop steward was sent on a union-sponsored eight-week course at Birmingham College of Technology and appointed to the work-study team, with a special remit to assist management and union to solve disputes arising from shopfloor problems.

Management appreciated the success of this move and decided to make use of the shop stewards more widely in preserving good industrial relations. This collaboration resulted in the adoption of a wage structure based upon job evaluation in which union and management participated.

Apart from the craft unions, a number of others had by this time recruited relatively small numbers of employees. The company felt that it would be more satisfactory to negotiate with one principal union only and accordingly, in 1959, entered into a formal agreement with the GMWU. This provided for joint consultation and led to the publication of an agreed employee handbook which laid down procedures to be followed in any dispute before a stoppage of work could take place.

By this time, virtually the same conditions had been extended to all the Ilford factories and there was increasingly effective cooperation in the creation and preservation of good industrial relations, with consequent beneficial effects upon productivity. The only difficulty was experienced temporarily upon the opening of the Basildon site in 1958, with the consequent influx of new employees from other industries.

By 1962, the personnel management structure had been consolidated under T. P. Lyons, as company personnel officer. He proposed a long-term wage agreement containing clauses designed to counter the wage drift then appearing in industry, while establishing a good measure of earnings security for employees. This attracted some publicity, as it appeared to offer a solution to the possibility, greatly feared at that time, of run-away inflation and general industrial unrest.

However, the union feared that such a wage plan, which provided a four-year schedule of wage increases, would lose them members because of the elimination of the element of free bargaining.

To counter this, the company agreed to issue a statement encouraging all employees to join the appropriate trade union and also agreed to collect union dues by deduction from gross wages. As a result, the wage plan was agreed and, in the words of the *Financial Times*, made Ilford the envy of industry.

This led, by 1965, to a union demand for 100 per cent trade unionism within Ilford. The company was opposed to the establishment of a closed shop, on the grounds that it was a denial of individual freedom, but signed an agreement in November 1965 to allow 100 per cent union membership. This differed from a closed shop concept principally because it allowed existing non-union employees to remain outside the union and prevented the union from expelling a member without company consent. However, the company stipulated that this agreement would be implemented only on condition that every union member signed a personal undertaking to abide by union rules and by negotiated agreements; if this undertaking were broken it would lead to termination of the 100 per cent agreement.

At this time, unofficial 'wild cat' strikes were increasingly common in British industry and the Ilford agreement was enthusiastically reported in the press as a way to assist the union in the control of their members. There was, however, much speculation about the difference between 100 per cent trade unionism and a closed shop. The *Financial Times*, in its 'Men and Matters' column on 29 October 1965, said it seemed like hair-splitting, but nevertheless complimented Lyons and the union on an astute move; Ilford were offering '100 per cent membership to a union renowned for many things but militancy and in return is assured of cooperation on productivity and a tough time on trouble-makers'.

However, the much-publicized agreement was never fully implemented. Union members claimed they had not been properly consulted and some managers had doubts about the proposals. Talks with shop stewards revealed that the desire for 100 per cent trade unionism was not as strong as had been supposed and the full implications had not been understood.

At the end of three months, less than half the necessary signatures had been obtained. By mid-1966, eight months after the signing of agreement in principle between the company and the union, three of the factories were virtually completely signed up, but Brentwood, the largest, had only reached 60 per cent. Union discussion later brought this up to 80 per cent, but the company felt obliged to insist that all members should sign the personal undertaking. Eventually this was implemented at three of the factories, but Brentwood had to be excluded.

About this time, members of salaried staff started to show an interest in becoming members of appropriate unions. Rupert A. Withers, the chairman, wrote to all monthly salaried staff in May 1967 pointing out that the General and Municipal Workers Union was the only one to which formal recognition had been granted. Staff associations had been formed within the previous 12 months with the object of gaining negotiating rights, but the company would only agree to their being consultative bodies and a means of better communication between management and employees. These bodies felt that they should have been consulted by management before the announcement was made, but soon decided to discuss the position with both the GMWU and the Association of Supervisory, Technical and Managerial Staffs which had recently been formed by amalgamation of the Association of Supervisory Staff, Executives & Technicians and the Association of Scientific Workers. In fact, some scientists in the company had been members of the AScW for many years, activity having been considerable in the years between 1939 and 1942, but salary negotiation procedures had never been discussed with management.

The staff associations had been restricted in their activities mainly to talks of interest to their members, including annual presentations by successive chief executives on the state and future of the company. There had also been some discussion on staff gradings and conditions of employment.

The Industrial Relations Act 1971 established that if a staff association were to act as a negotiating body on remuneration, it must be financially and administratively independent of the company employing its members. Staff association members were therefore asked by their committees whether they wished to continue membership or to join a union. The replies indicated a majority in favour of the latter course.

By this time, a number of employees had become members of ASTMS and opinion was moving towards membership of that union, a trend which was accelerated by the government wage freeze of 1972. When the freeze was implemented, the shop floor unions had just concluded a settlement with the company for an increase in wages, but no similar increase was offered to salaried staff as their annual review was not due for some months.

A ballot of monthly staff was therefore organized in December 1972, asking people whether they wished to join ASTMS. The result was a majority of two-thirds in favour and an Ilford branch of the union was set up for all monthly staff except those at Mobberley, in Cheshire, where they joined a Manchester branch of ASTMS.

However, at this stage the GMWU pointed out that the company had granted them sole recognition some years before and, although a joint negotiating committee had been set up, the company found itself unable to recognize ASTMS for negotiating purposes without breaking its agreement with the GMWU.

The position was further complicated in March 1973 by the company's decision to close the Ilford site and establish its head office at Basildon and a new research laboratory at Warley. ASTMS used this information to intensify its recruitment drive, but met with relatively little response.

Tony Axford, the chief executive, suggested that the GMWU and ASTMS should solve this problem themselves. Meanwhile, G. N. Fabb, a member of the staff who had joined ASTMS, submitted the dispute to the Industrial Relations Court. ASTMS supported this submission, but also approached the company and, following a meeting with Axford, discussed the situation with the other unions involved.

The case appeared at the Industrial Court under Section 51 (1) of the Act and was heard on 15 May 1973. It was adjourned for a month after hearing the cases presented by the various parties. A week prior to the second hearing, an inter-union meeting was held which led to agreement at the court that a reconciliation meeting be held immediately. As a result, a joint negotiating committee was set up for all monthly salaried staff, including those at Mobberley, with two seats allocated to the GMWU, two to the engineers (TASS), two to the electricians (EETPU), one to the staff association, and seven to the ASTMS.

This committee negotiated salaries with the company to a fairly high level of grading, but excluded the most senior grades. Subjects discussed included overtime payments, conditions of employment, flexible working hours, and job evaluation, as well as salary scales and annual increments. The staff

association subsequently disbanded and the joint negotiating committee was reconstituted with two MATSA, two TASS, and eight ASTMS members.

The relocation of work from Ilford to the other sites undoubtedly involved a larger number of employees than any other decision in the history of the company, though the establishment of the Brentwood site between 1902 and 1910 and the amalgamation of the 1930s must have been more traumatic for some of those involved.

When the company decided in 1973 to leave the town of Ilford, it tried to minimize the unavoidable problems presented to employees. A relocation-project team was set up with working groups to cover all major aspects of the move. Terms were negotiated to provide compensation for those unable to move to a new area, but an undertaking was given that employment would be found for anyone wishing to stay with the company. After three years, the move was completed successfully, as a result of involvement of all levels of employees concerned and careful attention to detail. Alfred Harman's original outlook was no doubt still apparent in the company attitude, but industrial relations and techniques of management had indeed changed from the old autocratic paternalism. The age of participation was dawning and, within a few years, the company had developed policies for two-way communications, joint consultation, and joint monitoring of the company's progress towards the achievement of its objectives.

12. Marketing the products

Harman had used press advertising for his services before launching into manufacture and continued to do so for his products. When he found distribution by carpet bag and dog-cart too time-consuming, he appointed Marion & Co. as his sole agents.

After a dispute with Marions over the tradename 'Britannia' Harman changed the brand of the plates to Ilford and halved the price to 1s per box of 12 plates $3\frac{1}{4}$ in × $4\frac{1}{2}$ in.

However, Harman's business success was not founded upon price-cutting. He had three basic lines of attack: to produce material of good specification to the highest quality; to extend and improve the range of products; and to use good advertising and trademarks.

His interest in quality and specification of the product explains the trouble he took to appoint, as early as 1888, a quality control manager and a research chemist—almost before any staff in the modern sense had been built up. Both were very capable, Acworth starting a new line of plates and helping to introduce papers before leaving Ilford, while Agnew, who reported directly to Harman, refused adamantly to allow any materials to leave the factory which were not up to his high standards. These two factors formed the basis of a business committed to high quality and technical progress.

Even before this in 1886, Harman had introduced the little paddle steamer, which survived in various updated forms until 1945—just 60 years! When printing-out paper was introduced as POP in November 1891, the paddle steamer occupied the centre of the O. The inspiration for this came from John Howson, Harman's first business manager, whom he appointed in 1889. Howson was a salesman with quiet charm, great originality and considerable initiative.

Immediately on joining, Howson started to write and publish *Photographic Scraps*, a free monthly magazine for the trade. It did not miss an issue until 1914, when it ceased publication as a wartime economy measure. It consisted at first of four pages dealing with technical points and items of interest about the products; in the late Victorian manner, it

also included comic pictures and jokes, often poor puns such as 'It is a simple matter to take a church—but photographing the churchyard is a matter of grave importance'. From 1894, it expanded to eight pages, in a coloured cover, and adopted a much greater air of dignity.

Howson was also responsible for the production, from 1890 onwards, of the *Ilford Manual of Photography*, written by C. H. Bothamley. It started as a 200 page volume bound in red cloth, costing 1s and 5000 copies were sold in the first two months; it continued, in improved editions, until 1960, when cumulative sales exceeded one million. Another of his ideas was the *Ilford Year Book*, which was a large pocket diary bound in morocco leather with pages for records of exposures made, 24 pages of useful hints and data and a photogravure illustration.

The scheme for lecturing to photographic societies which, in later years, developed into the Ilford lecture service was thought up by Howson.

He also offered medals for the best pictures made on Ilford materials at the various societies' exhibitions. The presentation of medals aroused criticism as to the propriety of degrading one of the fine arts by introducing a commercial flavour. As a result, in May 1890, the company announced its decision to withdraw the scheme and, 'to show the sincerity of its good will to photography', offered without conditions, a scholarship of £100 a year for three years to be awarded by the Photographic Society of Great Britain (later the Royal Photographic Society). This was a handsome sum of money at that time, but the society declined it, with thanks. The possible taint of dealing with 'the trade' was not to be risked.

From about 1884, the company had introduced a number of new materials. The original paper, known as Alpha, was a gelatino-chloride development paper which could be used only for contact printing, needed long exposures to artificial light, and had to be toned by means of a fixing bath containing gold salts. In 1891 it was largely replaced for contact printing by printing out paper (POP), which rapidly became a bestseller.

In May 1884, bromide paper had been introduced,

enabling 'enlargements to be made by electric light'. Professional photographers immediately seized on this new technique. A finished enlargement 32 in × 22 in cost about 9s. The paper was made in one speed, one contrast, and one surface. It was not baryta coated and contained no matting ingredient, so giving a slightly shiny print. By 1889, bromide paper was selling well in Rough and Smooth surfaces and Rapid and Slow speeds. The paddle-steamer trademark appeared on it; the price was 9s for 24 sheets $12\frac{1}{2}$ in × $10\frac{1}{2}$ in.

In 1889, the emulsion used for Alpha paper was coated on glass and sold as Alpha Lantern plates, which were produced, with many improvements, until 1939. Special Lantern plates using a bromide emulsion were introduced in 1891.

Bromide papers and POP were both introduced with a matt surface in 1893. In 1897, a dead matt bromide surface, called Platino Matt, came in, obviously an attempt to compete with the very popular Platinotype paper produced by the Platino-type Co., using platinum salts in place of silver. The latter was slow and could not therefore be used to make enlargements, so Howson clearly thought his bromide paper would prove popular.

By 1891, the company had decided that plates sensitive only to blue light had to be improved by dye-sensitizing to yellow and green. The Isochromatic Instantaneous, and Medium Rapidity plates so produced were not very successful.

In January 1894, an article in *Photography* attacked the concept of isochromatic plates. The editor was invited to Ilford to witness a demonstration and consequently agreed to amend his comments in the next issue.

However, in April of that year, the board was alarmed to learn that Tailfer's patent had lapsed. Ilford had a joint licence with B. J. Edwards under this patent, on which the sensitizing technique was based. It now expected competition and in September 1894 Lumière SA, in France, launched a new orthochromatic plate with a prize of £50 for results showing it to be superior to the competition.

Tests at Ilford showed the Lumière plate to have no yellow-green sensitivity and Harman considered that 'steps should be taken to open the eyes of the public to the fraud'. Howson arranged for a journalist friend to enter the competition but he found that the test objects supplied by Lumière were unsuitable for differentiation between the different types of plates. No action was taken.

Ilford improved the results obtained on its iso plates by the introduction of colour filters known as Ilford Isochromatic Screens. They were pieces of optical polished yellow glass, each in a holder and supplied with a leather case. The price was 7s 6d.

The Company was now in a relatively strong position in the plate market; although consistent speed and colour senstivity were hard to achieve, the plates were generally ahead of competition.

In 1893 the range of plates was advertised as shown in Table 7.

Plate	Relative Speed
Ordinary	1.0
Iso Medium	1.0
Rapid	1.3
Iso Instantaneous	2.0
Special Rapid	3.0

Table 7. Range of plates in 1893

From 1895 to 1897 five more plates were introduced and two flat films. The plates were named Process, Empress, Continental, Half-tone, and Chromatic; the films were Process and Empress.

At the same time, Harman agreed to introduce backed plates. He had previously opposed this step, despite the technical advantages, as the mixture of caramel and indian ink used was very unpleasant to handle. Harman is supposed to have said he would offer them only at double the price of unbacked plates but eventually he charged 25 per cent extra. Howson wanted to issue a disclaimer against responsibility for resultant faults in the hands of the user but, wisely, this was not agreed.

The introduction of Process and Half-tone materials indicated the growth of the use of photography for illustrations in newspapers and magazines. Eventually, Ilford was to make a speciality of materials for this market and, at one time, had as much as 80 per cent of the British business, as well as a large export trade.

The company had intended to restrict its range by discontinuing some of the older plates when new ones were introduced. However, dealers thought otherwise and most of the brandnames were continued for many years, even though improvements were made to the products.

At this time, the photographic manufacturers had a price agreement. Although Harman seems to have had freedom to fix his prices within a fairly wide range, he was forced to charge all backed plates at a higher price when he considered dropping the excess charge on Ordinary plates.

Great care was taken over packaging. Black boxes were used, with coloured labels to denote the different brands. Plates were packed in pairs, emulsion side inwards but separated by sheets of tissue paper or by slips of thin card inserted close to the edges on opposite sides. Wrapping materials were selected with great care to eliminate any which might fog the plates. Agnew's testing department carried out these tests as well as those on the finished goods. Waxed paper was normally used inside the box containing the plates but this had to be omitted from tropical packs as the wax melted. The use of edge slips in place of tissue paper also originated from problems with a mottle patterning produced by the tissue paper under very humid conditions in the tropics. As the Ilford materials behaved better than most of the competiton in the tropics, packaging was of great importance. Sales to India, China, and Japan rose steadily as a result.

Howson evidently kept close watch on his competitors. He contested a claim in a Cadett and Neale advertisement that their Lightning plates were 50 to 100 per cent faster than any others and they withdrew it. He also challenged the editor of *Amateur Photography* about a list of plate speeds in Wall's *Dictionary of Photography*, which he also published. The table was withdrawn.

Howson gave careful attention to customer complaints. Most of these concerned paper products, the commonest being about black spots and a yellow tint on POP. Both were found to arise from impurities, mainly in the base. Although specially pure paper bases were imported from Blanchet Frères and Kleber of Rives and from Steinbach of Malmedy, trouble was experienced with small particles of copper, brass, and iron in the paper or in the baryta coating which was applied by the papermaker. These particles reacted with the emulsion to form black specks of silver. The yellow tint of POP was produced by traces of chloride in the barium sulphate of the baryta coating. The paper also suffered physical defects, such as creasing. Complaints of holes in the paper were traced to the habit of customs officers of sampling rolls of paper by boring holes in them with an auger!

By 1896, the product range was selling well. The average monthly sale of plates was about 480 000, calculated as equivalent of whole-plates ($8\frac{1}{2}$ in × $6\frac{1}{2}$ in). The Ordinary plate accounted for about half of this figure. Sales turnover rose from £11 000 per month in 1896 to £17 000 in 1899, mainly as a result of the success of Empress and Special Rapid (SR) plates and the continuing growth of POP and bromide papers.

The largest contribution to revenue was made by POP—£7500 per month, against £900 for bromide paper and £3200 for Ordinary plates.

The profit was also good. In Knobel's notebook for 1896 he details the cost of producing SR plates: 4800 dozen whole-plates, sold by the company for £816, cost £543 to make, resulting in a 50 per cent mark-up. The breakdown of cost is shown in Table 8.

	Costs		
	£	s	d
Salts and gelatin	141	7	6
Glass	215	0	0
Wages	59	3	0
Profit-sharing bonus	7	9	11
Packing	16	15	4
Overheads	104	0	0
Total	543	15	9

Table 8. Cost of producing SR plates

The net profit of the company rose from £32 000 (27 per cent of capital) in 1892 to £47 000 (39 per cent of capital) in 1897. The dividend was 20 per cent, except in 1897 when $27\frac{1}{2}$ per cent was declared.

In November 1896, a meeting of photographic manufacturers was proposed in order to devise rules for regulating the trade. At that time, prices and discounts were commonly set in many industries by agreement between manufacturers. The Association of Manufacturers of Photographic Plates, Papers and Films came into being with an agreed convention on 1 April 1897. The companies signing the convention were:

Birmingham Photographic Co.
Britannia Works Co.
Cadett and Neale
Eastman Photographic Materials Co.
B. J. Edwards and Co.
Elliot and Son
European Blair Camera Co.
Imperial Dry Plate Co.
Marion and Co.
Mawson and Swan
Morgan and Kidd
Paget Prize Plate Co.
Sandell Works Co.
R. W. Thomas and Co.
Wellington and Ward

The following declined to join:

Austin Edwards
Gem Dry Plates
Otto Scholzig
Wratten and Wainwright

All but Edwards, Imperial and Paget also signed an agreement not to sell POP under 15s per quire (24 sheets, 17 in $\times$ 24$\frac{1}{2}$ in) or 1s per packet (24 sheets, 6 in $\times$ 4$\frac{1}{4}$ in). Although Imperial and Paget refused to sign, they agreed not to undersell the others; Edwards signed a month later.

The agreement was issued in two parts, one for dealers, the other for manufacturers. A sheet common to both documents set out the rules governing the sale of photographic materials, which stated that they should only be sold subject to the following conditions:

1. In original, unopened packets.
2. Retail, not under manufacturers' published price lists.
3. To professional photographers, with not more than the following discounts:
   Plates and films (rollable films excluded)
   £2 worth per month 5 per cent; £5 worth per month 7$\frac{1}{2}$ per cent; £10 worth per month 10 per cent; £25 worth per month 15 per cent—all plus 5 per cent for settlement before the last day of the month.
   Printing out and bromide papers
   One quire or its equivalent in cut sheets and upwards, not more than 10 per cent.
4. Carriage paid by the manufacturers on £5 worth of plates or £4 worth of papers, sold to dealers and professionals, and on all amounts within Carter Paterson and Co.'s district.

The copy of the rules sent to dealers was accompanied by a statement of the advantages of the scheme to both dealers and manufacturers.

Attached to the manufacturers' copy of the rules was a list of conditions to be applied:

1. Goods would not be supplied to any dealer who broke the rules.
2. Goods would not be supplied to any photographer in the UK contrary to the rules.
3. No plates or POP would be sold or listed below the 1s basis nor any bromide papers below the current list price.
4. No plates, films, or papers would be introduced at prices lower than those charged by the agreeing manufacturers.
5. The agreement was binding only if all British manufacturers signed, unless those signing agreed to the contrary.
6. The agreement to remain in force for one year from the date of signing.
7. If the agreement were broken by any signatory it would become void.
8. The signatories to form and become members of the Association of Photographic Plate, Paper, and Film Manufacturers for the purpose of carrying out the rules.

Bishop (Marion) was elected chairman of the association and Howson (Britannia Works) was the secretary. In January 1898, Howson reported that the convention was working smoothly. He also announced he was resigning the secretaryship at Harman's request.

After this, competition increased. Other British manufacturers improved their products and a rising flood of materials was imported from the Continent. Apart from Lumière materials, these were generally inferior but also much cheaper. Eastman had also started to intensify his efforts to promote his Kodak business in England. The dividend fell to 10 per cent in 1903, 8 per cent in 1904 and 6$\frac{1}{2}$ per cent in 1905.

Ilford weathered the storm of competition at home by increasing its exports, especially to India and the Far East. If it had not been for this, the company might not have survived the difficult period between 1899 and 1914. The company also made some attempt to improve its product range but without much effect.

Its ambivalent attitude is illustrated by its approach to three segments of the market open to it and skilfully built up by Eastman: roll and cinematograph films, cameras, and colour materials.

The move from monochrome to colour photography was clearly expected by a large number of people. Hundreds of inventors lost fortunes trying to perfect commercial processes. Harman could have entered this market early, as did Lumière with considerable success. Professor John Joly, one of the pioneers, approached Harman in 1897 with his colour screen plate.

The process would have worked well as a development of Ilford's plate expertise, though panchromatic plates would have had to be produced. Harman evidently felt the process too difficult to commercialize and turned it down. It was to reappear in the Ilford range, nearly 40 years later, in modified form, as Dufaycolor film.

The Ilford approach to film was even less adventurous. In 1899 the Blair Camera Co. approached Ilford with a view to selling their company. They made roll and cinematograph films and held a patent for coating and drying film base. After a price had been agreed, Knobel inspected the plant and turned the deal down. The following year, he turned down an offer from Goldberg Films for base-making equipment. Several other approaches were also turned down; in 1903 the whole question of making films was rejected by the board.

115

An Ilford roll film appeared in advertisements but no record remains of its origin and it was a neglected sideline until after 1918.

This attitude is difficult to understand. The Lumière family in France were making a great success of their cinematograph film business, while Eastman was establishing a worldwide amateur business with his roll films. This must have been obvious but Ilford evidently felt that they should confine their efforts to glass plates and concentrate upon the professional, commercial, and graphic arts, markets.

This would also explain their attitude towards cameras. Roll-film cameras were looked upon with disdain by serious photographers—the snapshot hobby was a frivolity—though plate cameras were recognized to be heavy and clumsy. R. and J. Beck had brought out the Frena camera, holding forty notched sheets of film in a magazine, and Ilford did make flat films for it for a time. These cameras were made in Germany, where the move towards mass-produced hand cameras was starting, although the UK made the best brass-bound mahogany cameras.

Harman decided he could improve on the Frena camera and took out a patent but never fully exploited it.

In 1899 the company accepted an offer of a similar flat-film camera from Arthur Charles Smith and Albert Arthur Smith. The patentees received a royalty of 4s 6d per camera. This was made in Germany and marketed as the Ilford camera. It sold for £5 (or 8 guineas with a superior Ross anastigmat lens) but sales ceased in 1908. No roll film camera was offered until more than 40 years later.

Meanwhile, the company struggled to introduce new products into its range. One of the successes was the introduction in 1908 of non-stress papers, an invention of Wilford Lean. Until then, development papers had shown black streaks if subjected to friction. Lean conceived the idea of coating the surface with a thin protective layer of plain gelatin. Ilford bought the rights for £20. Within a few years all manufacturers had copied the idea.

Another innovation was the self-developing plate which incorporated the developing agent in the

Figure 33   The first Ilford camera: a magazine box camera for sheet-film, 1903. (Courtesy Science Museum, South Kensington.)

116

emulsion and needed only to be processed in a weak solution of sodium carbonate. However, this material, the Amauto plate, did not keep well and was discontinued. The idea had to wait until Phenidone had been invented 50 years later, when it could be applied to paper products. This was an era of curious product names—the Wellington self-developing plate bore the name 'Watalu'!

The most valuable innovation was in the X-ray field. Camera plates had been offered for use in X-ray work since 1897, the SR being the most popular of the Ilford range. The board saw the potential for a special plate and marketed the Ilford X-ray Plate in 1907 based upon a formula purchased for 30 guineas from T. Thorne-Baker. It was soon improved by Renwick and sold at twice the price of camera plates, 12 in $\times$ 10 in—17s 6d per dozen, though doctors received a discount of 15 per cent and hospitals 25 per cent. This plate was an instant success and dominated the British market until it was replaced by X-ray film in 1923, which, in turn, enjoyed a very large share of the market.

Dental X-ray films were introduced as early as 1912, as glass plates were unsatisfactory for use in the mouth. After a while, the advantages of coating on both sides of the base, thus increasing the effect of the X-rays, was realized. By the time the Ilford X-ray film came on the market in 1926 this type of film was normal.

During the period just before the First World War, experiments in marketing were taking place. Ilford and most of its British competitors had always offered a discount to any *bona fide* photographic shop. Kodak, on the other hand, had appointed only selected Kodak agents, whose numbers were restricted by the needs of each district. Thus each was assured of a worthwhile level of business and had an incentive to offer Kodak goods.

The Ilford board set itself to emulate this system. It brought out a new plate, the Versatile, in three speeds, which was claimed to make photography easier for the amateur. The distribution of these was restricted to special agents, through whom other dealers had to buy them. The trade was unenthusiastic. Agents had to stock more lines and those not selected as agents threatened to discontinue business with Ilford altogether. The amateur felt that plates made for professionals were probably better. The scheme was abandoned in 1915 and Versatile plates disappeared.

Another interesting feature of Ilford sales activities was that it never employed travelling salesmen. These were introduced by T. M. Illingworth when he joined the board in 1920. Illingworth travellers had always

been active and, following the purchase of the Illingworth company they were expected to sell Ilford products as well as their own. The psychological pressures were too strong and, in August 1921, after a year's trial, the scheme was dropped. Instead, Ilford supplied Illingworth with plates under their brand label. The Illingworth Fleet Plate proved extremely popular in Fleet Street, and later all over the United States, until plates were replaced by film.

Ilford then arranged with Houghtons, the largest photographic wholesaler in the UK, to concentrate on the sale of its products on the understanding that Ilford would not itself employ travellers. This arrangement lasted only two years, after which the company built up an increasingly large sales force.

Export was still the company's strongest area but it had also been unusual to visit overseas distributors. It was Illingworth again who broke this tradition by visiting India, China, Japan, Australia, and the United States in 1922. In 1929, a special representative was engaged for the Far East, Irwin V. Scott.

Although Ilford and Imperial had been the first to enter overseas markets and had, in general, secured the best agents, all the manufacturing companies acquired by Ilford had appointed agents and, after the merger, the best had to be selected. Wellington and Ward had premises in Paris, Amsterdam, Bombay, and Calcutta, Apem had a company in Copenhagen, while Apem, Wellington, Imperial, and Illingworth had joined in 1930 to form an Italian company in Milan. In Holland, Imperial had a strong agency.

Gradually, new selling companies were set up in Denmark, Holland, Belgium, France, India, and, later, in Australia. Distributors were chosen for Austria, Switzerland, Italy, Norway, Sweden, and other countries outside Europe.

At home, provincial branches were established at Birmingham, Dublin, Glasgow, Leeds, Manchester, and Newcastle. Later, in 1950, Belfast and Bristol were added. These handled goods, serviced equipment and gave some technical service.

Technical developments, led by Frank Renwick under Sir Ivor Philipps' business guidance, produced some remarkable products. The Brentwood factory concentrated from 1923 on the new double-coated X-ray film and at one time Ilford held almost 90 per cent of the British market, as well as having a considerable export business.

Dye sensitizing of emulsions for camera materials was also beginning to play an important part. From 1910, Ilford had been able to offer a reliable panchromatic plate. However, the dyes came from Germany and during the First World War work was

Figure 34   Transport: top left, the earliest vehicle used by the company—a Foden steam wagon; above, a van used by Rajar Ltd; top right, an early motor vehicle used by the Selo factory at Brentwood.

done at Cambridge University with Professor (later Sir) William Pope to produce competitive sensitizers. The outcome of this, and later work by Frances Hamer at Ilford, was a range of excellent panchromatic plates, including one specifically designed for the graphic arts industry.

Following the consolidation of the mergers, Ilford decided to attack the amateur market seriously. Roll films had been sold for some years under a variety of labels but in 1932 Selochrome film was produced with higher speed, good orthochromatic sensitivity and anti-curl and anti-halo characteristics. Although greeted with doubt by the trade, this film caught on well. Continental markets sent in substantial orders and soon the business had grown to considerable proportions.

It was decided at once to produce a Selo panchromatic film. This led on to Hypersensitive Panchromatic films.

The Leica camera had been introduced in Germany some years earlier and at first used lengths of 35 mm film cut from motion picture stock. Ilford realized fairly early that 35 mm 'miniature' cameras were to be a permanent feature of the industry and prepared to make special fine-grain films. The naming of these posed a problem but G. A. Peck, the advertising manager, suggested calling the existing film simply HP and following it on in 1938 with HP2. This was made in Agfa Karat cassettes as well as conventional 35 mm cassettes and cut lengths. It was followed later by HP3, using gold sensitizing in manufacture, which for over ten years, was the most popular fast fine-grained film in the world. Similarly, Selo Fine Grain Panchromatic Film became Selo FP2 to be followed later by Ilford FP3.

One of the most spectacular introductions of this period was the Ilford Infra-red plate, marketed from 1932. Olaf Bloch, who was as much a showman as a scientist, demonstrated the plate at the Royal Photographic Society by photographing the audience in total darkness by means of infrared lamps. He also demonstrated the technique of detecting forgeries in documents, showed how haze could be eliminated in long-distance photography, produced a number of medical photographs of superficial veins invisible in normal white-light shots, and demonstrated the use of infrared photography in the textile industry.

The popular press hailed this as a major discovery and Ilford hit the headlines as never before. *The Times* ran a series of photographs of great beauty showing landscapes taken with the infrared plate, including one of the French coast across the Straits of Dover, which caused one daily paper to state that war would no longer be possible with such a means of observation!

Experiments were also made with new papers. One, known as 605, was a development paper which produced results similar to POP. It sold briefly on the continent but it was unsuitable for enlarging and hence out-of-date before it started.

A much more successful introduction was Plastika, a medium speed warm-tone development paper designed to a specification provided by the sales department. Most products were designed by research on the basis of their ideas of the needs of the customer. Plastika gave very delicate tones and, from October 1936, it sold well until the demand for warm-tone paper changed and cold blacks were increasingly preferred.

The business in the printing industry was also going well. Ilford plates were greatly liked, not only in the UK but round the world. In October 1932, F. J. Tritton was engaged as process department manager to foster this business. As a result, a range of plates for line and halftone work and gravure was built up which remained a large business until the advent of dimensionally stable film base some 30 years later. Ilford were unable initially to obtain polyester base of sufficiently high quality and spent some years experimenting with polystyrene and polycarbonate bases which were not really competitive.

Tritton and his assistant E. T. Wilson took out the first patent for halftone contact screens in 1937 but the invention was not successful with the then available high-contrast emulsions. The patent was allowed to lapse and the idea subsequently picked up by Kodak and marketed by them with the newly developed 'lith' films in the late 1950s. The combination was such a success that the contact screen rapidly became a standard throughout the printing industry worldwide.

Films had traditionally been produced on cellulose nitrate ('Celluloid') base until 1930. In 1929 the celluloid base of X-ray negatives caught fire in a hospital in Cleveland, Ohio and turned the building into a ranging furnace. The US authorities prohibited the use of highly inflammable film base and other countries soon followed. By 1932 Safety X-ray Film was on sale, produced on cellulose acetate base. This was soon extended to graphic arts films, motion picture film, miniature films, and, finally, to roll film.

This move, forced by safety considerations, was soon turned to a sales advantage because cellulose acetate, especially when coated with Saran resin to improve its water-resistant properties, proved an easier material to use than the old nitrate.

Ilford had been making motion picture films since 1923 but Ramsden encouraged the development of the business from 1932 onwards. W. A. Balmain was

Figure 35   A light aeroplane used by Ilford for advertising Selo films in the 1930s.

appointed to head this business with R. S. Liddle as sales executive. Liddle had worked for S. Guiterman & Co., where his father had been instrumental in supplying Ilford with its film base. Offices were opened at National House, Wardour Street, London, in the heart of the British motion picture business.

Liddle appreciated that the cine trade demanded, above all, a reliable product of very consistent quality. A cine studio and testing department were set up at Brentwood to allow the film to be examined under working conditions. The European market was attacked as well as the British one. In general, the new fast negative films were found to be more profitable than fine-grain cine positive film, which needed to be produced in huge quantities if uniformity of quality was to be maintained.

To keep pace with the new technological advances, the company increased its advertising and sales promotion. So far, this had largely been carried out through the Ilford Gallery in High Holborn, originally the Wellington Gallery established in 1914. This was designed by a well-known architect, George Walton, as a pictorial display centre at which no actual business was transacted. Practical demonstrations were given and technical service of all kinds. When Ilford acquired it in 1930 the old, now somewhat shabby, mauve and grey decor was removed and the Ilford Gallery started life as a shop which also held topical exhibitions. It was managed by E. Scott Job.

Exhibitions were also supported, notably stands at the Annual Photographic Fair at the Horticultural Hall.

All the companies involved in the Ilford merger had 'specimen publicity departments' where prints were made to illustrate the variety and quality of the products. In 1930 this work was concentrated in the old Imperial factory at Cricklewood with Kenneth Gaseltine in charge. His father had been works manager there and he was an enthusiast for photography and a good teacher. So the Ilford photographic advertising department became a showpiece and a demonstration and training centre.

Similarly, the department of radiography and medical photography started in 1935 at Tavistock House under Miss Kathleen Clark, became a centre for medical demonstrations and training.

Although technical demonstration and exhibitions continued during the Second World War, and Kathleen Clark's department was particularly valuable, normal commercial activities were greatly reduced.

When the war ended, a vigorous new marketing approach was started by T. M. Illingworth, assisted by George Dorman, advertising manager, and James Mitchell, who later became sales director.

The first step, in 1945, was to drop the old image, including the paddle steamer, and redesign the packaging, letterhead, and advertising material.

Design Research Unit, run by Milner Gray, produced a striking new colour-scheme, typeface, and layout for the products, especially the range of materials for amateurs. Gray introduced the company to the idea of a single logo applicable to all goods, which was then quite a revolutionary idea.

New advertising agents were engaged for amateur products—Everett Advertising—who ran a series of advertisements in newspapers, journals, on posters and the sides of buses and in point-of-sale display features. This culminated in the Ilford 'Films for Faces and Places' campaign, the most successful in the history of the company. It made Ilford a household name and was quoted along with other famous slogans such as 'Guinness is Good For You'. Samson Clark continued to handle the advertising of technical products.

Coupled with this, Ilford entered seriously into the amateur camera market, the Sportsman range being easily the most popular.

The success of the new marketing approach reached a peak about 1955. After that, selling became more difficult and Ilford found themselves handling a very large range of goods including the Azoflex diazo copying process and magnetic tapes, both outside normal photographic business.

Enormous efforts were made to market improved products, but the graphic arts business, which had been so buoyant in the days of glass plates, had collapsed with the inability of the company to offer materials on polyester base. Furthermore, the colour film business was proving highly expensive to organize. The whole amateur market was found to be expensive in advertising and distribution.

In 1961, it was decided to try an experiment by setting up a techno-commercial department. This was designed to couple technical development of products with marketing, so that the maximum use of the company's technical resources would be achieved in providing a market range attractive to the customer. Each major product group had a separate manager with specialized technical knowledge, who could link research, development, sales, and technical service.

A detailed study was made of the market and the technology of each product group. For example, in the X-ray group, studies were made of: the available base materials, triacetate, polycarbonate, or polyester; the methods of machine processing, 'dunking' or roller processing; the future of the rapid processing system then being introduced; the possibility of packaging film in bulk without interleaving; the methods of automatic film changing; and the probable future of the use of silver X-ray emulsions as against other processes.

This aggressive approach produced useful results. Very successful new processes such as Ilfoprint paper with its associated processing machines, improved bromide papers, new graphic arts film, and better X-ray films resulted. However, the rate of growth of sales was not significantly improved and the new organization was costly.

The company was clearly trying to develop and sell a larger range of products than it could manage. The result was retrenchment. The system was changed again in 1965. The marketing of colour film was slowly altered, following the Monopolies Commission report. The Azoflex and magnetic tape business were both sold and other operations streamlined. During this period a new bromide paper range was introduced under the brandname Ilfobrom. The new papers were so well received that Ilford's share of the UK market alone increased from 15 per cent to over 50 per cent inside two years.

From 1969 to 1972 profits improved and marketing was established on a more orthodox product management basis. Apart from the technical stimulus provided, the techno-commercial department had pointed the way to the concentration of effort into logical product groups. Previously, the commercial departments had been entirely sales oriented with activities split into customer segments—dealer, professional, industrial, medical, and so forth. Now the split was more nearly productwise—X-ray, graphic arts, microcopying, black and white camera materials, monochrome papers, colour materials, etc.

This was consolidated by Hans-Ruedi Hug, the commercial managing director, from 1972 to 1975, assisted by John S. Fraser, who became marketing director in 1975. The move of head office to Basildon in 1976 enabled the accommodation allocated to the product groups to be tailored to the organization and the technical service department was rehoused there with much-improved experimental facilities.

By this time, the company had developed a new image as a specialist in black and white photography. A complete range of packaging had been developed in black and white, coupled with specialist advertising. The expertise in fast fine-grain camera materials had continued, with materials such as HP5 and FP4 ranking high in the list used by press, professional, and hobbyist photographers. The same group welcomed

Figure 36   Development of the paddle-steamer trademark over 50 years (see also Fig 3): 1901, 1908, 1913 and 1930–45.

Ilfospeed papers, with their ability to produce good enlargements quickly, and the new Multigrade papers launched in 1978. X-ray materials and new radiographic screens were enabling hospitals to obtain better radiographs with lower doses of X-rays. At the same time, colour photography was still represented by the very successful development of Cibachrome products out of the Ilford Group Company in Fribourg. Also from Fribourg, an improved range of graphic arts products was developed which enabled Ilford to commence the re-establishment of itself as a major supplier to the printing industry.

Meanwhile new fields in specialized industrial and commercial photography were opening up, such as microfilm, where Ilford were able to exploit their strong monochrome emulsion technology.

The overseas companies were linked to the Ilford Group of Ciba-Geigy by stronger ties than ever and exports continued to rise throughout the world. In 100 years, distribution had moved from agencies supplied by the dog-cart and steamer to a network of subsidiary companies and distributors, contacted daily by telephone and telex and supplied, when needed, by airfreight.

THE TECHNOLOGY OF COLOUR PHOTOGRAPHY

Modern colour photographs have been evolved after many years of research and experiment from the time when Clerk Maxwell demonstrated the first colour prints in the 1850s. Two types are now in common use: 'reversal' films, which provide positive transparencies which may be viewed in the hand or by projection; and 'negative-positive' films, the latter provide negatives which are reversed from the original scene in both tone and colour values. From these negatives, colour prints are made, either by contact or, more usually, by enlargement.

For many years, the 'additive' system of construction was used. This produced transparencies by a relatively simple reversal process. It relied upon the use of a tiny mosaic pattern of primary colours on a screen through which the picture was exposed and later viewed.

The additive system was replaced by another, known as the 'subtractive' system, from the 1930s, although it had originally been described by du Hauron in France in 1862. The subtractive system forms images in layers of film. Effectively, there are three layers, which record respectively the bluish, greenish, and reddish elements in the scene. For this reason, such films are known as 'tri-packs'. Early films were sometimes in separate layers, processed independently and later superimposed; all modern films are 'integral tri-packs', having the layers coated successively on a single base layer. This is true both of reversal and negative-positive materials; the latter comprises both a film tri-pack, used to make the negative in the camera, and a paper tri-pack on which the negative is subsequently printed.

Tri-packs can be either of two types, substantive or non-substantive. In the former, the light-sensitive layers incorporate 'colour couplers' which when processed after exposure, produce a visible coloured image (positive or negative, as the case may be). Non-substantive films contain no colour couplers; these are introduced in the course of processing in order to produce the colours in the final film.

A totally different type of material, used only for printing directly from transparencies, is known as 'silver dye-bleach' film. This is also an integral tri-pack but the dyes are incorporated in the light-sensitive layers in manufacture and are bleached out, imagewise, instead of being formed during processing.

13. Colour photography

Attempts to achieve natural colour photographs date back to the earliest days of photography. J. Clerk Maxwell gave a demonstration of the feasibility of colour photography to the Royal Institution in London on 17 May 1861. Before Harman founded his company, Louis Ducos du Hauron, Charles Cros, and others had devised methods of taking colour photographs but little progress could be made before good colour-sensitizers were available.

One of du Hauron's ideas had been the screen-plate process, in which the surface of the photographic plate was covered with small red, green, and blue elements which analysed the image into its constituent primary colours. Professor John Joly of Dublin produced the first practical application of the principle in 1894 (BP no. 14161) and Harman was one of the manufacturers to whom he tried to sell his invention.

Joly first suggested forming the screen from strands of film, dyed in each of the three primary colours, laid in sequence on a varnished plate, or in the form of a fabric woven from transparent coloured fibres. However, the patent he offered Harman in 1897 (BP no. 17900) described a machine to rule the glass surface of the plate in fine parallel lines of colour. Panchromatic plates were needed for the process and these had been produced by Vogel as early as 1884; by 1897 a number of sensitizing dyes would have been available to Harman.

Harman turned this down, either because he felt there was no commercial future in colour or, more likely, because he thought the process too difficult to commercialize. It was taken up by others, notably by Dufay and by C. L. Finlay of the Thames Plate Co. Both of these were pioneers of processes later used by Ilford. Finlay worked between 1905 and 1914 with G. S. Whitfield, son of the founder of the Paget Prize Plate Co.

In 1904, Louis Lumière, working in France, had published an account of his new 'screen process'. From 1907 onwards, both he and Agfa, in Germany, marketed materials using a mosaic screen (or 'réseau') composed of microscopic dyed potato starch grains, scattered over a varnished sheet of glass, which was afterwards coated with emulsion.

In 1908, Louis Dufay was granted several patents relating to a similar process which employed a mosaic screen ruled on the surface of the glass in place of the potato starch grain réseau.

Finlay did not produce his process until April 1913, when it was demonstrated to the Royal Photographic Society by G. S. Whitfield's son, G. E. Whitfield, who was works manager of the Paget factory at Watford and remained there, latterly under Ilford ownership, until after the Second World War.

The distinctive feature of the Finlay process was that the colour screen, otherwise similar to that used by Dufay, was separate. It could therefore be used many times over and with any panchromatic plate. The exposed plate, separate from the screen, was processed just like any normal monochrome plate. After drying, it was printed to produce a conventional transparent 'lantern slide', which was bound tightly in contact with a 'viewing screen' similar to that through which the negative had been exposed. The full colours of the picture could then be seen in the transparency.

Because the expensive colour mosaic was separate, the Finlay process was cheaper than its competitors; taking screens were 8d, viewing screens 8d a pair, and panchromatic plates 1s to 1s 4d a dozen.

The Lumière material, under the name Autochrome, remained on the market until after the Second World War, although it had been discontinued by the time Ilford became involved with Lumière SA in 1964. Finlay plates were sold until 1933 when Ilford had become involved in the manufacture of Dufaycolor film, a material evolved from the original Dufay plate of 1908, using film base ruled mechanically with a colour réseau.

All these processes produced attractive colour transparencies which could be viewed against a source of light or projected in a 'lantern'. They could not provide prints on paper. This objective was not fully achieved by any company associated with Ilford until after 1950.

Ilford realized soon after starting film manufacture at Brentwood in 1921 that colour photography was more than a technical curiosity. They cast around for practical processes and, in 1928, participated in the manufacture of a subtractive type of negative-positive colour 'tri-pack' roll film for a small concern, Colour Snaps Ltd, which carried out the developing and printing itself. A tri-pack consisted of three separate films, rolled up together, each sensitive to one of the primary colours. After processing, each film was printed in a complementary colour and the resulting prints brought into register to provide a single print in full colour. The process proved too difficult to operate. Only small numbers of prints were ever made and the company was wound up in 1930, after less than two years in operation. Their technical manager, F. J. Tritton, later joined Ilford Limited in another capacity.

By 1934, it had been decided that the Dufaycolor film process held out the most promise. Although the tiny mosaic was difficult to print on film base, the subsequent operations of sensitizing and processing were relatively simple. Processing could, in fact, be carried out by any competent amateur photographer.

Hence, from 1935, Ilford produced, in conjunction with Dufay-Chromex, additive reversal colour roll films and professional motion picture film. Printing of the screen pattern of red, green, and blue elements on the film base before coating required high precision equipment and a clean atmosphere. The operation was carried out by Spicers, in a factory at Sawston near Cambridge. The printed rolls of base were sent to Ilford at Brentwood for emulsion coating.

The main drawback to Dufaycolor—as with any other additive process—was that the screen pattern became rather obtrusive on enlargement, especially in the high magnification used in the cinema. Very powerful projection lamps were needed because of the inherent loss of light; with an additive process, the maximum amount of light reaching the screen is only one-third of that applied, the rest being absorbed by the réseau.

Another drawback was that duplication of the films, essential for the cinema industry, was very difficult. From 1930 to 1936, G. B. Harrison and R. G. Horner worked on this problem but without completely overcoming it. However, the material was the most successful, commercially, of all the mosaic screen processes and a number of full-length professional motion picture films were produced on it, as well as very many newsreels, including those of King George V's Silver Jubilee and his funeral and the coronation of King George VI. Dufaycolor was also widely used by amateurs as roll film, 35 mm film and 16 mm cine film.

From 1935 onwards, the search for new sensitizing dyes led the organic chemical research scientists to test certain materials as possible colour couplers for use in chromogenic systems similar to those covered in Kodak and Agfa patents issued at that time. In view of the commitment to Dufaycolor, little work was carried out but a testing service was inaugurated under L. V. Chilton, assisted by S. Welford. Colour couplers, later to become of some importance, were patented in 1938, but no further work was carried out. Kodachrome and Agfacolor were heavily covered by patents and it was 1938 before Ilford decided that chromogenic processes might replace Dufaycolor within a few years. Some attention was therefore turned to alternative processes which might be within the resources available.

Various systems were examined, including one offered by the Veracol Film Syndicate. D. A. Spencer, managing director of Colour Photographs Ltd, acted as a consultant to Ilford at that time. His Vivex process had become technically very successful and Veracol was an attempt to adapt Vivex to motion picture production. Work continued, in parallel, to try to achieve good positive prints from Dufaycolor masters. Veracol started as a two-colour process and was later developed into a three-colour process intended to compete with Technicolor. However, it never progressed beyond the experimental laboratory stage.

The Second World War intervened and, from 1939 to 1945, government directives prevented any colour research work being carried out.

When the war ended, Ilford was quickly at work to try to make up the time lost. A small team was set up in the Rodenside Laboratory, headed by R. B. Collins. H. O. Dickinson was in charge of emulsion chemistry, R. R. Robinson the layer-assembly and processing techniques and R. Stapleton the testing methods. They considered the possibility of a process similar to Agfacolor, because of the simpler processing, but decided that the Company did not possess the resources to make the substantive colour couplers needed, even with the information provided by the British Intelligence Objectives reports from Germany. W. H. Dimsdale, then joint managing director, suggested trying a process more like Kodachrome, in spite of the formidable patent barriers to be overcome.

By 1948, only three years after starting the project with virtually no knowledge of many of the basic requirements, the team had produced a non-substantive colour transparency film, named Ilford Colour 'D'. It avoided the Kodak patents by the use of a colourless layer containing silver sulphide, which produced an effective light barrier during the first development of the film and thus allowed the material to be reversal processed by re-exposure of the red sensitive layer. Hence it was also referred to as the 'barrier layer process'. Its speed was the same as Kodachrome (ASA 8) and it provided a somewhat soft but very pure colour, which was much liked by some users, especially technical photographers engaged in biological and agricultural work. Processing facilities were retained in the research department and adjustments were made to compensate for slight batch variations. As a result, the quality was very consistent. A process for duplicating transparencies was also set up, using a masking system which gave excellent results.

Although some work was carried out on negative-positive chromogenic systems, the resources available did not allow the development of colour negative film, with associated printing paper. So Ilford embarked upon a programme to produce prints from the Colour 'D' transparencies. A survey of the possible processes pointed to silver dye-bleach as the most promising direct positive system.

Attempts failed to produce successful prints on silver dye-bleach materials supplied by Dr Bela Gaspar, from the United States in 1947. However, subsequent work on an Ilford version of this type of material showed promise under the guidance of Harrison and Collins. The azo dyes required for the new product were worked out by Dr Keller of Geigy and made by them in Switzerland. Prints of acceptable quality were produced by 1949. These were the first good prints to be made by any manufacturer direct from transparencies in a single step.

By 1952, Ilford decided it was ready to launch an entirely new service, offering colour prints from 35 mm transparencies—either Ilford Colour 'D' or Kodachrome. Jack H. Coote joined the Company to establish the laboratory and recruit the staff. The new service was set up in a building owned by the Britannia Works Co., at Rosedale Road, Richmond. High-intensity printers, with Xenon lamps, and specialized processing machines were designed.

Within a year or so, the annual output of silver dye-bleach colour prints had reached more than one million, at a time when colour negative materials were still unknown to the amateur photographer outside the United States. Prints were produced at Richmond until 1960.

Meanwhile, work had been proceeding on the improvement of the barrier layer process. For some time, Kodak had been using a different method of re-exposing the individual emulsion layers during reversal processing and by 1960 their patent protection in the method had expired, so that Ilford

could use a similar method to achieve a material simpler to manufacture and easier to process than the barrier layer film. A speed of 32 ASA was achieved; this was suitable for the 35 mm film but 8 mm was introduced at 25 ASA, the highest convenient speed for 8 mm cameras. Both were marketed in 1962 under the name Ilfochrome.

Ilford had hoped to be the first to market colour films of such speeds but it took longer to perfect than had been anticipated and Kodachrome II, at similar speed levels, was marketed before Ilfochrome.

Throughout the immediate postwar years, ICI had been working at Blackley, near Manchester, on a colour negative film and a paper on which to print it. The information on which ICI based their research was obtained from the Agfa records obtained by the British Intelligence Objectives Sub-committee at the end of the war. They were aided by a small team of scientists, some of whom had worked on Agfa colour products in Germany.

When ICI obtained a share of the Ilford equity in 1959, this technology was passed on and it was decided to market the products under the name Ilfocolor.

For a time, work was proceeding on five colour products: Colour 'D', Ilfochrome film, Ilfocolor film, dye-bleach print material, and Ilfocolor paper. All these films and print materials were processed and printed in a new colour processing laboratory at Basildon. This range over-extended all the departments concerned: research, production, testing, and processing. Colour 'D' was discontinued when Ilfochrome was introduced but processing still had to be carried out for some years, as customers used stocks of material. After much discussion, it was decided that the silver dye-bleach print material required more research and production effort than the company could afford and it was discontinued in favour of Ilfocolor negative film and printing paper. These were rapidly improved, with a continuous series of modifications.

In 1962, CIBA AG demonstrated in Switzerland a silver dye-bleach print material on which they had done extensive research. Ilford re-entered this field by an agreement with CIBA to assist them with emulsion technology and coating methods. However, the printing of amateur transparencies was not revived. For a short time, silver dye-bleach material was again coated at Brentwood but it was soon decided that all further work on improvement and production of this product should be carried out in Switzerland. At first, it was called Cilchrome (the 'cil' being derived from 'CIBA' and 'Ilford') but this was later changed to Cibachrome.

In May, 1965 a fresh effort was made to increase the sales of colour films. The colour negative film was improved and renamed Colorprint and the substantive reversal film was marketed in two versions, called Colorslide and Super Colorslide. So for some years Ilford offered a wide range of colour products.

The 35 mm version of Colorprint material—the first colour negative film to be sold in the UK in this format—was returned from processing with a contact print strip. This proof strip was intended to assist the amateur to choose the negatives to be enlarged. The idea was well received because of the difficulty of judging colour negatives without printing them, which normally involved the extra cost of making enlarged prints.

The Wholesale Photofinishers' Association had already complained that its members were precluded from competing for the processing of the bulk of reversal colour film sold in the UK because it was sold at prices inclusive of processing. They now assumed that, because the proof strip had to be made on expensive specialized equipment, Ilford was trying to follow the same route for colour negatives. They referred the whole matter to the Monopolies Commission for investigation.

The Monopolies Commission's findings in 1966 put Ilford in a difficult situation. Strong representations were made to the Board of Trade stating, among other points, that:

1. Although negative-positive processing was not simple, its difficulties could not be compared to those encountered with non-substantive films. To obtain acceptable results, the techniques laid down by the manufacturer had to be followed closely.

2. It was not always convenient or economic for photofinishers to alter their processing baths and printing methods to cope with the peculiarities of each manufacturer's product. Hence, a photofinisher might produce excellent results on one material but have totally unacceptable standards when handling others.

3. The position of the brand leader was less serious because photofinishers were prepared to put in a processing line, with associated quality control, provided there was an adequate volume of business to justify it.

4. As the colour market was dominated by one manufacturer, Ilford was obliged to offer the customer some advantages to induce them to purchase their film. These included the contact strip print, which offered novel advantages to the consumer. All these advantages would be eliminated if the Commission's views were upheld, leaving the company in a vulnerable position.

The Board of Trade rejected Ilford's representations; on 8 August 1966 it issued a notice enforcing the recommendations of the Monopolies Commission on the points concerned.

Largely as a consequence of these changes, it was decided to discontinue the sale of branded Ilford colour films, although research and production continued on colour negative film and chromogenic printing paper, which were produced specially for the Film Corporation of America. Even so, the company's facilities were stretched too far and, in 1970, the whole effort was concentrated upon Cibachrome, apart from research work to explore other types of material.

14. Engineering development

Because the photographic industry is a relatively small one, large-scale specialist equipment is not available on the open market. The larger companies, including Ilford, have therefore designed and made their own, apart from standard items available from other industries.

Originally, Harman and others cleaned and coated their glass plates by hand. From 1890 mechanization proceeded steadily. By then, Ilford plates had a large share of the British market and were being exported. With such a volume of business, hand methods must have become impractical; glass-washing machines and drying equipment were soon in use. Glass-cutting machines were introduced in 1894.

A glass-washing machine had been designed by Harman himself (BP no. 18349) in 1888. It passed the plates between pairs of rollers, sprays, and rotary brushes. One of the early machines handled the glass vertically but later ones were horizontal. A machine designed by Edwards and made by R. W. Munro Ltd, of Bounds Green, London, was also used. This employed flat badger bristle brushes operated by a reciprocating mechanism across the plates at 90 strokes a minute. The drive rollers were covered with sulphur-free rubber. After brushing, the plates were polished with eccentric pads fed with whitening. Later types included a heated tunnel to dry the plates but Harman had them placed in racks by hand and dried in warm rooms or even, in the early days, in the open air by the river Roding. Munros produced specialized plant for the photographic industry for about 60 years and have since designed and manufactured scientific equipment. The use of hot soda solution for cleaning, in place of plain water, was soon adopted as also was a final pair of rollers to apply the substratum needed to enable the emulsion to adhere firmly to the glass.

The emulsion was produced in earthenware pots, as it was for the following 70 years or so. After production, it needed washing before coating. Before it could be washed it had to be shredded; this was done by forcing the jelly through a sieve or perforated plate. James Cadett appears to have been the first to suggest hydraulic power for this. A high-pressure water service was common in Victorian industry and was used to operate lifts and even very large pieces of plant, such as the bascules of Tower Bridge, London. Cadett's equipment had a capacity of over 2 gal/min and used water pressure of 75–100 lb/in^2.

All the early equipment suffered from problems over the sensitivity of photographic emulsion to metallic contamination, especially from copper and iron. Much industrial equipment was then made of copper or brass. Cadett's equipment, and that of most others of the period, used copper or bronze very heavily plated with silver. A few were constructed from solid silver. Cadett's shredder had a perforated plate of sterling silver or nickel about $\frac{1}{4}$ in thick, perforated with $\frac{1}{16}$ in holes at a separation of about $\frac{1}{8}$ in. A rubber disc was used on the face of the piston, as in an air pump. This expanded under pressure and ensured that no emulsion was left clinging to the walls of the cylinder and so wasted.

Ilford installed the first hydraulic shredder in 1909. Early models were made of solid silver, later ones in Xylonite 2 in thick, until the advent of suitable grades of stainless steel provided a more satisfactory alternative.

Coating of the warm emulsion from teapot-like vessels was soon replaced by better systems. The first machine for coating plates was devised in 1879 (BP no. 4607) by Sir Joseph Wilson Swan of Mawson and Swan in Newcastle but was never put into production.

In 1884, Swan's design was improved by B. J. Edwards (BP no. 8643) and Harman started by renting three of these machines from Edwards for £200 per annum. They were evidently satisfactory, as he later bought them outright. The early Edwards machine was capable of coating about 1000 plates an hour but, by 1930, the machines had been so improved that a skilled team could coat 3600 an hour. An improved coating head designed by Swan in 1885 (BP no. 8917) does not appear to have been used by Ilford.

Other machines available employed Cadett's pump system, Smith's weir system, or the slot system. It is interesting that the last, though little used for plate coating, was eventually selected as the basis for later precision film-coating methods. Ilford plate machines

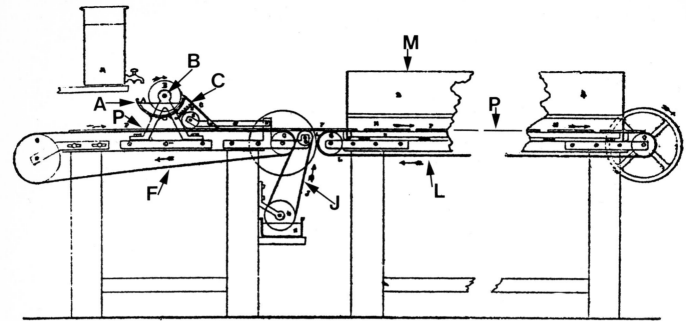

Figure 37   Edwards' plate coating machine, 1884. The emulsion ran into a trough A containing a metal roller B. One end of a scraper C rested against the roller as it rotated, taking off the emulsion and delivering it to the plates P, which were carried forward by an endless band F and delivered to another endless band L, which passed through a chamber M cooled by ice. Below the plates was a band J which washed the backs of the plates.

ultimately used a weir with a constant level device and a metering pump.

Edwards' system consisted of a roller running in a trough fed with emulsion (Figures 37 and 38). The film of emulsion picked up on it was scraped off by a blade and ran down an incline onto the plate. In later models, a strip of flexible material was used to conduct the layer from the incline onto the surface of the plate. The best material was found to be thin wet-strengthened paper such as airmail writing paper. Control of coating thickness was achieved by varying the rate of revolution of the roller and the speed of the belts on which the plates passed under the coating head. In the early days, the machines were hand-cranked. Later, small steam engines were used to drive them, until electric motors came into use.

To avoid waste of emulsion the plates were fed onto the moving belts by hand, butted end to end and controlled by lateral guides. Soon after coating, the plates met a second series of belts, travelling faster than the first, which plucked them apart, breaking the continuous film of emulsion on the surface. The plates then passed through a chilling tunnel, cooled with ice, where the emulsion was thoroughly set, before being placed on edge, by hand, into racks and transferred to drying rooms (Figure 39).

The method of chilling first used by Harman was air cooled by ice. Later, a stream of chilled water was used, the surface of which just touched the backs of the plates. Following the introduction of chilled water setting, more critical control of coating speeds was needed. Eventually, this was achieved by a special expansion pulley, patented by H. W. Horton in 1921 (BP no. 17422). Many years later, when refrigeration plant had reached a higher stage of development, chilling was achieved by jets of air impinging upon the back of the glass, which gave plates of better uniformity.

The racking of plates at the end of the machine before transfer to the drying room was a skilled operation. The plates were held by the edges only, on the tips of the fingers, and had to be handled quickly. This was primarily to prevent the warmth of the hands remelting the emulsion locally, though high machine speeds also necessitated deft work. This method was used by most manufacturers until plate production was replaced by film, though the Agfa plant at Wolfen, Germany, later had more sophisticated machines, using racks on trolleys running on rails, with six tracks through a drying tunnel. This was said to have been designed by a model railway enthusiast. At Ilford, the racks were placed by hand in heated rooms with a circulation of air which, in later years, was filtered to ensure cleanliness.

Figure 38   The feed end of an Ilford plate machine, which operated from the early part of the century until the Second World War. On the right is E. C. Dodd, later head of paper research at Mobberley.

Figure 39   The 'racking' end of the machine shown in Fig. 37. The plates, with emulsion coat set but not dry, were lifted quickly off the end of the moving belt and placed in a rack for transport to the drying room. With panchromatic plates, this delicate operation was carried out in total darkness.

Figure 40   An early four-head plate cutting machine made by Munro; it was still in operation when the Ilford plate factory was closed in 1975. (Courtesy R. W. Munro and Co., Ltd.)

Ilford was fortunate in discovering, at a very early stage, the application of controlled air conditions to the difficult problem of plate drying and this later helped the design of dryers for film machines. In consultation with Haslams of Derby, a leading firm of refrigeration engineers, Ilford constructed a cooling battery in an airtight enclosure. This housed a large water tank cooled by refrigerent circulating through coiled pipes. Above the tank was a series of steel plates, 8 ft high and spaced 3 in apart, which were cooled by the water constantly circulated from the tank below. Low velocity air was circulated from the drying rooms through this battery, by means of well-insulated ducts. The air was thus dehumidified by cooling and cleaned before being recirculated to the drying rooms. Additional cleaning was achieved by means of fabric filters. The drying rooms were heated by steam pipes which were independently controlled.

Later, Hall and Kay blanket filters were introduced and became the standard air intake filter at all Ilford factories. The cotton fabric used was pretreated with a solution of silver nitrate before the material was stretched over the filter frames. This was an Ilford invention for the removal of gaseous sulphur compounds in the air. Prior to the Clean Air Act, contamination from sulphur fumes was a great menace and coating would often have to stop in foggy weather, but as pollution in the air lessened and with the introduction of modern filtration methods this problem was gradually eliminated.

The plates were 'cut' by scribing a straight line on the glass side with a diamond and then cracking them into two pieces along the line, by gently bending the plate from the glass side. Originally a special cutting board was used which centred the plates and guided the diamond so that each plate was accurately cut into two halves. R. W. Munro devised a machine which did this quickly and accurately and which could be rapidly adjusted for different plate sizes, based on a design by W. J. Wilson of the Paget Prize Plate Co.

135

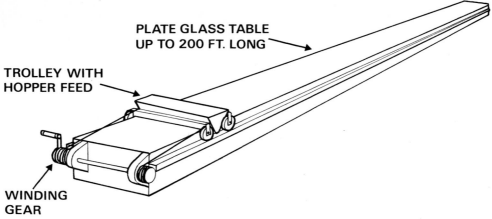

PLATE GLASS TABLE UP TO 200 FT. LONG

TROLLEY WITH HOPPER FEED

WINDING GEAR

Figure 41   Diagram of an early film base casting and coating machine. The hopper was wound along the plate glass table.

(Figure 40). It was found that, with these machines, it was possible to scribe the glass from the emulsion side as the diamond was capable of cutting through the emulsion layer to the glass underneath. With the older method, the emulsion layer along the scribed line was stretched when the plate was cracked, which led to frilling of the emulsion along those two edges during processing. The new method avoided this as the layer was already severed and the emulsion layers were bent towards each other.

The new machines also removed any glass or emulsion dust. The plates were then placed together in pairs by hand, back to back, and each pair separated by channel-shaped pieces of card along two opposite edges, before being packed in fours or sixes in black paper and boxed.

The earliest method of coating film, used by Kodak (and by Lumière of the eventual Ilford companies) combined the film-casting process with the coating (Figure 41). The cellulose nitrate solution was poured from a V-hopper, mounted on a trolley, on to sheets of plate glass laid on a long table, up to 200 ft in length. The joins between the sheets were filled with lithage cement or tin foil, carefully polished. The hopper was drawn over the table, leaving a layer of solution on the glass bed. The room was warmed and fans turned on to remove the solvent. The surface was then treated with a mixture of ethanol and ether. Finally, the hopper-trolley was used, in the dark, to apply a coat of emulsion which was set and dried before the whole assembly was carefully stripped from the glass and rolled up.

The Lumière brothers' system in France, used for their cinematograph film, employed glass tables, 60 m long; one of them was still in the Lyon factory when Ilford became involved with them in 1963.

Ilford did not attempt to produce film in roll form for many years. Harman himself never seemed convinced that film had a future comparable with that of glass plates. He did produce some flat film but this was coated in individual pieces, like plates, by the 'sticky back' process. For this, sheets of cellulose nitrate, usually 10/1000 in thick produced by slicing from a thick block, were polished between heated metal platens and attached to glass sheets by means of a tacky mixture of gelatin and glycerine, with some sugar syrup added. The substratum solvent was applied by hand with a pad and the film coated in a plate-coating machine. After drying, it was cautiously stripped from the glass in humid conditions to avoid the generation of static electricity.

This method of coating film was used by Ilford until it was decided to produce film in roll form. A start was made in 1908 when S. Guiterman & Co. Ltd, of London submitted quotations for film base in 300 ft lengths 21 in wide. N. L. Scott & Co., London, were approached for a machine and replied:

Messrs. Ilford Ltd.,
Warley Common,
Brentwood,   February 17th, 1909
Dear Sirs,

We are in receipt of your letter of 16th inst., and beg to say that the Coating Trials which we are now making with the Celluloid Coating Machine referred to, are of quite a private nature, and not open to inspection. Owing to the success of these trials we are designing a machine on an entirely new principle and if you are likely to be interested in it we will communicate with you further when the same is completed.

We may mention that we are not amateurs at this

business having constructed or had experience of nearly every machine in Europe, while, (apart from the Kodak Co.) the bulk of the Cinematograph Film at present produced is coated on our machines.

Yours faithfully,

N. L. Scott & Co.

Marketable film was not produced until 1914, when war intervened; production in any volume started only in 1921.

Paper had been coated from the web from the earliest days. The coating of paper for various other industrial purposes was, of course, a well-known operation and photographic coating was not strikingly different, apart from the exclusion of white light. Silver bromide printing papers were patented by Swan in 1879 (BP no. 2986) and were in general use from 1880 onwards. It is not recorded exactly when Harman started to coat papers, nor what equipment he used. He was certainly producing material for sale by 1884, the year in which Eastman started coating paper from the web in Rochester, USA. At that time, fully equipped paper coating and drying equipment was already available from both British and German sources. By 1900, there were two paper-coating machines in the Ilford factory, both made by Masson Scott & Co.

From about 1894 an underlayer of baryta (barium sulphate) in hardened gelatin was used to improve the quality and gloss of prints. Harman probably bought his paper base already baryta coated. His suppliers were the Coloured Paper and Glue Co., Blanchet Frères and Kleber (Rives paper), and Steinbach (Saxe paper).

The emulsion (or the baryta) was applied to the paper base by simple 'dip coating' that is, by dipping the paper in the coating liquid while the paper was travelling round a roller. The speed of travel, which was only a few feet per minute, determined the thickness of the coating. Originally, the paper was 21 in wide and the machines were hand-cranked. Later, paper of 44 in or 54 in width was used and more uniform machine drives developed. More sophisticated coating methods, such as air-knife and slot coating, were not developed until after the Second World War.

Dryers were of the festoon type (Figure 42); loops of paper were carried through drying tunnels on horizontal poles. This simple technique simulates mechanically the action of hanging washing on a line and originated in the textile industry about 1870, the early machines being made by Mather & Platt Ltd. The principle was applied to paper as soon as the invention of photoengraving brought a demand for papers coated with clay or satin white. Mather & Platt supplied a number of the early machines used by Rajar at Mobberley and probably some used by Harman at Ilford.

Festoon dryers were later almost universally used for some years in the photographic industry for both paper and film. In Ilford they ranged from one only 15 ft long, installed by Paget Prize Plate for the manufacture of collodion self-toning paper, to some tracks 600 ft long. The early ones were mainly of wooden construction. Some used turntables to alter the direction of travel, the ones at Brentwood having a 300 ft two-legged track which brought the dry loops back to a point near the coating head, so that coating and reeling-up of the dry web could be done by the same crew (Figure 43). This also limited the distance for which the poles supporting the loops had to be carried to bring them back to the start.

Most of the early festoon machines were open to the room but later ones were enclosed, with a good supply of conditioned air. All festoon machines had the advantage of a natural 'magazine capacity' to enable the coating and reeling heads to be stopped while drying continued. This was utilized at one time at Mobberley (Rajar) to enable the web to be slit into small rolls continuously at the end of the dryer.

An interesting variant, used at Watford (Paget Prize Plate) was the 'kangaroo' track, which moved the poles intermittently by ratchet action in place of continuous motion on a chain. Unfortunately, it was very apt to contaminate the paper by producing dust.

Ilford realized by 1922 that the festoon dryer was not entirely suitable for film production. Drying was slow, as the air velocity had to be kept low to avoid physical damage to the loops. Drying cycles of up to four hours were common. The poles tended to produce marks. Other manufacturers tried to avoid these by using oval poles or double poles, by using large cylinders covered with felt or by rotating the poles intermittently. A festoon track of the last type was used by Tellko SA and subsequently by Ciba-Geigy at Fribourg, Switzerland.

Festoon machines performed adequately for paper products and were kept in use at Mobberley after Ilford closed the Illingworth, Paget, Imperial, and other plants. They were also used for some years for baryta coating at the Cassio Photographic Co. at Watford, owned jointly with Wiggins Teape Ltd. However, film clearly needed a better technique.

In 1922 a very remarkable engineer, W. H. Smith, had been appointed as works manager of the Selo works at Brentwood. His answer to the problem of

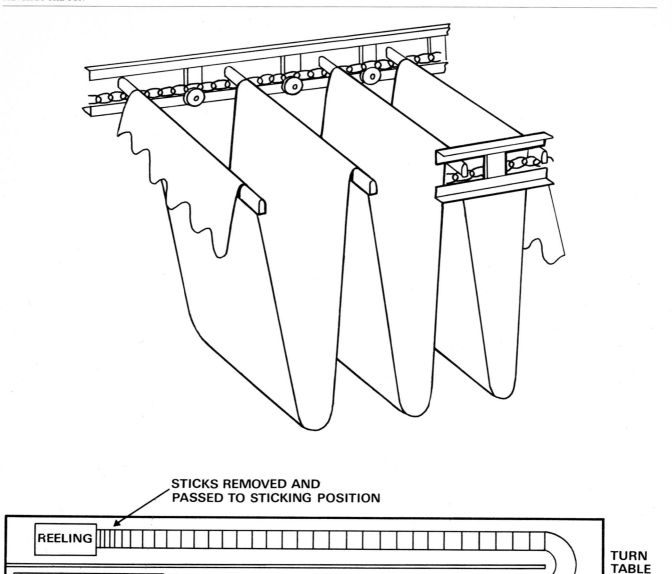

**STICKS REMOVED AND
PASSED TO STICKING POSITION**

REELING

STOCK
COATING
SETTING

STICKING

TURN
TABLE

*Figure 42   Diagram of a festoon drying track. The film or paper is hung in loops over poles which are
carried by a track through the drying chamber.*

drying film was to produce a spiral dryer called a
'spider' from its similarity to a spider's web, when
viewed from the side.

He had taken over two festoon coating tracks
moved in 1920 from the Rajar Works at Mobberley.
These had wooden frames with rollers running on
centres to support the film. The rollers tended to drop
out with the movement of the frames and their festoon
system also scratched the back of the film. Two new
machines were therefore installed, built mainly by
Dixons of Letchworth, and utilizing Smith's universal
fittings.

The machines used cellulose nitrate film purchased
from the Celluloid Corporation of America through
their UK agents Guiterman (the Celluloid Corporation later became American Cellanese). The name
'Celluloid' was their registered trademark and led to
the use of the name 'Xylonite' by British Xylonite,
from whom Ilford later bought base and with whom
they eventually set up the joint company Bexford to
manufacture film base materials.

An etching substratum of solvent ether was applied
just before coating. Drying was by steam pipes on the
floor of the festoon track. Electric fans were later fitted
but had to be modified when they were found to cover
the film with dust. Buckets of water were stood on the

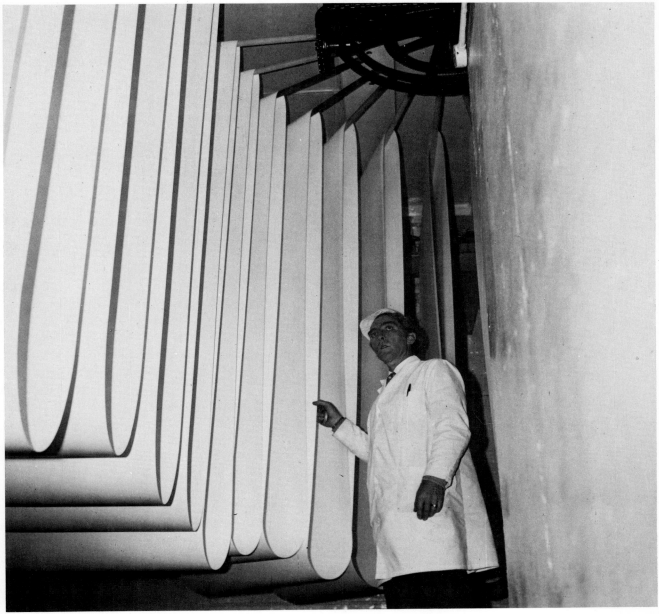

Figure 43   The turntable on one of the Mobberley festoon dryers.

steam pipes to humidify the air and thus prevent the film curling too badly; in bad cases, thin laths were pegged across the film as it dried.

Emulsion was applied by running the liquid down an inclined glass plate nearly radial to the roller round which the film passed, a method introduced by C. S. Whitfield, who was then managing director of Selo.

Smith believed a compact drying frame was needed to replace the festoon track if dirt, curling, and stick-marks were to be overcome. He designed and made a four-turn (60 ft capacity) spiral dryer. Such dryers had been used by Imperial from about 1911. After coating, the film was fed into the frame which was then wheeled into a drying room. Smith converted this system into a continuous dryer attached to the coating machine. This produced clean, high-quality film and was followed in 1924 by a spider machine with a capacity of about 600 ft. Both of these suffered from the disadvantage that film had to be rewound from the spiral on to a core when dry.

The system was obviously successful, however, and H. Horton, chief engineer of Ilford, approached Dixons to devise a cheaper method of construction, though their system was not ultimately adopted. By the end of 1924 one of the festoon tracks had been

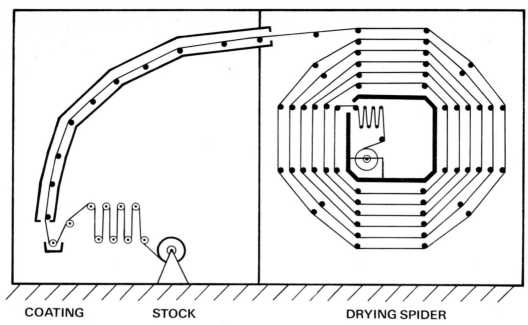

COATING   STOCK   DRYING SPIDER

Figure 44   Diagram of a spider dryer, as used for film manufacture at Brentwood. From the coating point, on the left, the film was fed into a large spiral in the drying chamber, finally being reeled up in a room within the hub of the spiral. This was a highly economical method of drying film.

dismantled and a separate subbing operation had been introduced.

The year 1925 saw big changes. A new spider machine was designed and constructed to Smith's specifications. This used double width (that is, nominally 42 in) base, had automatic tension control for the web (believed to be the first in use in the industry) and reeled up the dry film continuously in the centre of the spiral. (Figure 44.)

These early spiders, like the festoon tracks, operated at low speeds, some at only 5 ft/min and none above 15 or 16 ft/min, and had very simple drive and air-supply arrangements. However, the method was a great improvement upon festoon dryers. The film was, above all, very much cleaner, especially when the floor, walls, and ceiling were washed down weekly with glycerine solution. Experience showed that it produced better film and was also a very economical method of drying. The principle was developed until, by about 1960, highly sophisticated machines of this basic type with two coating points, were running at speeds of about 100 ft/min for a continuous 24 hours, 7 days a week.

Smith also designed an ingenious machine to coat X-ray film with two layers on each side of the base simultaneously. The web was held at the edges by rollers of truncated cone shape and followed a sinuform path through the dryer. The machine produced good film, of which some was sold for about two years, but it was not finally adopted as it was more

difficult to use than the spiders and base of very high quality was needed to avoid waste. The concept was far ahead of its time and, if pursued, might have led to financial gain for the company when, in later years, the economics of X-ray film production became a key issue. In fact, X-ray film was coated on a spider machine, to avoid pole marks, from 1926 onwards. It had to be run through the machine four times—once for the emulsion and once for the protective non-stress layer, on each side of the base.

At this time (1925–28) there was no adequate public supply of power. Each plant in the group had its own generating plant, the one at Brentwood being a Bellis Morcom 2-cylinder compound steam engine, run from a Lancashire boiler at 65 p.s.i. and driving two 220 volt d.c. 50 kw generators. A 50 hp National gas engine, with a smaller generator, was available as a standby but never had to be used.

In the early days, most of the film was produced for the cinematograph industry. Apart from film for normal photographic processes, it was also produced dyed amber, blue, or red, for sunshine, moonlight, or firelight effects. A Dixon 35 mm slitter was used, with a variety of perforators, Cinechrome, Debrie, and Bell & Howell. When George Hudson joined the company from the British Film Co. of Ashtead ('Brifco') in 1926, he obtained secondhand B & H machines and the Cinechrome machines were discarded. In 1928, the public electricity supply reached Brentwood but the old generators were kept on standby in case of power

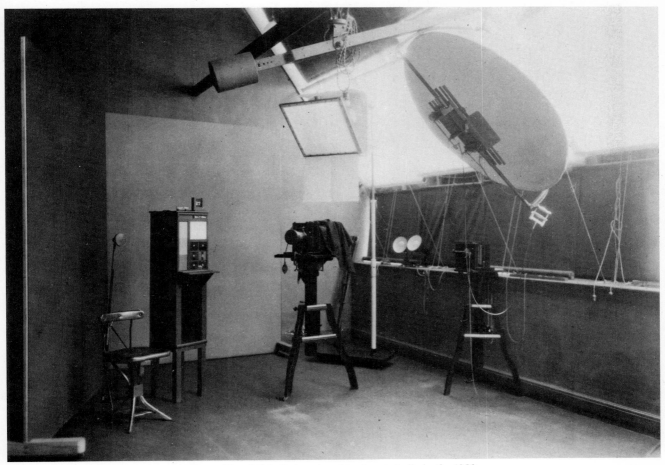

Figure 45 A Selo Ltd testing department studio in the 1930s.

failure. This always seemed to happen when 1000 ft rolls of cine film were being coated!

Increasing quantities of roll film were also produced. Originally, spooling was slow, as the film was susceptible to static damage at high speeds. Gradually the machines were improved and, from about 1940, increasingly automated. The duplex paper wrappers were made on a hand press after slitting on a Munroe slitter; in 1956, a fully automatic machine was designed and built by Chambon Ltd. About 1930, hand cartoning gave way to two machines of American origin for the two most popular sizes 120 and 116. Separate brand labels were used for Imperial, Ilford, Illingworth, Rajar, Apem, and Gem, until Selo was introduced as the sole brand.

Changes again took place between 1930 and 1933. All engineering work at Brentwood was amalgamated under W. Cornell with John W. W. Smith as assistant works engineer. The established channel of liaison with the chief engineer at Ilford was maintained. From this emerged a plan for a central engineering department.

A new cine film department and a new sensitometric testing laboratory were built (Figure 46). Before long, special Dufaycolor printers were developed, designed to eliminate moiré patterns. But the biggest change was a temporary reversion to festoon drying.

The spider type of coating machine was not suitable for drying paper, though some machines in the Austin Edwards factory at Warwick (designed by an engineer who joined them from Ilford) were used for handling double-weight paper (card) for a time after Ilford bought the plant in 1953. The alternative was to use a flat-bed machine. One was used by Leto, who were subsequently taken over by Wellington and Ward, from about 1914 to coat collodion self-toning paper. However, collodion is much more easily dried than gelatin, which needs a higher velocity of air than could be provided in the early days.

From about 1950, air-filtration systems had been improved to allow even higher velocities to be attained. As the name 'flat bed' suggests, the paper was originally run on a horizontal set of rollers, but the use of a convex path was afterwards found to prevent the pronounced edge-curl which led to damage producing troublesome breaks in the paper web. The air impinged on the paper from slots or nozzles fairly close

141

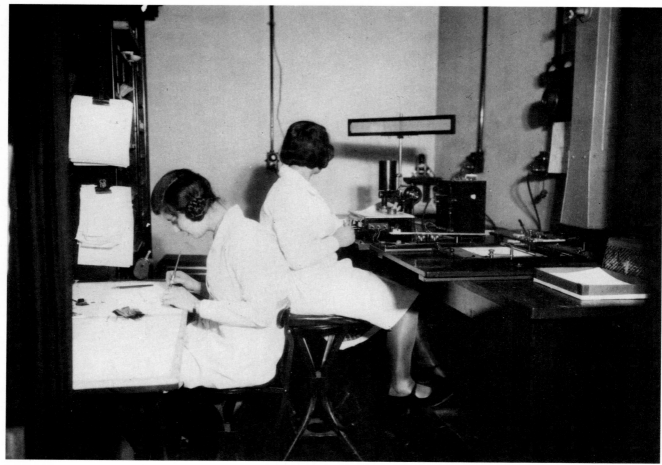

Figure 46   The Selo sensitometric testing department opened in 1938.

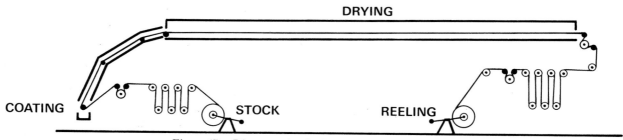

Figure 47   Diagram of a single-coat flat-bed drying system.

to the surface and this also kept the web flat. Such dryers came into operation at Mobberley in 1956, as a result of collaboration between A. G. Horton and E. Cameron, in consultation with J. D. Whittaker of the Greenbank Engineering Co., Blackburn, who constructed the machines. Shortly after, air-knife coating was introduced with a new flat-bed dryer. This increased the output to such an extent that, in 1960, a similar coating head was installed on the previous flat-bed machine.

Based on the experience at Mobberley, a small flat-bed dryer with air-knife coating was designed for sale to Valca SA, Spain. This was installed in 1965 to

enable them to produced Ilford designed products. 'Know-how' deals with the Polish photographic industry also involved the design of similar, but larger, plant for film and paper production.

Experience with the Mobberley machines later led to the introduction of large new machines at Brentwood and at Fribourg, all having high-capacity flat-bed dryers and the capability of cascade coating in addition to air-knife application. (See Figure 48.)

After the end of the Second World War the increasing complexity of manufacturing machinery involved the development of more advanced instrumentation and control systems. In particular, G.

Figure 48   A modern flat-bed dryer used for film production at the Brentwood factory in 1975. The horizontal casing contains the film web, travelling at high speed, with zones of air at different temperatures and levels of humidity along its length.

H. Farrington, who was consultant engineer during this period, introduced advanced pneumatic systems, while E. Cameron evolved numerous novel and elegant techniques for improved machine drives, air-floated and suction-supported webs, and air jet sensing for steering the web. Cameron was also responsible for the introduction of low dew-point air for setting, high-speed methods of drying and the introduction of a range of improved monitoring instruments.

The change in methods of application brought about some changes in emulsion technology. In simple dip or slab coating, the thickness of the emulsion coat is determined by gravity and by the viscosity of the solution. Coating speeds higher than 20–30 ft/min could not be used because the necessary dilution required an uneconomically large dryer to evaporate the large amount of water in the coating. This water was not only present to give a low-viscosity solution

but also because washing of the emulsion with water, to remove unwanted salts, was almost universal. The shreds of emulsion tended to absorb water, which was difficult to remove before coating.

The Selo factory at Brentwood did not suffer from this problem, as they had never used water washing. The flocculation process they employed had been in use by the Paget Prize Plate Co. from their early days but had been neglected by most other manufacturers. The more concentrated solutions produced in this way allowed the emulsion to be coated at higher concentration but the higher viscosity restricted the coating speeds possible at Brentwood with dip-coating methods. The original flocculation process suggested by Wratten in 1887 used industrial alcohol alone. When anionic wetting agents became available much later they were used in conjunction with spirit by Brentwood and afterwards licensed to Du Pont and others. The volume of spirit used remained large,

143

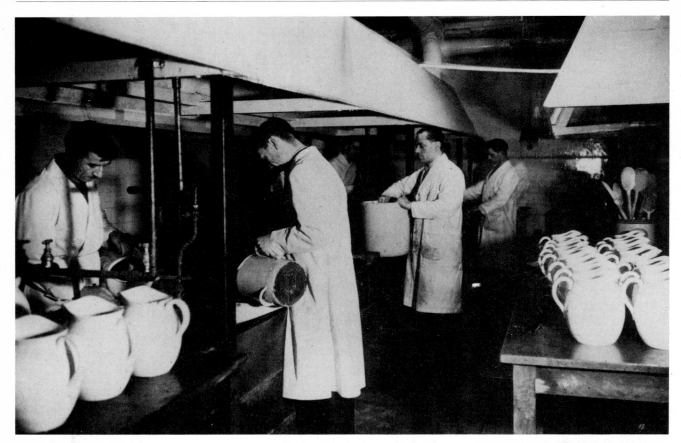

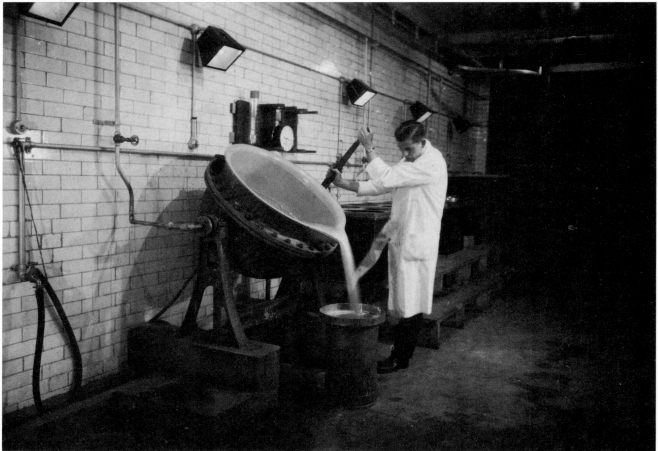

Figure 49   Emulsion making: Top left, The original 'jug and bottle' method. Bottom left, Larger volumes of production; pans surrounded with warm water jackets to maintain temperature. Above, An hydraulic shredder, showing the perforated plate through which the emulsion was forced. The demonstrator is C. S. Hall, later the manager of the Ilford plate factory. Overleaf, The control panel of an automated emulsion production system at Brentwood in 1970.

however, and a still was introduced to recover the waste alcohol. This soon had to be enlarged, the new plant having high columns capable of producing pure spirit at proof strength.

The use of the flocculation method, giving more concentrated emulsions, enabled smaller drying units to be used coupled with improved methods of application. These included the use of air-knife-, reverse-roller-, slot-, and cascade-coating; with air suction applied in some cases. Ilford engineering research concentrated on these methods from 1953 onwards, leading to the first accurate control of coating weight, so essential to the manufacture of colour products. The demand for multilayer colour film caused the need for high-capacity drying to increase still further.

Looking back, the progress in emulsion application methods had been from the sloping glass plate, devised by S. Whitfield to try to improve coating from very viscous emulsions, to a W. H. Smith modification, in which the glass plate was supported on a warm-water

tank and held tangentially under the coating roller. Emulsion was fed from a water-jacketed pan to maintain constant temperature. About 1929, Horton designed a low-level emulsion pan with an immersed mechanical pump. Various methods of dip coating were tried. By 1941, this had been replaced by a trough containing a weir, which held back and diverted any bubbles in the emulsion. Finally, from 1955, slot coating was used to meter emulsion accurately onto the base at high speeds and, from 1958, air-knives were used to restrict the coating weight.

As a result of Brentwood experience with film, the Mobberley factory also abandoned water washing from 1957 onwards and adopted flocculation techniques for paper emulsions, coupled with air-knife coating and high-capacity flat-bed dryers. Precipitation with sodium sulphate was used to avoid the many problems in the use of alcohol.

The new developments in emulsion technology and the growing volume of output finally led to the end of emulsion-making in small batches. (See Figure 49.)

Pots, and later relatively small 'kettles', had been used to make emulsion since Harman founded the company. Ilford had tended to cling to this method because of its belief in the high consistency of the product which could be achieved by the blending of relatively small batches.

By 1960, it was clear that an automatic system was needed. The process of emulsion making was understood better and instruments had become available which enabled conditions to be controlled to much finer limits. Accordingly a gravity-feed system, controlled by punched tape, was installed at Brentwood in place of the old hand line. This mixed and dissolved the raw chemicals and then emulsified, ripened, flocculated, washed, and digested the film emulsions; large vessels were used with automatic control of times and temperatures. The emulsion was finally run into stainless steel pans and chilled until needed for coating. A continuous flow system was tried experimentally for a time at Mobberley but it was found in practice that a batch system, which gave time for detailed testing and fine adjustment of exact properties, was superior.

Meanwhile, the growing volume of production of paper and film products had necessitated the use of high-speed automatic chopping and packaging machines. Ilford had designed fully-automatic roll-film and cassette-spooling machines from 1950 onwards. The introduction of the 126 cartridge by Kodak had later necessitated the design and production of special injection-moulding tools and of complex automatic machines for spooling the film and filling the cartridges. The advent of magnetic sound had involved the design engineers in equipment for striping the cine film with magnetic lacquer.

Electronics were being used to an increasing extent. Contact proof printers provided fully automatic printing of a continuous band of colour negatives, while an electronic tone masking printer was used for duplicating colour transparencies.

The early days of hiring machines from B. J. Edwards were indeed forgotten.

Appendix 1. Harman's early premises in Ilford

The address of Harman's house, when he first moved to Ilford in the 1880s, is given only as South Park, both in *Kelly's Directory* (1882) and in the *Voters' List* (1885). At that time, South Park was a group of 18 houses on the southern boundary of Valentine's Park. Of these, 10 were located on the south side of the lane, later called Park Avenue, and the other 8 were in Cranbrook Road, 4 on each side of the junction with the lane.

In an article in the local paper on the occasion of the company's diamond jubilee in 1939, A. J. Haynes stated that Harman lived on the corner of Cranbrook Road and Park Avenue and that four houses, including 'The Lodge' and Harman's house, had been de-molished to make way for a cinema in the early 1930s.

When Ilford houses were numbered for the first time, the four south of the junction became 83 to 89, 85 being 'The Lodge', and 89, on the corner, being 'Elmhurst'. The last, therefore, seems most likely to have been Harman's residence. Harman probably rented it, as he is not mentioned in the deeds of the property.

The cinema referred to by Haynes was never built. The site remained empty for many years after the Second World War; eventually, 'The Cranbrook' public house was built there.

In 1886, Harman moved to 'The Limes', New London Road, Chelmsford. He stayed there a few

Figure 50   A view of Cranbrook Road, Ilford, as it was in Harman's time. His house, 'Langsett', was on the left, behind the trees, just before the church.

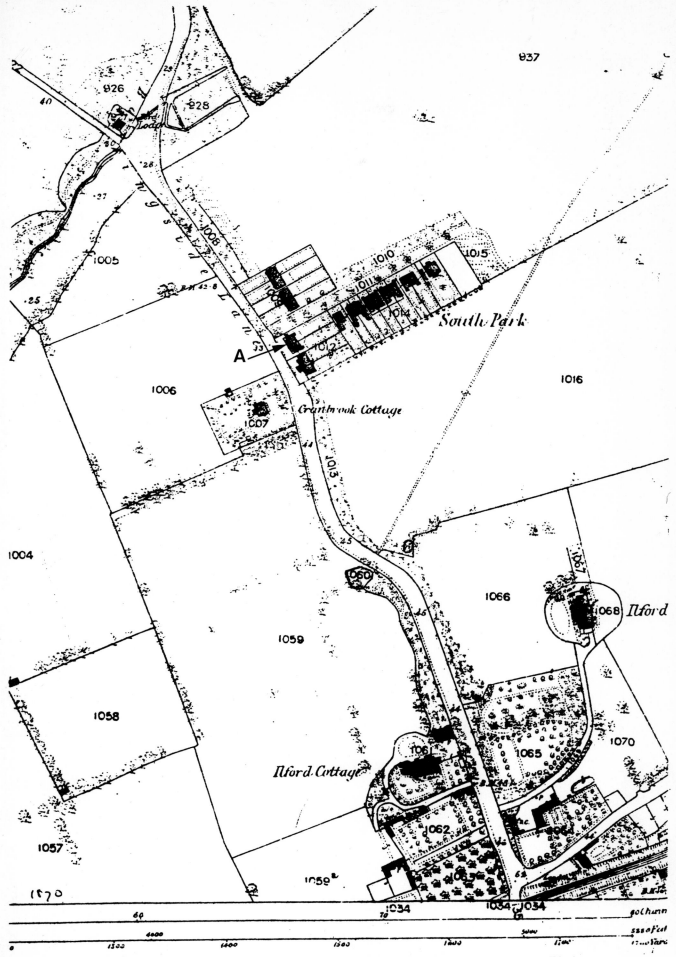

*Figure 51   Map showing the Cranbrook Road area of Ilford in 1881. The railway station and Ilford
Broadway are just off the bottom of the plate. Harman's house is marked 'A'.*

Figure 52   A map of the Clyde Estate, where Harman set up his factory. The first cottage he rented is marked 'B'; the seven houses in Grove Terrace are at 'C'. Back Street is now Roden Street and Grove Terrace is called Uphall Road.

years and then moved back to Ilford, to 'Langsett', Cranbrook Road. 'Langsett' became 61 Cranbrook Road. The site is now occupied by Chieseman's furniture store, on the corner of Wellesley Road.

Harman made his early plates in the basement and ground floor of 'Elmhurst'. He may have done experimental work at 'Langsett' but it was never used for the manufacture of plates. When he moved to Haslemere in 1894, 'Langsett' was sold to a Mr Hammond.

Appendix 2. Britannia Works Institute

As a consequence of the decision to expand the factory in 1893, No. 5 Grove Terrace, which contained the mess room for employees, was no longer available for that purpose. Harman stated that he was willing to purchase land and erect a building to replace the old mess room, for a sum not exceeding £2000, provided that it was maintained by the company. He suggested that the Institute should contain two rooms for the caretaker and one large room spacious enough for meetings and entertainments; Mr Hughes should look for a plot of land near the dairy.

Two plots of land were purchased from Dr Shimeld in June 1894 for the Institute, which was completed by 23 November 1895 when the annual shareholders' meeting was held there. The official opening did not occur until Wednesday December 18.

That day, the factory was closed early and a dinner was arranged for 6.30 pm; only shareholders and invited guests were present. After the dinner, there was a concert at 8 pm, to which all employees earning more than 13s per week were invited. Mr and Mrs Knobel took part and Mr George Rousby was asked to organize a short dramatic performance with such outside assistance as he thought proper.

Figure 53   The Britannia Works Institute as it was soon after erection.

Figure 54   The Britannia Works Institute as it was when the Ilford site was vacated in 1976.

Initially, it was agreed that the company would meet the expenses, but finally Harman agreed to pay for the dinner personally. He also made a deed of gift of the Institute to the company.

The Institute rooms were opened to the members on December 27 and a committee of 12 was elected to manage the Institute.

The first committee consisted of:

W. Anderson	W. C. Shepherd (Sec.)
A. Bell	W. M. Smith
P. J. Coyle	W. Taylor
W. J. Glasscock	H. J. Tillett
A. W. Lindsell	W. Underwood
M. Poole	W. White

The directors and secretary also sat on the committee as *ex officio* members.

The subscriptions to the Institute, payable in advance, were 2d per week for those over 16 and 1d per week under 16, for employees, and 1s per month for outsiders.

The object of the Institute was: 'to provide recreation and instruction for employees of the Britannia works and such others as the committee chooses to elect'.

Beer and provisions had to be consumed on the premises. Gambling was prohibited. The company provided £10 to start the Institute fund, to be kept as a balance at the bank; it provided tea and coffee urns, a clock, cooking utensils, an umbrella stand, a looking glass and towels; it took responsibility for gas, coals, rates, taxes, and the caretaker's wages. A little later the company agreed to provide six dining tables, six card tables, and a bookcase with cupboards for games.

A request for a billiard table was referred to Harman, who suggested that a quarter-size table would answer the purpose. The committee, however, was adamant that only a full-size table would do and the board were inclined to agree. Harman still resisted the idea, tartly commenting that it appeared that the desire was to use the Institute chiefly as a billiard room. Ultimately he relented and even agreed to pay for a full-size table for the Institute, to be the property of the company.

By the end of January 1896, complaints were received from the committee that the stove used to heat the hall was inadequate. Again the matter was referred to Harman who replied that he believed that the stove was improperly used and undertook to consult Underwood (a committee member and senior engineer). In the meantime, Knobel had taken professional opinion and was advised that at least two more stoves were required. It was not until the following November that an extra stove was purchased at the cost of £15 6s 0d.

During 1896, the euphoria which had accompanied the opening of the Institute disappeared; disagreements between the board and the Institute committee increased. Knobel reminded the board that Harman intended that the Institute should be self-supporting, as far as possible, and therefore all expenditure should be included in the Institute accounts. The books had

Figure 55   The interior of the Institute in the early years.

not been kept in accordance with this idea and the company secretary was asked to ensure that they were kept in the proper manner; the committee would be allowed to spend up to £4 on any single item without reference to the board.

By June, Knobel was expressing surprise that 75 members were in arrears with their subscriptions in spite of the rule that all subscriptions should be paid in advance. As the subscription was payable weekly, many members paid their subscription only for the week in which an event occurred which they wished to attend.

A special meeting of the board and the committee was held on 11 August 1896 to discuss the management of the Institute. Taylor, on behalf of the committee, suggested that it would be better for foremen to collect the subscriptions and hand them to the caretaker. They had not purchased books for the library as they had been advised not to spend money for unnecessary objects; with reference to the provision of instruction, they did not feel competent to provide this. Furthermore, they were dissatisfied with the way the caretaker carried out his duties.

Knobel replied that the caretaker was the servant of the committee; if there had been irregularities then the committee was clearly to blame. Harman and the directors appreciated the difficulties in the way but they had been sadly disappointed with the management of the Institute; it would be a deplorable state of affairs if it led to the closure of the Institute.

He suggested that the extension of the library was an absolute necessity and one which ought to receive their careful attention. As to the collection of subscriptions, the way suggested by the committee would doubtless be satisfactory but the directors could not take official cognizance of it. The Institute was intended as a place of recreation and instruction and this must be adhered to. Instruction did not necessarily mean anything which was dry and unpalatable, but dissolving views, interesting lectures etc., would be a step in the right direction. The objects of the Institute were certainly not fulfilled if they simply interested themselves in billiards and card-playing.

The caretaker was then sent for and severely reprimanded. However, he obviously did not improve his ways and was dismissed in October. The opportunity was taken by the board to draw up a list of instructions of the caretaker's duties:

1. He was to live in the Institute and not be absent any night without special leave from the committee.

2. He was to keep the Institute clean internally and externally and always to be present: during breakfast and dinner hours; in the evening from 6 o'clock until closing time; on Saturday afternoons; and at other times as specially desired by the committee.

3. He was to take charge of all fires and lights with due regard for economy, especially of gas.

4. He was to collect only payments for refreshments. The control of the library and the collection of subscriptions and payments for billiards were transferred to the committee.

Knobel asked Hughes whether he had ever noticed any member under the influence of liquor; Hughes replied 'No'. He also asked whether any of the songs sung at the smoking concerts were even slightly indecent or suggestive. Hughes replied that although he did not take exception to them himself he would not like his wife or daughter to hear some of them. The board therefore warned the committee that nothing should be permitted at any entertainment which might deter the wife or daughter of any member from attending and enjoying the performance.

By the beginning of 1897, there were 91 members of the Institute, 64 men, 8 boys, and 19 outsiders. A new system of subscription payments was in force but it was felt that some would-be members could not afford to pay the half-yearly subscription in advance and it was suggested that the company should advance the money and deduct it monthly from the wages.

The income and expenditure account for the Institute for 1896 showed a deficit of £24 7s 8d and that the Institute owed the company £35 11s 11d. The committee was asked to pay the £35 11s 11d to the company but the board agreed to hold a sum of £70 per annum at the disposal of the committee, which could be drawn quarterly in advance. The board objected to payment of money prizes for billiard and card tournaments, as all gambling was strictly prohibited. It ordered that future prizes should be other than money.

As the years passed, interest in and membership of the Institute waned. In 1907 an offer of £2000 was made for the Institute by the Ilford Social Club, which was not accepted. Three months later the billiard table was sold for £10 to the 'Cross Keys', Dagenham.

Leonard Randall and Co. offered to rent the Institute in 1909. A meeting of employees was called to discuss the matter and after much argument it was decided to run the Institute as a working men's club. Ilford, Limited agreed to meet the running costs of the Institute building, provided they did not exceed £52 per annum, and to contribute £25 towards the cost of coal for heating and gas for breakfast and lunches. A loan, at four per cent interest was granted for the purchase of a new billiard table. The name was changed from the 'Britannia Works Institute' to the 'Britannia Works Club'.

Britannia Works Club Tariff 1909

Whisky	2½d per ¼ gill
Brandy	2½d per ¼ gill
Bitter Ale	1½d per glass
Tea, Coffee or cocoa for breakfast or lunch	½d per cup
Small pot of tea	2d
Bread and butter	½d per slice
Bread and cheese	1½d
Tobacco	4d per ounce
Will's Gold Flake cigarettes	3d per 10
Marcella cigars	2d each

What the change involved is not recorded, but by the end of 1910 the membership had doubled to over 200 and a profit of £144 was made, after repayment of the loan, the purchase of a second billiard table, a bagatelle table, and additions to the library. The company paid for redecorating the rooms and installing new heating apparatus.

In 1911, a Benefit Society, run separately from the Club, was formed to meet sickness and funeral expenses incurred by its members. Any money left in the fund at the end of the year was shared out among the members. In 1913, the subscription was 6d per week; sickness benefit paid was £21 and each member received £1 3s 3d at the end of the year. The annual report listed not only the sickness benefits paid to the members but also the nature of their complaints, which must have proved embarrassing at times. This practice was continued until 1939 after which only the benefit received was listed.

The existence of the Institute building was threatened in 1923 by an offer, from the Loxford Social Club in Roden Street, to exchange premises. This was seriously considered for a time, as the company wished to possess the Loxford premises which were adjacent to the factory. Finally, the board was able to purchase the Loxford Club for £2000. Another offer, made in 1935 by Randalls, surveyors of Ilford, to purchase the Institute for £3500 was rejected and the Institute was saved once again.

The Institute survived until 1972, when a new Social Club, with restaurant and bar, was built on the Sharpe's market site and the old premises were sold to a furniture company. By this time, Ilford had social centres, with restaurants and bars, at all the main sites, catering for a very wide range of employees' interests.

Appendix 3. Phenidone

One of the most important discoveries by Ilford scientists was that of the photographic developing properties of 1-phenyl-3-pyrazolidone. This chemical, first made in 1890, was found in 1940 by Dr J. D. Kendall at the Rodenside laboratory to possess useful properties in processing. As a sole developing agent, it gave very low contrast, with a tendency to fog, but the situation was quite different in combination with hydroquinone. Developers containing these two agents were highly active, had a short induction period and gave their best performance using a quantity of the new developing agent which was only 10 per cent of the amount of metol necessary in conventional metol-hydroquinone formulae.

No further work was done immediately, partly because of wartime pressures of work and partly because the chemical was expensive to make.

Early in 1950, G. F. Duffin, in connection with other work, synthesized 1-phenyl-3-amino pyrazoline from phenylhydrazine and acrylonitrile, a chemical which had become available cheaply after the war. He realized that this would be an inexpensive route to 1-phenyl-3-pyrazolidone. Even so, the photographic developing properties of the chemical might have remained a laboratory curiosity if it had not been for the acute sulphur shortage of 1950–51, which reduced the supplies of metol. Ilford therefore decided, late in 1950, to economize on metol by replacing it with a smaller quantity of the new chemical in its range of packed developers. Formulations were prepared on the basis of work by Dr A. J. O. Axford.

The new developers were liked and it was decided to name the new material 'Phenidone' and to publish information, which Dr Kendall did on 3 October 1951 in a paper *Chemical Shortages and the Efficient Use of Processing Chemicals*, before the Royal Photographic Society. At the same time, his associates Duffin and Axford evolved a better synthesis from acrylic ester and phenylhydrazine.

A more detailed study of the behaviour of Phenidone-hydroquinone developers showed they had advantages in their own right: better keeping qualities, slower exhaustion, no tendency to induce dermatitis, and the ability to provide highly concentrated developing solutions. The last property proved of great importance; the modern range of high-concentration developers would be impossible without Phenidone.

Soon after the announcement of Phenidone, it began to be used by the majority of other manufacturers of photographic developers. The scale of synthesis of the material became too big for Ilford to carry out; manufacture was passed over to Geigy in Switzerland and in Manchester, England.

One of the largest users in the late 1950s and early 1960s was Gevaert, Belgium. They were one of the pioneers of diffusion transfer photography applied to document copying; the use of Phenidone was essential to the optimum performance of their products. Since then, Phenidone has been widely used in diffusion transfer processes and in many formulations, especially for rapid processing of films and papers.

Appendix 4. List of the company's products

This list of products—by no means complete—includes a selection of speeds to indicate the progress that the emulsion makers have made during the century.

The H & D system of speed numbers was in use from 1890 until it was replaced by the DIN system (1934) and the BS and ASA systems (1947). At the beginning of the 1960s, the ASA system was modified to yield speeds which were twice as great as those on the old ASA system.

For a variety of reasons it is difficult to equate one system with another, but an attempt has been made to express all speeds in the new ASA numbers in order to make comparisons easier. (*Ilford Manual of Photography*, Alan Horder, Ilford Limited, 5th edition, 1958.)

The speeds given are those the products had when introduced. The speeds of those materials, which were in production for many years, were often increased during the products' life span.

Plates

		New ASA
'Britannia' Dry plate	1879	—
Ilford 'Ordinary' (replaced Britannia plate)	1885	4.5
Rapid	1885	5.5
Special Rapidity	1888	9.5
Alpha Lantern	1889	—
Special Lantern	1891	—
Isochromatic Medium Rapidity	1891	4.5
Isochromatic Instantaneous	1891	9.0
Special Rapid (SR)	1895	13.0
Process	1895	0.55
Empress	1895	9
Chromatic	1897	4.5
SR used for X-rays	1897	—
Half-Tone	1897	3
Backed plates introduced	1897	—
Monarch	1903	3.5
Rapid Isochromatic	1905	9
Zenith	1905	3.0
Amauto	1905	—
X-ray	1907	—
Alliance	1909	—
Versatile Rapid	1910	20
Versatile Most Rapid	1910	30
Versatile Ortho	1910	20
Panchromatic	1910	8
Rapid Chromatic	1911	20
X-ray Screen	1911	20
Kings Own	1912	20
Extra Fine Grain	1915	4
Screened Chromatic	1916	20
Rapid Process Panchromatic	1918	8
Rapid Panchromatic	1918	20
Zenith Extra Sensitive	1919	32
Press	1919	32
Special Rapid Panchromatic	1919	32
Zenith High Speed	1920	42
Iso Zenith	1923	56
Special Rapid Extra Sensitive	1925	32
Zenith Super Sensitive	1928	52
Soft Gradation Panchromatic	1928	56
Golden Iso Zenith	1929	110
Auto Filter	1929	32
Iso Record	1930	40
Hypersensitive Panchromatic	1931	160
Infra-Red	1932	—
Thin Film Half-Tone	1933	0.8
Record	1935	40
Double-X-Press	1935	120
Press Ortho	1935	56
Nuclear, R1 and R2	1935	—
FP 1	1937	—
HP 2	1937	—
Selochrome	1937	125
FP2	1937	200
Salon H Pan	1938	—
Trichrome	1938	—
Ordinary	1938	—
Contact Lantern	1938	—
Warm Black Lantern	1938	—
FP 3	1942	250
Thin Film Halftone Pan	1942	—
Ortho Process	1942	—
HP 3	1942	400
Soft Ordinary	1945	6
Litho Negative	1945	—

	Year	New ASA
Ortho Halftone	1945	—
High Resolution	1947	—
Astra	1947	—
Q	1947	—
Long Range Spectrum	1947	—
FP Special	1949	80
Electron	1950	—
Photo Mechanical	1950	—
Nuclear	1952	—
HP S	1952	800
Orthotone	1952	—
Formalith	1952	—
High Contrast Thin Film	1953	—
Fast Ordinary	1959	16
Formalith Pan	1960	—
Diapositive	1968	—

Flat Film

		New ASA
Empress	1895	8.8
Process	1895	0.55
Special Rapid	1900	13
Monarch	1906	35
Chromatic	1906	4.5
Rapid Isochromatic	1906	9
Studio Supersensitve	1925	45
Universal	1925	30
Panchromatic	1930	30
Universal Ortho	1930	—
Fine Grain Panchromatic Film Pack	1930	30
Selochrome Film Pack	1935	50
Commercial Ortho	1935	20
Portrait Ortho Medium	1935	30
Portrait Ortho Fast	1935	60
Hypersensitive Panchromatic	1935	160
Portrait Pan	1938	160
Fine Grain Ordinary	1938	—
Hyperchromatic	1938	125
Hyperpanchromatic	1938	200
Press Ortho	1940	—
HP 2	1940	200
FP 2	1940	—
HP 3	1943	250
Ordinary	1945	—
FP 3	1946	125
HP S	1953	800
HP 4	1964	400
FP 4	1968	125

Roll and Miniature Films

		New ASA
Ilford Daylight Loading Roll Film	1915	—
Roll Film	1922	—
Ilford Ultra-rapid Roll Film	1925	28
Panchromatic Roll Film	1930	32
Fine Grain Panchromatic Roll Film	1935	28
Hypersensitive Panchromatic Roll Film	1935	160
Selo	1937	64
Selochrome	1937	100
Selo FG Pan (FP)	1938	80
HP 2	1938	200
FP 2	1939	80
Selo Ortho	1940	64
Selochrome CF	1941	—
HP 3	1941	250
Infra Red	1942	—
FP 3	1946	125
PAN F	1948	50
HP S	1954	800
HP 4	1960	400
FP 4	1968	125
HP 5	1976	400

Colour Film

		New ASA
Colour Film D	1948	20
Colour Film A	1949	—
Colour Film F	1956	—
Ilfachrome Film	1960	20
Ilfacolor Paper	1960	—
Ilfacolor Film	1960	32
Colortrack Film	1961	—
Ilfochrome	1962	32
Ilfocolor	1962	32
Colorslide	1965	—
Colorprint	1965	—
Colorcine	1967	—
Super Colorprint	1968	64
Cibachrome Graphic	1968	
Cibachrome Print D	1969	
Cibachrome Transparent	1971	
Cibachrome Print A	1976	
Cibachrome Copy Paper	1977	
Cibachrome Copy Film	1978	

Cine and Aerial Film

Cinematograph Film	1923
Selo 16 mm. negative	1935
Selo 16 mm. positive	1935
Selo 16 mm. reversal	1935
HP 3	1943
Pan F	1946

FG Pan Pos	1953	High Definition	1939
Hyperpan	1953	Brytex Leaves	1941
HP 3	1953	Kryptoscreen paper	1942
N	1957	Lead Screens	1942
FP 3	1958	High Voltage	1952
HR	1959	Fast Tungstate	1960
Mark V	1965	Super High Definition	1974
HRT	1965	Rapide (rare earth)	1976
A	1965		
FP 4	1969		
L	1975		

Microfilms

Graphic Arts Films

Micro Neg.	1941	Process	1895
Micro Neg. Pan	1952	Thin Base Process	1935
COM 1	1973	Process Pan	1942
Ilfodata B	1974	Contact	1942
HS	1975	Litho Neg	1942
Surveillance	1975	Line	1942
HR	1976	Ortholine	1942
COM 2	1977	Panchroline	1945
COM 3	1977	Rapid Ortholine	1948
Ilfodata A	1978	Slow Contact	1949
		Formalith	1952

Industrial X-ray Films

		Photomechanical	1955
Industrial A	1942	Formalith Diaback	1952
Industrial C	1942	Formaline	1960
Industrial B	1943	Separation	1960
Industrial F	1953	Orthoset	1960
Industrial G	1958	Photolettering	1963
		Inverpos	1963

Medical X-ray and Dental X-ray Films

		Pan Masking	1963
		Ortholith (Formalith) SP4	1967
		PTS (Ilfoset)	1967
X-ray (Plate)	1909	Ilfolith	1968
Dental-Standard	1911	Ilfoline	1970
Dental-Contrast	1923	Ilfostar	1971
Standard X-ray Acetate	1939	Ilforep	1971
Ilfex	1940	Ilfoline PL4	1973
Red Seal Acetate	1944	Ilfolith Contact	1975
GX	1945	Ilfolith Graphic	1976
HPX	1945	Ilfolith Special	1978
Personnel Monitoring	1951	Repro IRF4	1978
Ilfex (Improved version)	1953		

General Purpose Papers

Dental-Fast	1960	Bromide paper, Slow and Rapid,	
Gold Seal	1962	Rough and Smooth	1884
Red Seal Polyester	1965	Bromide Opals	1884
Rapid R	1967	Alpha paper	1884
Type S	1974	POP (printing-out paper)	1891
Ilfex 90	1975	POP pink-base paper	1892
Rapid E	1976	POP mauve-base paper	1893
		POP matt paper	1893

X-ray Screens

		Bromide matt paper	1894
Ilford Standard Tungstate	1917	Bromide Platinomatt Surface ('PMS')	
Fluorazure	1938	paper	1897

POP Special, for hard negatives	1899	Roll Head Type C	1955
Platona platinum paper	1899	Ilfoprint	1963
Kalona, self-toning gelatin paper	1902	Ilfobrom	1967
Bromona, cream tinted paper	1906	Ilfomar	1973
Collodion paper	1908	Ilfospeed	1974
Intona, self-toning POP	1910		
Hyptona, self-toning collodion paper	1910		
Therma, tropical POP	1911	**Other Papers**	
Chlorona	1933	X-ray Paper	1907
Studio Neg. Card	1938	Photomechanical	1938
Plastika	1939	Orthotrace	1939
Seltona	1938	Ortho Stripping	1941
Tintona	1938	Document	1943
Enitone	1938	Reflex	1947
Dry Transfer	1938	Autopos	1949
Outdoor Neg. Card	1938	Inverpos	1952
Selo Contact	1938	Ilfacopy	1959
Bromoil	1938	Formalith	1959
Multigrade	1940	Photolettering	1970
Ilford Contact—Industrial Contact	1947	Teletransmission	1972
Press Bromide	1952	PTS Phototypesetting	1974
Carbro Bromide	1953	PRC Phototypesetting	1976
Negapos	1953	Repro IRP	1978
Kenprint	1955	PTI 110 Photolettering	1978

Appendix 5. List of directors of the company

The directors of the private company, formed in 1891, were A. H. Harman, T. Hughes, J. Howson, and F. J. Jenks.

The list below records the directors from 1898, first of the Britannia Works Co. (1898) Ltd and then of the subsequent company, Ilford, Limited.

A. H. Harman	1902–1904
E. B. Knobel	1898–1907
J. Howson	1898–1900
D. W. G. Keppel	1898–1902
T. Hughes	1898–1903
Lord Crawford	1898–1900
Maj.-Gen. J. Waterhouse	1901–1903
Maj.-Gen. G. F. Blake	1901–1903
C. J. Cox	1901–1903
R. D. Lewis	1903–1940
J. Kemp-Welch	1903–1936
A. R. Smith	1903–1908
A. Ashmole	1903–1924
Maj.-Gen. Sir Ivor Philipps	1906–1940
Col. F. W. Evatt	1908–1946
F. J. Jenks	1915–1930
T. M. Illingworth	1920–1957
Major Blundell Mein	1924–1937
Lt.-Col. V. B. Ramsden	1930–1936
F. F. Renwick	1930–1943
B. L. Drake	1930–1950
W. H. Dimsdale	1936–1971
J. P. Philipps	1937–1965
Lord Milford	1940–1949
Sir Philip E. Haldin	1941–1952
G. B. Harrison	1945–1963
J. Mitchell	1945–1963
W. E. Metcalfe	1946–1959
Lord Rockley	1949–1966
Sir Laurence Merriam	1950–1964
Sir Frederic Hooper	1952–1960
L. H. Williams	1958–1967
Dr J. Avery	1958–1964
R. A. Withers	1959–1968
F. W. Hutchinson	1960–1969
G. A. Jones	1960–1969
S. T. Ferris	1961–1967
Lord Harvey	1964–1972
Dr W. A. Cowdrey	1965–1967
J. L. Porter	1965–1969
Dr A. J. O. Axford	1966–1975
J. D. Rose	1967–1969
P. Erni	1967–1971
A. E. Frost	1967–1969
J. E. Duffy	1969–1974
A. A. S. Rae	1969–
G. A. Jones	1971–1977
H.-R. Hug	1971–1974
Dr L. von Planta	1971–1974
Dr H. Schramek	1971–
Dr W. A. Lustenberger	1971–1974
Dr B. Messikommer	1971–
Dr N. Tarköy	1971–1972
J. C. Cooper	1972–
W. K. Wenger	1973–
T. W. Parton	1973–1978
Dr H.-J. Heller	1974–
F. W. Hutchinson	1975–
J. S. Fraser	1975–
Dr F. Trautweiler	1975–
N. R. Wynn	1976–

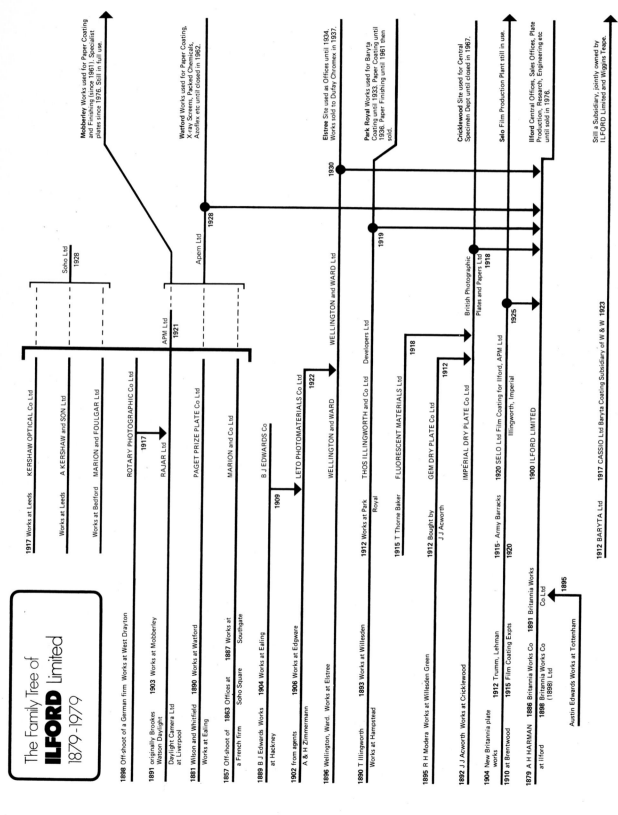

The Family Tree of
ILFORD Limited
1879-1979

1898 Off-shoot of a German firm Works at West Drayton

1891 originally Brookes
Watson Daylight
Daylight Camera Ltd
at Liverpool

1903 Works at Mobberley

Mobberley Works used for Paper Coating and Finishing (since 1961). Specialist plates since 1976. Still in full use.

Soho Ltd
1928

1917 Works at Leeds   KERSHAW OPTICAL Co Ltd

Works at Leeds   A KERSHAW and SON Ltd

Works at Bedford   MARION and FOULGAR Ltd

ROTARY PHOTOGRAPHIC Co Ltd

1917
RAJAR Ltd

1881 Wilson and Whitfield   **1890** Works at Watford
Works at Ealing

PAGET PRIZE PLATE Co Ltd

Watford Works used for Paper Coating, X-ray Screens, Packed Chemicals, Azoflex etc until closed in 1962.

Apem Ltd

APM Ltd
1921

1857 Off-shoot of   **1863** Offices at   **1887** Works at
a French firm   Soho Square   Southgate

MARION and Co Ltd

1889 B J Edwards Works   **1904** Works at Ealing
at Hackney

B J EDWARDS Co

1902 from agents   **1906** Works at Edgware
A & H Zimmermann

1909
LETO PHOTOMATERIALS Co Ltd

1922

1896 Wellington, Ward.   Works at Elstree

WELLINGTON and WARD

WELLINGTON and WARD Ltd

Elstree Site used as Offices until 1934. Works sold to Dufay Chromex in 1937.

1930

1890 T Illingworth   **1893** Works at Willesden
Works at Hampstead

1912 Works at Park
Royal

THOS ILLINGWORTH and Co Ltd   Developers Ltd

Park Royal Works used for Baryta Coating until 1933. Paper Coating until 1936. Paper Finishing until 1961 then sold.

1915 T Thorne Baker

FLUORESCENT MATERIALS Ltd

1918

1919

1895 R H Modera   Works at Willesden Green

1912 Bought by
J J Acworth

GEM DRY PLATE Co Ltd

1912

1892 J J Acworth   Works at Cricklewood

IMPERIAL DRY PLATE Co Ltd

British Photographic
Plates and Papers Ltd
1918

Cricklewood Site used for Central Specimen Dept until closed in 1967.

1904 New Britannia plate
works

1912 Trumm, Lehman

1915 Film Coating Expts

1915 Army Barracks

1920

1920 SELO Ltd Film Coating for Ilford, APM Ltd
Illingworth, Imperial

1925

Selo Film Production Plant still in use.

1879 A H HARMAN   **1886** Britannia Works Co   **1891** Britannia Works
at Ilford   **1898** Britannia Works Co   Co Ltd
(1898) Ltd

1900 ILFORD LIMITED

Ilford Central Offices, Sales Offices, Plate Production, Research, Engineering etc until sold in 1976.

1895

Austin Edwards Works at Tottenham

1912 BARYTA Ltd   **1917** CASSIO Ltd Baryta Coating Subsidiary of W & W 1923

Still a Subsidiary, jointly owned by ILFORD Limited and Wiggins Teape.

1928

References

The main sources of reference for the preparation of this book have been the board minutes of Ilford Limited, the Britannia Works Co. (1898) Ltd and the companies acquired over the years. Use has been made of the companies' annual reports, of ledgers and other material (now mainly deposited at the Science Museum Library, South Kensington, London) and of committee minutes remaining on file, mainly covering the years 1960–77. A number of unpublished internal histories have proved useful, including *Our First 75 Years* by A. J. Catford, *Phew! Said the Visitor*, a description of the Selo Works between the wars, *The Works* by C. N. Potter, and a short technical description of engineering development in the photographic industry by W. H. Dimsdale.

Other specific references, selected to provide more information on the chapters indicated, are given below:

Chapter 1. Introduction
History of Photography, J. M. Eder (trs. E. Epstean), Columbia University Press, 1945.
Photography, Theory and Practice, L. P. Clerc, Pitman, 1937.
The Birth of Photography, B. Coe, Ash and Grant, 1976.
Light, F. Bray, Ed. Arnold, 1930.
Greek Science, B. Farrington, Penguin, 1944.
Masters of Victorian Photography, J. Hannavy, David and Charles, 1976.
Sir Joseph Swan, K. R. Swan, Longmans, Green, 1946.
Sir Joseph Wilson Swan, FRS, A Memoir, M.E.S. and K.R.S., Benn, 1929.
Brit. J. Phot., 8 Sept. 1871, p. 422.
Idem, 4 Nov. 1887, p. 697.
Idem, 18 July 1873, p. 348.
Idem, 18 Dec. 1873, p. 599.
Idem, 19 June 1914, supplement.
Idem, 17 August 1877, p. 384.
Idem, 29 March 1878, p. 146.
Idem, 21 March 1879, p. 133.
Idem, 22 Aug. 1879, p. 895.
Brit. J. Phot. Almanac, 1877, p. 95.
Monthly Fluctuations in the Price of Bar-Silver, 1833–1970, Sharps, Pixley Limited, 20 Fenchurch St., London.

Chapter 2
Brit. J. Phot. Alamanac, 1864 p. xiv.
Idem, 1865, p. xx.
Idem, 1867, p. xxxv.
Idem, 1868, p. xxviii.
Idem, 1874, p. xxx.
Idem, 1875, p. lxxix.
Idem, 1877, p. cii.
Photographic News, 8 Aug. 1873, p. 378.
Idem, 8 Aug. 1873, p. 381.
Idem, 15 Aug. 1873, p. 395.
Idem, 22 Aug. 1873, p. 407.
Idem, 2 Feb. 1877, p. 59.
Prov. Pat. No. 2174, 30 May 1878.
Brit. J. Phot., 8 Sept. 1871.
Idem, 8 Sept. 1887, pp. 27 and 42.
Kelly's Directory for Surrey, 1915, p. 212.
Haslemere Parish Mag., March 1900.
Ilford, Past and Present, Sir E. Torker, 1901.

Chapter 3
Ill. London News, Diamond Jubilee Number. (1897)
Daily Telegraph (London) Centenary Number, 1855–1955.
History of the British Economy, 1086 to 1970, B. Murphy, Longmans,
Brit. J. Phot. Almanac, 1875, pp. 2, xli and xlii.
Idem, 1879, p. lxxiv.
Idem, 1881, p. cviii.
Idem, 1883, pp. 77, 121, 163, 177, 192, 224, 239, 252.
Idem, 1886, pp. 414 and 779.
Brit. J. Phot., 20 June 1888.
Photographic Scraps, 1891.

Chapter 4
Britannia Works Co., company registration nos. 57395, 68713, 35433, and 68713, Public Records Office.
Leaves From My Life, H. Osborne O'Hagan, John Lane, The Bodley Head, 1929, vol. 1, pp. 401–08.

Chapter 5
The Photographic Researches of F. Hurter and V. C. Driffield, London, 1920.

Chapter 6

Photographic Emulsion Technique, T. Thorne Baker, Boston, American Photographic Publishing Co., 1948.

Ilford Manual of Process Work, L. P. Clerc, London, Ilford Limited, 1925–53.

Phot. J. (W. H. Mills and Sir W. J. Pope), 1920, vol. 60, pp. 182–202 and 253–267.

Idem (O. Bloch and F. F. Renwick), 1920, vol. 60, pp. 145–147.

Idem (O. Bloch and F. M. Hamer), *The Optical and Photographic Properties of a Series of Typical Cynanine Dyes*, 1928, vol. 68, pp. 21–33.

Idem (F. J. Tritton and E. T. Wilson), 1939, vol. 87, pp. 71 and 396.

Chapter 7

The Photographic Industry in Germany during the Period 1939–1945, W. H. Dimsdale, 1949, BIOS Overall Report no. 19, London, HMSO.

Phot. J., Nov. 1940, pp. 434 and 435.

Chapter 8

Colour Film; A Report on the Supply and Processing of Colour Film, 1966, The Monopolies Commission, London, HMSO.

The Times, London, 13 Sept. 1977, 'Questions of Site and Size', E. Fordham.

PLATES – No More, A. T. Gill, Royal Phot. Soc. Historical Group, 1976.

Chapter 11

The Guardian, London, 29 Oct. 1965, 'Ilford Sets a Union Precedent'.

Daily Telegraph, London, 29 Oct. 1965, 'Ilford's Closed Shop'.

Daily Mirror, London, 29 Oct. 1965, '100 pc union bid to cut strikes'.

Financial Times, London, 29 Oct. 1965, 'Ilford Pact with NUGMW'.

Observer, London, 31 Oct. 1965, 'TU break-through'.

Tribune, London, 5 Nov. 1965, 'What Tribune Thinks'.

Tribune, London, 19 Nov. 1965, 'Ilford: 100 per cent trade unionism or closed shop?'

Statist, London, 19 Nov. 1965, 'No Closed Shop' (letter to editor from L. G. Wright and T. P. Lyons).

City Press, London, 29 Oct. 1965, 'Now the Ilford Plan: New Problems for Marxists'.

Chapter 12

Selo Text Book of Amateur Photography, 1925(?)–1939, Ilford Limited.

Infra-Red Photography, S. O. Rawling, London, Blackie, 1935.

Phot. J. (O. Bloch), 1932, vol. 72, pp. 334–40, 'Developments in Infra-red'.

Evidence by Infra-red, London, Ilford Limited, 1934.

J. Roy. Soc. Arts, 1937, vol. 85, pp. 651–72, 'Applications of Photography to Scientific and Technical Problems'.

Chapter 13

Colour Photography in Practice, D. A. Spencer, Pitman, 1938.

The Dufaycolor Process, Elstree, Dufay-Chromex Ltd, 1936.

Lumière Filmcolor, 1933, Thos. K. Grant Ltd.

Farbenfotografie mit Agfacolor Ultra Filmen und Agfacolor Platten, 1935, K. von Holleben, Agfa AG.

The Ilford Book of Colour, L. Gaunt, London, Focal Press, 1963.

B. J. Phot., 10 May 1929, pp. 273–4, 'How Colour Snapshots are Made'.

Idem, 7 June 1929, p. 23 (supp.), 'Developing Coloursnaps'.

Idem, 1 Aug. 1930, p. 31 (supp.) 'Colour Tripacks'.

Chapter 14

Phot. J., Nov./Dec. 1976, pp. 292–296, 'Plates, Ilford, England'.

R. W. Munro Ltd.; 1864–1964 Centenary, London, R. W. Munro Ltd, 1964.

Index of names

Subject index

Printed and bound in Great Britain by Jarrold & Sons Ltd, Norwich